Le Grand Richards Speaks

With all my heart and soul, I bear you my witness of the divinity of this work, that God the Eternal Father has decreed its destiny. It is built on the foundation of apostles and prophets, with Christ our Lord as the chief cornerstone, and he is guiding his Church today, and will continue to do so until he comes in the clouds of heaven as the holy prophets have declared, and I leave you that witness in the name of the Lord Jesus Christ. Amen.

LeGrand Richards

LeGrand Richards Speaks

by
LeGrand Richards
of the Council of the Twelve
Inspirational Talks by the
author of
A Marvelous Work and a Wonder

Compiled by
G. LaMont Richards

Published by
DESERET BOOK COMPANY
Salt Lake City, Utah
1976

Library of Congress Number 72-76068
ISBN 87747-469-9

Copyright © 1972 by
DESERET BOOK COMPANY
Printed in the United States of America

Contents

v

VI. Prophets and Patriarchs

VII. The Promise of Eternal Life

Introduction

"How's your father, LaMont? Is he still going strong?" "Where has he been traveling lately?" "Is he writing another book, like his *Marvelous Work and a Wonder?*" "When is someone going to publish a book with your father's great sermons?"

A proud son, I am happy to give the latest report on the youthful activities of Father, who is now in his eighty-seventh year. He has recently come home from South America, Africa, Australia, and will leave soon for the Orient. By assignment, he has just divided another stake of Zion. He talked at the BYU devotional. He spent an hour with the missionaries in the Missionary Home. He just returned from the temple, where he performed marriages for young couples who had made appointments months in advance. He is on the way to the hospital to visit a sick friend. He is in private conversation with one who is broken-hearted and in need of kind words. He is on special assignment from the First Presidency on matters relating to business. He is writing to a missionary grandson. He is reading the scriptures. He is studying reports regarding the next stake he is to visit, and preparing the challenges for the stake and ward leaders.

When Father was eight years old, his father, George F. Richards, a patriarch in Tooele, Utah, at the time (he later became an apostle and was president of the Council of the Twelve Apostles at the time of his death), gave his son LeGrand a patriarchal blessing from which I quote:

> Thou hast not come here upon earth by chance, but in fulfill-
> ment of the decrees of the Almighty to accomplish a great labor in
> the upbuilding of God's kingdom, the salvation of mankind, and
> to prove thyself, that thou mayest become exalted in the Lord's
> kingdom. . . .

And thou shalt be exalted among thy fellows, and if thou shalt live for it, thou shalt preside in the midst of the Lord's people. Many shall seek thy counsels and be benefitted and blessed thereby. The power of God shall be made manifest through thee and thy ministrations. Under thy hands the sick shall be healed, the bowed down shall be cheered up and comforted, and many shall receive blessings at thy hands, both spiritual and temporal.

Father was promised that if he would live for it, he would "preside in the midst of the Lord's people." He later wrote, "My heart is full of deep gratitude unto the Lord for the opportunities that have come to me to thus preside. It has been my privilege to preside over quorums of deacons, teachers, and priests; to preside over auxiliary organizations both in wards and stakes; to preside over three wards and one stake of Zion; to serve on two stake high councils; to preside over two missions of the Church; and as a General Authority, to be honored to serve as the Presiding Bishop of the Church and as an apostle of the Lord Jesus Christ."

My father was called to be the Presiding Bishop of the Church on April 6, 1938. He was serving at the time as bishop of the University Ward in the Emigration Stake, having been called to that responsibility following his release as president of the Southern States Mission. I recall the day clearly. I was informed by a fellow student at the University of Utah that he had heard on the radio that Father had been called to serve as the Presiding Bishop. I left class and raced to the Tabernacle just in time to watch him go to the pulpit. He stopped at the row of the apostles and embraced his father, George F. Richards. Then he spoke:

I have had the privilege, my brothers and sisters, of standing before you upon various occasions in general conference, but I have never felt so humble as today. I feel very grateful that the Presidency of this Church and the General Authorities have had confidence enough in me to nominate me to be appointed to this new position, and I feel grateful to you, the Latter-day Saints, for your sustaining vote. I love these men and I love the Church, and I am sure the Lord knows that there isn't a place in the world that I wouldn't go, because of my love for it, and testimony of the gospel.

I am very happy to be associated with the Latter-day Saints. I am grateful for every opportunity of service that has come to me in the past. I feel that the Lord owes me nothing. All I have done for the Church I have done because I love the Church and because I love the Lord. . . . I am willing to give all I have, and all the Lord will give to me, to help this work roll onward and upward to the destiny which I know the Lord has decreed for it. . . .

I want to say to you that there is no achievement that can ever come in the lives of my own children that will be so pleasing to me as to know that their lives shall be lives of service to this great church.

For thirty-three years Father has been serving in the spirit of his promise and dedication. "I am willing to give all I have, and all the Lord will give to me, to help this work roll onward and upward to the destiny which I know the Lord has decreed for it."

A newspaper reported a reception honoring Elder and Sister Richards, at which President David O. McKay enumerated four virtues that characterized the life and mission of Elder Richards: faith, loyalty, cheerfulness, and willingness to serve. "He always radiates faith—a faith which is the source of strength and testimony," President McKay declared. "You feel when in his presence that the dearest thing in the world to him is the gospel. It is that which makes him strong as a leader and as a missionary."

The dearest thing in the world to Father *is* the gospel, building and establishing the kingdom on the earth. His inspirational messages have been read and heard throughout the entire world. At the April 1971 general conference he related his long service and mentioned that he had stood in the Tabernacle pulpit during a general conference more than any living man in the Church except President Joseph Fielding Smith. This was his seventy-fourth time to speak in a general conference.

LeGrand Richards was born at Farmington, Utah, February 6, 1886, one of fifteen children of George F.

Richards and Alice A. Robinson. The family moved to Tooele and were prominent in farming and church activities in that community.

After graduating from the District School at Tooele in 1901, LeGrand enrolled in the Salt Lake Business College, where he was instructed in English and mathematics by President J. Reuben Clark, Jr. They little realized that later they would be a team in managing Church temporal affairs, Father as the Presiding Bishop and President Clark as a counselor to Presidents Heber J. Grant and George Albert Smith.

The following is from LeGrand Richards' journal:

In February, 1905 I was taken with a lameness in my right knee, the same being greatly enlarged by a watery joint. The Doctor put my leg in a plaster cast which I wore for six weeks, walking on crutches during that time. It was while in this condition that I received a call to go on a mission to The Netherlands. When I reported at the office of The First Presidency in answer to the call I had received to go on a mission, the brother in charge asked me what I was there for. When I explained that I was there to answer the call I had received, he replied: "It looks to me like you ought to go home and take care of yourself." I assured him that I would be ready to leave at the appointed time in April. He said he would book me for then, but that if I were not able to leave at that time I could let him know and my mission could be deferred. . . . Father blessed me for my mission, and among other things he said, "I bless you with strength of body and of limbs, that you may not become lame and be overtaken with sickness," and I went at the appointed time and cannot remember that I lost a day of work during my mission because of sickness.

I left for my mission to The Netherlands April 17, 1905, and spent the first eighteen months in the Mission Office as secretary of the mission. . . . I arose around four o'clock each morning to study the language and to get my office work done, that I might find time in the afternoon to go tracting, and in this way, it was not long until I had all the investigators I could take care of. . . . The Lord blessed me with great success in my mission, so that at the close thereof, I counted some forty people who had joined the Church who I felt might not have done had it not been for my mission.

On April 9, 1906 . . . I received a letter from my father dated March 24, 1906, from which I quote, "I had a remarkable dream

last night. I dreamed of seeing the Savior and embracing him.
The feelings, I cannot describe, but I think it was a touch of heaven.
I never expect anything better hereafter. The love of man for
woman cannot compare with it. May we be faithful and make every
sacrifice necessary to obtain that blessing, to live in His presence
forever." The following day, a telegram from the First Presidency
reached our office for President Grant, who was due there the next
day from Berlin, announcing the appointment of three members
of the Twelve (President Grant was an apostle at the time,
presiding over the European mission); the telegram read,
"Richards, Whitney and McKay appointed," and while it did not
say which Richards, I immediately associated this announcement
with the feelings I had always had as a boy and the dream my
father had just received· a few days before his call, and I was sure
it was my father. Upon President Grant's arrival the following day,
he invited me to be his guide a day at The Hague, to show him
and Sister Grant the sights in honor of my father's call.

In his journal Father also recorded the following:

In our home, when I was a boy, we never speculated on the
fact that my father might some day be called as one of the General
Authorities,. although in my heart I always felt that he would be
some day. I recall an experience that occurred on our dry farm
in Tooele while I was a boy. My cousin, Stephen L Richards, who
became an apostle and first counselor in the First Presidency of the
Church, had come to spend the summer with us. He was a young
man, I was a boy. . . . While we were eating one day, my father
turned to Cousin Stephen and said, "Stephen, which would you
rather have, my farm or your father's knowledge of medicine?" To
which Stephen replied, "If Father's knowledge of medicine were
law, I would rather have it." As time has passed, I have regarded
this as quite coincidental—that day, on that dry farm, were three
future members of the Quorum of the Twelve Apostles of the
Church. . . .

Returning home from his first mission in Holland,
Father spent a few months checking annual reports at
the office of the Presiding Bishopric. He then took a
permanent position as bookkeeper for a stock brokerage
firm until the spring of 1909, when he went to Portland,
Oregon, to assist in promoting the Portland Cement
Company.

Prior to moving to Portland, Father courted and won a beautiful young schoolteacher, Ina Jane Ashton, daughter of Edward T. and Cora Lindsey Ashton. They were married May 19, 1909, in the Salt Lake Temple. Father tells in his own words concerning his love and appreciation for Mother and his family.

Ina has been a wonderful wife and companion. Eight children have blessed our union, five girls and three boys, six of whom are still living, and at time of printing of this book there are 29 grandchildren and 51 great-grandchildren. Our children are as follows:

Mrs. Werner Kiepe, Salt Lake City (Mercedes)
Mrs. Reed E. Callister, Glendale, California (Norinne)
Mrs. Harold R. Boyer, Salt Lake City (Marian)
Jane Richards, born in Holland and died at the age of three
LeGrand Ashton Richards, died through an accident in 1932 at age 16
George LaMont Richards, Salt Lake City
Mrs. J. Glenn Dyer, Washington, D.C. (Nona)
Alden Ross Richards, Salt Lake City

I gladly share with my dear wife full credit for all we have been able to accomplish together, for she has been willing to follow me wherever duty has called me. At times she has expressed the thought that I must belong to the wandering tribe of Israel, I have moved around so much. She went with me to Portland, Oregon, then to Holland where we presided over the mission together; then to California where we presided over the Glendale Ward and the Hollywood Stake; then to Atlanta, Georgia, where we presided over the Southern States Mission, and now in my present position. She cannot keep up with me—in fact, it is hard for her to even know where I am much of the time, I am away so much. But in it all, she has been uncomplaining and willing and a helpful partner, and a wonderful mother to our children. She has at times remarked that the children belonged to her and I belonged to the Church. Because so much of my time has been required in my church duties, the raising of the children has been largely left to her, with the result that I am so very proud of each of our children and their faithfulness and accomplishments. The Patriarch seemed to understand that my wife's life would be filled with responsibility, for a year before her marriage, after telling her of some of her responsibilities, he said, "For the time is not far distant when thou shalt be called to labor among those upon whom much responsibility rests."

Not long after his return to Salt Lake City from Portland, Father, who was associated with a lumber firm and on the eve of a great financial opportunity, was called to preside over the Netherlands Mission, replacing Sylvester Q. Cannon (whom he succeeded again years later when he was named Presiding Bishop of the Church). The following describes in Father's words some of his experiences in The Netherlands:

Accompanied by Sister Richards and our three little girls, we left Salt Lake November 13, 1913, for Rotterdam, Holland. We were just getting the work well under way when the first world war broke out in August 1914. The whole country was immediately in an uproar. The Germans entered Belgium and the Dutch were afraid that any day they would enter Holland. . . .

Since communication with Germany was cut off, we became the contact point between America and Germany, and we received numerous cablegrams daily asking us to try to locate students and missionaries in Germany, giving us their last address, and as the missionaries and students left Germany, nearly all of them came through Holland and called at the mission office, and in some instances, we were able to arrange transportation and finances for them to return to America.

Elder Hyrum M. Smith of the Council of the Twelve was then president of the European Mission, and he instructed me to make every preparation in the mission so that the missionaries could be evacuated upon a moment's notice if so instructed. We therefore organized all the branches under local leadership. I suggested to President Smith that should the call come to evacuate the missionaries, it would please me if we might be permitted to retain two elders for each district, and that I might be permitted to remain to look after the mission. Accordingly, on October 3, 1914, we bid farewell to all our missionaries except two for each district. I was also privileged to remain with my family.

We were close enough to hear the roaring of the cannon upon many occasions. . . . During our stay in Holland, we had a little girl born to us. We left Rotterdam with some of the Saints and Elders on June 21, 1916. Because of mines in the waters, we sailed up around the British Isles with a convoy vessel following us for the first day or two in case we should strike a mine. We landed in New York harbor on July 6, 1916. Upon our arrival, we received a telegram from my father informing us that he had been called to preside over the European Mission, so about ten days after we reached Salt Lake he left for his mission.

Upon returning from his second mission to Holland, Father engaged in the real estate business in Salt Lake City, until January 1930. In January 1926, while serving as bishop of the Sugarhouse Ward, he answered the call for experienced missionaries. Those issuing the call stated that bishops and stake presidents were not exempt for short-term missions. The family now had grown to five girls and three boys. Seven of us with Mother were left while Father went east to be a missionary for the third time.

Father records the short-term mission in these words:

I found conditions there much different than I had been accustomed to in my two previous missions in Holland, for in Holland we were baptizing people in the larger branches nearly every week, and in the city where I was assigned to labor in the Eastern States Mission there had been two elders and two lady missionaries laboring most of the time, and I found they did not expect to get baptisms, but seemed contented in making friends. At least, so it seemed to me. . . . I found that it had been five and a half years since they had had the baptism of a convert in that branch. I was given a new companion and we went right out tracting from door to door in an effort to demonstrate that converts could be made if the gospel were properly presented to the people. Accordingly, the night before I left that mission, we baptized five new converts; two weeks later the elders who followed me baptized five more, and before the end of the year, the baptisms from our investigators totaled twenty.

After Father reestablished himself in the real estate business in Salt Lake City, the family moved from Sugarhouse to a home on the east bench. We were not to be blessed to stay here long, for Father was called in by President Grant and asked to make an exploratory trip to Southern California to see if he could successfully find employment. President Grant desired Father to move to that area so that he could be called to preside over the Hollywood Stake. The family took residence in Glendale, and not long after that, in 1930, Father was named bishop; by the end of 1931 he was sustained as president of the Hollywood Stake.

In January 1934, the family was on the move again. Father had been called to preside over the Southern States Mission with headquarters in Atlanta, Georgia. Accompanied by Mother, Nona, Alden, and myself, we traveled by car across the Southwest to our new home and his fourth mission for the Church.

In the Southern States Mission, Father brought the missionaries in from the rural areas to the big cities— Miami, Tampa, Jacksonville, Montgomery, Columbia, and others, where today there are now stakes and wards. Father records:

> When we left the mission, we left a number of districts organized as miniature stakes. I told the Saints that they were like Jacob of old. One day his name was Jacob, the next day his name was Israel; but he was the same man only with greater responsibility. I said, "Soon the brethren will come here and organize these districts into stakes and change the branch presidents from branch presidents to bishops and district presidents to stake presidents." It was not long after that that President Callis and Elder Harold B. Lee organized a stake of Zion at Jacksonville, Florida, and soon thereafter one was organized at Columbia, South Carolina.

Before leaving the mission, Father wrote an outline for the missionaries, called "The Message of Mormonism." It was a lesson guide for investigators, and with urging from those who had used it successfully throughout the Church, he enlarged the outline upon his return to Salt Lake City and published, as his great contribution to missionary work, the now highly circulated book *A Marvelous Work and a Wonder.*

The family returned to Salt Lake City, where Father once again entered the real estate business. In January 1938 he was called to preside over the University Ward of the Ensign Stake. In the April general conference of this same year he was sustained as the Presiding Bishop of the Church. He was set apart by President Grant in the upper room of the temple. Marvin O. Ashton was set apart as his first counselor and Joseph L. Wirthlin as second counselor. To quote Father:

This call came as a great surprise to me, and I felt very humble in accepting it. When President Grant set me apart to preside over the temporal affairs of the Church, I thought that was a tremendous assignment, but when he set me apart to preside over the Aaronic Priesthood, that seemed to me to be of far greater importance.

Shortly before I left the Southern States Mission, I dreamed one night that I met President Grant on the street, and everything seemed so real, and he invited me into his office, telling me that he had a special blessing for me. When I awakened I could only remember how thrilled I was, and when he set me apart as the Presiding Bishop of the Church, the thought came to me immediately that that was the special blessing he had for me, of which I had dreamed before leaving the mission field.

At the April 6, 1952, conference of the Church, President McKay called Father to fill the vacancy in the Council of the Twelve. This was President McKay's first appointment as the new president of the Church. Thus, Father followed his father, George F. Richards, and his grandfather, Franklin D. Richards, as members of the Council of the Twelve.

With fourteen years of experience as a General Authority already, Father enjoyed immediate success as he traveled throughout the Church, visiting stakes and missions, inspiring leaders and missionaries, and with love securing commitment to future dedication to goals of achievement.

His *Marvelous Work and a Wonder* book has and is converting thousands and his *Israel, Do You Know?* and *Just to Illustrate* are being used widely today in missionary work.

G. LaMont Richards

Advice to Youth

1

Youth's Triumph Over Temptation

As I go through the Church and parents ask me what I think about sending their daughters to the Brigham Young University, I tell them that it is the most wonderful place in the world. More young people of quality can be found together there than in any other place. But I tell these parents that it is just like a herd of sheep—there is always a black one here and there in the herd. I let them know that we have a few who creep into our school there, and I tell them to prepare their children to come armored so that they will know how to protect themselves against the few wolves in the herd. I mean that with all of my heart.

I think the devil is just as anxious to try to destroy the lives of our young people as the Lord is to try to save them. Satan works overtime—he works day and night, particularly at night when it is dark. I tell young fellows that if they never take their first cigarette, they will never need to worry about the second one, and if they never take their first glass of beer, they will never need to worry about becoming an alcoholic.

Let me say a few words about petting. You know, to be honest, just a few years ago I had to ask one of the brethren what that word meant. Now if petting is

what they say it is, then I think it is the first step toward
a life of sorrow and disappointment that an individual
can take. If you never engage in petting, you will never
need to worry about losing your virtue.

I want to tell you from my own experience that as
near as you will ever get to heaven in this world is when
a young man kneels down before the altar of God in
the temple with a girl who is sweet and clean, and the
young man is sweet and clean with her. I kept company
with my wife for a year after I came home from my mission before I married her, and I can truthfully say that
I never touched her once in a way that would make her
think that I was motivated by an unholy desire. Then,
when we knelt before the Lord in that holy temple and
I took her in my arms and knew that she was all mine
—well, you just cannot get any nearer to heaven than
that in this world.

You never need to be afraid then of anything coming to light. But what if there were a lot of hidden skele-
tons in the closet; what if I had a lot of things that I
knew that she didn't know and she had a lot of things
that I didn't know and that she knew? Then there would
not be that unity, that love and understanding.

Elder Melvin J. Ballard used to say we would be
successful if we could just help our young people over
"Fool's Hill." Many of our young people are traveling
up that hill now. It will only last for a few years during
their courtship, and if they can keep themselves sweet
and clean, they have nothing to worry about. But if they
do not, it will worry them all the rest of their lives. I
know that is true because I have so many young people
come to me in their troubles.

I want to refer to a little story President David O.
McKay once told. He related the story of a mother who
sent her son into the service. She said, "John, I want you
to come back to me just as clean and sweet as you are
now or else do not come back at all." The officer ac-

companying the boy said, "Why, lady, you must not expect that of your boy." She replied, "I do expect it of him." I am sure that the mother and father of each young person expects the same thing of their son or daughter.

When I went on my first mission, my father told me that he would rather receive me home in a casket than to know that I had lost my virtue or had robbed a woman of hers. I never forgot that—I would have given my life rather than to have disobeyed that instruction from my father. When we were down in the South and I presided over that mission, one of our sons was going west to go to college. He and I sat up together until the wee hours of the morning, and the last thing I said to him as we embraced each other was, "My boy, you know how your father was reared. The same instruction that I got from my father goes for you, and I hope that you will never disappoint me." He said, "Daddy, I do not think you will need to worry." And he never did give us cause to worry.

Young people, you have an eternity to live. Did you ever stop to think how long eternity is? Oh, if you can just get over Fool's Hill and not get caught—if you can beat the devil to his job! Do you know that your parents are praying for you, the Church prays for you, and the Lord cannot answer these prayers better than through you?

Let me just say this to the boys: You could be the instruments in the hand of the Lord in answering the prayers of your loved ones and the parents of girls if you would protect their virtue even with your own lives. Girls could answer the prayers of the parents of the boys if they would just use their influence to protect them against the temptations that could mar their lives.

You remember that Alma, in talking to his son Corianton, told him his departure from the way of virtue was the greatest sin in this world next to the shedding of innocent blood or denying the Holy Ghost. (Alma 39:5.)

Not one of our wonderful young people would ever want to be guilty of a sin as grievous as that. One way to be sure that you never are is to be sure that you never engage in petting.

I would not want you to get the wrong idea! I did kiss my wife "good night" when I was sure we were going to marry, but I did not kiss her like you see in these movies that move every passion in a man or a woman. I would kiss her like I would kiss my mother or my sister. Now, boys, if you never kiss your girl with more emphasis and enthusiasm than you kiss your mother goodbye, you will never lose your virtue. If you will just remember that one thing, it will be all you will have to do to make sure that you never engage in petting. It is worth it! You could not buy it with all the wealth in the world.

I had a young girl in to see me not long ago, and she said, "Brother Richards, is there any way in this world that I can get my virtue back again?" I said, "No, it is gone forever." I know that we believe in forgiveness of sin, but it is so much better if the Lord does not have to forgive us and if we do not have that to worry about because we keep ourselves clean.

When I was a young man out in the little country town where I was reared, one of the brethren was called to speak. (We had a lot of the old, long-bearded men who used to preach from Genesis to Revelation—we could go home and tell our parents what they preached about without even waiting to hear them. This time we had something new.) This man brought a two-by-twelve plank, a sack of ten-penny nails, and a hammer. He drove all of those nails in that plank, and then he pulled them out, one by one. He said, "You see, they were there, but they are not there anymore. However, the holes are there." He then preached a sermon on the holes, and I want to tell you that made an impression upon me I never forgot. I can now go back to the little town where

I was reared as a boy, and I can talk to the mothers and the grandparents about how to rear their children and their grandchildren without being afraid that two old women of my age would be sitting down in the corner of the chapel with their heads together, saying, "Ah, but you had ought to have known him when *we* knew him as a boy!" That would be the holes in the plank.

None of us ever know what is ahead of us—what kind of a position we may be called to. When I used to come in from the country and visit with my Uncle Stephen and his boys over in Sugarhouse, I can tell you to this day one of the lessons that I learned in that Sunday School. If somebody had told me that someday I would be the bishop of that ward, I would have thought that was the craziest thing that anybody could say. But I did become the bishop of the ward, and from there on I have had a few positions in the Church. You don't know what is ahead of you. You can afford to forgo the apparent pleasure or whatever you call it that you get out of petting, for if you never engage in petting, you will never need to worry about losing your virtue. You will be worthy of any position the Lord has in store for you throughout the eternities to come if you will just keep close to him and his church, and keep yourself clean.

Sometime ago I was invited to talk to a high priests quorum in my own stake. The president of the quorum wanted to pick me up. I said, "Oh, no, I will meet you at the church." "No," he said, "I want to pick you up." Well, I learned a long time ago that if you let someone do something for you, he gets to like you better and you like him better too. You cannot love people you do not know. So I let him pick me up.

On the way to the church, he told me this story. He said, "I was driving down Main Street one night during the war [he worked for Salt Lake City] and I saw a boy in uniform in the hands of a wicked woman.

Something said to me, 'You rescue that boy!' So I parked my car and I went over and took that boy by the arm, and I said 'You come with me.' She said, 'Oh, no, you don't—he is mine.' I told her, 'There is a policeman on that corner that will take care of you.' "

He got no further resistance. He drove that boy around until he had sobered him up, took him to a hotel, paid his night's lodging, and left him his calling card. In a few weeks he received a letter from the mother of the boy back in Virginia which read like this: "Why you did what you did for my boy, I cannot understand. He was never in the hands of a wicked woman before. He had never been drunk before, but that day I prayed for him as I had never prayed before." You see, the only way the Lord could answer that prayer was to put it into the heart of this man to stop and rescue that boy!

I was down in Mexico some years ago, and a doctor who has since been a mission president told me this little story. He said that there was a boy in the town whose mother was a widow. That boy wanted to go on a mission until it just hurt so much that he asked his mother if she would fast with him for forty-eight hours, that the Lord would open the way for him to go on a mission. They fasted and they prayed. As they were about to close their fast, a knock came at the door and one of the brethren came in and said, "Sister So-and-so, you know, I have been thinking that I ought to be doing something for the great missionary cause of the Church. I do not have a son to send on a mission, so how would you like to let me support your boy in the field?"

That boy had faith, and with his faith and the help of his mother and their fasting, the Lord moved upon that man to go to that home and offer to send that boy on a mission. Now in that same sense, all boys can be instruments in the hands of the Lord to answer the prayers of girls' parents at home in sending them back to them sweet and clean. And girls can be the instruments in the hands of the Lord in sending the boys back the same.

Some girls are sort of clinging vines—they cannot keep their hands off from the boys. I had a mother come to see me who told about her boy who had always wanted to go on a mission. He saw all of his buddies go on missions, but he went out with a girl who just could not leave him alone. So they got into trouble. He had wanted to study medicine, but now it got to the point where she did not even want to support him in his schoolwork. Finally he said to her, "I hate you. I hate you more than anybody that lives." All this came about because she just would not let him alone until it had ruined his life and his ambitions and the things that he expected to accomplish in life. We never know what the end is going to be, and so we cannot afford to play with fire. If we do, we are liable to get burned.

Some time ago I read a statement in one of our Salt Lake newspapers that told about a young man who had committed suicide. The report said he was discouraged, but his father told me that the real reason he committed suicide was because his body was being wasted away from venereal disease from immoral living. You see, we pay the price, for it comes to us in one way or another.

During World War II, as I was on my way back from LaGrande, Oregon, I was in the men's dressing room on the train (this was before we traveled by plane) and there was a doctor in the uniform of his country who was just returning from the islands of the Pacific. Something was said about the Mormons, and he started in on a tirade against the Mormons and Salt Lake City that was the filthiest thing I had ever heard (I have never repeated it to anybody). When he was talked out, I turned to him and said, "Doctor, it may interest you to know that my home is in Salt Lake City and that I am a member of the Mormon Church, and I *know* that you do not know what you are talking about. I am going to tell you why. I have a magazine here in my briefcase with an article from the office of the Surgeon General of the

United States, telling the percentage of men and boys in the armed forces, married and unmarried, who are immoral during the time of their service."

Then I said, "I have a letter here from the superintendent of a hospital in Salt Lake City indicating that they had given the Wasserman test to 7,000 Mormon boys. Out of those 7,000 tests, they had found only three that had any trace of impure blood—and they tell me that can happen even if you have not been immoral." I continued, "Doctor, I challenge you to duplicate a record like that anywhere in this world, outside of a Mormon community! You can't do it, and you know you can't."

"Well," he said, "I will have to say this: Over in the islands of the Pacific, everybody lets their hair down."

"But," the doctor continued, "there was one little Mormon girl there from Salt Lake City that no man could touch. She said, 'I left my home clean, and I am going to return the way I left it.' "

I have never met that girl, but in my heart I have asked God to bless her and her posterity. I thought of the experience of Joseph who was sold into Egypt. You remember how Potiphar's wife tried to seduce him until he fled from her, upon one occasion, and she grabbed his cloak. He knew that she would use that as evidence against him and that it might mean death or imprisonment. He was imprisoned and almost put to death. But as he fled from that wicked woman, he was not thinking of the injury to his body. He said something like this, "How could I do that wicked thing and thus offend God?" (Gen. 39:7-9.) I have often thought that when the patriarch tells us that we are descendants of Joseph who was sold into Egypt, how honored we should feel to think that we are descended from that noble man. In days to come, the sons and daughters of that little girl in the South Pacific who said, "I left my home clean, and I am going to return the way I left it," will arise and call her blessed even to the latest generation.

Speaking of the holes in the plank, some years ago, I was riding on a train in Idaho. I thought everyone else had left the train when in came the brakeman and sat down by me. He said, "Aren't you Brother Richards from Salt Lake?" I said, "Yes, sir." Then this was his story: He had filled a mission; he had kept himself sweet and clean; he had married a woman whom he thought was clean—she even got a temple recommend by not telling the truth. He said, "I discovered that she was unclean when I married her. What am I going to do? Am I going to stick with her and be loyal to my marriage vows? Can I trust her to plant in the hearts of my children the standards that were planted in my heart by my parents? Tell me, Brother Richards, what must I do?" Well, there are the holes in the plank that you have to live with after it all happens.

Some years ago I read in a magazine a little article called "The Mistake." It told about a young couple, who, after the night of their high school graduation, went out together and made a mistake. Satan whispered in their ears that everything could be covered up, but they found through their own experience that this was not true. I copied the last paragraph of the article; here it is:

" 'I am sorry, darling, for everything.'

" 'Don't be,' he said. 'We are in it together, and we will get out of it together.'

"But later upstairs, long after he was asleep, long after the house and the street outside were quiet, Janet turned her head and buried her face in the pillow to stifle the sound the sobs made, because it was not true, as people had said, that you could make a mistake and pay for it. You make a mistake and then you settle down as she and Ken were doing to live with it for all the rest of your life."

This comes back to what Brother Ballard said: "If we could just help our young folks over 'Fool's Hill.' "

I had a couple come in my office and this was their

story: Before they married she had had an affair and she had even given birth to a child out of wedlock. She did not tell her husband when she married him. He found it out when they already had three children. When he came he said, "Well, now, Brother Richards, what are we going to do? Can I ever forgive her enough to stay with her and be true to my marriage vows?"

Then I thought, "Isn't it pitiful that just for that brief period of courtship the girl should have made a mistake like that!" She might have had an eternity of happiness with her companion if she had not made the mistake. That was one of the holes in the plank that the preacher told us about when I was a boy. I hope that none of you will ever get any holes in your plank.

When I was president of the mission back in the South, we converted a very wonderful woman—a school-teacher. She had loaned a book to one of her students and when it came back it had one of our Articles of Faith cards in it. It impressed her so much that she wanted to know more about the Church, and she was soon a member of the Church—a wonderful woman.

I met her later at a conference, and at the close of the meeting she came up and said, "President Richards, I am going to get married. What do you think of that?"

I said, "I think it is wonderful. Do I know him?"

"No," she said.

I said, "Is he a member of the Church?"

"No, he is not a member of the Church."

Down there I didn't dare tell her that she shouldn't marry out of the Church. I didn't know where she would find a boy in the Church, except our Mormon missionaries—and we had "hands off" signs hanging all over them. So I said, "Well, now, there is something I would like to say to you. You are a sweet, clean, lovely woman, and you could no more find happiness with an unclean man than you could mix oil and water—they don't mix together. In your courtship you will know whether he would take advantage of you if you would let him. You will know whether he is clean or not. Another thing, he must be a prayerful man because, as wicked as this world is today, I wouldn't trust any man to be true to his wife and kiddies if he didn't believe in God and that some day he will have to answer to God for his life here upon this earth."

I said, "He must be willing to let you rear your children in the Church, for, knowing as you do that we have the truth restored from heaven—a marvelous work and a wonder—you would be a very unhappy woman if you had children and could not rear them in the Church. If he measures up, let me know when he joins the Church."

Well, I didn't see her until I went back about four months later for a conference. At the close of the meeting she came up and stretched out her hand to shake hands with me.

I shook hands and said, "Name, please."

"Oh, I am still Miss So-and-so," she said.

I said, "What became of the marriage?"

"He didn't come up to your specifications!"

She had had the courage to turn him down.

I told that story over in Alabama a short time after that, and at the close of the meeting a little seventeen-year-old girl came up to me and said, "President Richards, if I had heard that story six months ago I would have been an unmarried woman today."

It did not take that little seventeen-year-old Mormon girl long to find out that she could not find happiness with an unclean man.

Some time ago a young man called me and said, "Is this Bishop Richards?"

I said, "Yes, sir."

"Well," he said, "I am in trouble."

I said, "What is your trouble?"

He said, "I have been keeping company with a girl

for three years and she heard you preach the other night, and now she won't go out with me anymore."

I said, "Why won't she?"

He said, "Because I am not active in the Church."

I said, "Good for her! I am glad to know that there is at least one girl in Israel who would listen to an old man like me. Now, what are you going to do about it?"

He said, "What can I do?"

I said, "Get active in the Church and then go back to her."

He said, "How can I?"

I said, "You go and talk to your bishop and if he doesn't help you, you come back to me."

He hasn't been back, so I guess the bishop helped him out.

I picked up this little story down in Los Angeles when Sister Richards and I were there just a few years ago. We met a young lady who was the daughter of one of the families who lived in our stake when I was the stake president. She went to BYU to go to school, and she started keeping company with boy who had been baptized in the Church but didn't do anything in the Church. I don't know whether he was at the "Y" or whether she just picked him up in Provo. Anyway, when he got serious with her, she said, "I will never marry a man who does not honor his priesthood and do his duty in the Church. I am going to be able to point to my children and say, 'You follow your father.'"

He was not willing to pay the price, so their courtship ended there. (My, I admire a girl who knows what it takes to find happiness!) In a little while she started keeping company with another young man, and finally they were engaged and their engagement was announced in the paper. A friend of this first suitor sent a copy of the announcement to him back in Chicago. When he read it, he called up this girl all the way to Los Angeles. He said, "I can't live without you. If you will just call off that engagement and give me another chance, I will do anything and everything you ever ask me to do in the Church."

To make the story short, when we met them down there in Los Angeles, he was a counselor in the bishopric. I have checked on him since, and he is now the bishop of his ward.

I tell girls that "you can get a man to do anything in this world if you will just use the gifts and the charms with which the Lord has blessed you, and if you will keep yourselves sweet and clean, so they can admire you. And you can live in the clouds—you know that little song in *South Pacific* that if you don't have dreams, your dreams can't come true." My wife and I—and she is an angel— I don't mind telling you that I have never heard an un- clean word or thought from her in her life, and we have lived together for over sixty years. We lived in the clouds. We planned during our courtship the kind of a home we wanted and the family that we wanted and how we wanted to raise them and so forth. Thank God that they are all active in the Church and sweet and lovely today.

My wife wouldn't like me to say this, but I like it. When we had been married thirty-five years, I said, "Mother, what do you think we will be doing in thirty- five million years from today?"

She said, "Where did you get that crazy idea? It makes me tired to think of it."

I said, "You believe in eternal life, don't you? In the Book of Mormon we read that 'time is measured only to man, but with God there is not such a thing as time—it is one eternal round.' The Prophet Joseph illus- trated this by taking a ring. He said that when you cut it, there is a beginning and there is an end. As long as you do not cut it, there is no beginning and no end." Then I said: "Mother, if you believe that, you and I ought to be pretty well acquainted with each other in thirty-five million years from today."

I have a little talk on how long eternity is that makes thirty-five million years look just like the snap of your fingers. We cannot comprehend it nor understand it. If we could, do you think we would let a few years of courtship stand in the way of our becoming kings and priests unto the most high God, to rule and reign with him forever over our own kingdoms to be projected throughout the eternities to come? And yet many of us might sacrifice our right to such a privilege.

The Lord said, through the apostle Paul, that our bodies are tabernacles of the Holy Spirit, and he that defileth the body, him shall God destroy. The Lord has given us the great principle to permit us to be parents, to raise a family, and to have a kingdom, and he doesn't expect us to abuse it.

I like this poem from Ella Wheeler Wilcox, who was a great writer:

"It is easy enough to be virtuous
When nothing tempts you to stray,
When without and within no voice of sin
Is luring your soul away.
But it is only a negative virtue 'til it is tried by fire
And the soul that is worth the blessings of earth
Is the soul that resists desire."

I do not know why the Lord made temptation such a strong thing in a person's life, but don't kid yourself that you are the only one who has it. Temptation comes to all of us unless we are unfortunately born, and triumph is the only way for us to prove that we are worthy to stand in the presence of God the Eternal Father; Jesus said, "For blessed are the pure in heart, for they shall see God."

Remember this little statement from the Doctrine and Covenants: "Let virtue garnish thy thoughts unceasingly; then shall thy confidence wax strong in the presence of God and the doctrines of the priesthood shall distil upon thy soul as the dews from heaven." Then he goes on to tell us all the things that might be ours.

With all my heart and soul I say to you, as President McKay said, "I think our young people are the finest young people in all this world." With all the power of the priesthood that I bear, I pray God to bless all of our youth and preserve them from mistakes that would cause them great sorrow in life and prevent their having any holes that will worry them all the rest of their lives.

You boys give your lives, if you need to, to protect the virtue of girls; and you girls give your lives, if necessary, to protect the virtue of boys. I promise you, as a servant of the living God, that in the eternities to come you will thank God from the bottom of your hearts if you follow that advice. If you never indulge in petting, you will never need to worry about losing your virtue or the promises of God that await the faithful of his children.

2

"Choose You This Day Whom Ye Will Serve"

Jesus, the great teacher, in order to help men choose the proper course of life, the road that would bring them eternal happiness, said:

"Enter ye in at the strait gate: for wide is the gate, and broad is the way, that leadeth to destruction, and many there be which go in thereat:

"Because strait is the gate, and narrow is the way, which leadeth unto life, and few there be that find it." (Matthew 7:13-14.)

To every individual comes the responsibility of choosing his way: the wide and broad way that leadeth to destruction, or the strait and narrow way which leadeth unto life—and, I should like to add, to respect, achievement, and happiness.

With this in mind, I call attention to three of many problems with which our youth are faced. The first I mention is the growing practice of profanity. Our young people are particularly susceptible to it. During the war many communications were received from men in the armed forces containing alarming statements such as this:

"I have been amazed, astonished, and disgusted at some of the things I have seen and heard in the six weeks that I have been with Uncle Sam. I never expected to hear the swearing and vile talk that I have heard, not in a so-called Christian country. Where have the parents been to let a generation grow up so morally wrong?"

And to this question might be added: Where have the teachers of our youth been, and have we of the clergy done all that we might have done?

The Lord has never rescinded the commandment that he gave to Israel of old through his great prophet Moses:

"Thou shalt not take the name of the Lord thy God in vain; for the Lord will not hold him guiltless that taketh his name in vain." (Exodus 20:7.)

Have we as parents taught our children this great commandment in sincerity, so they may have reason to feel their parents believe the Lord meant what he said? It is difficult to understand how a person may truly approach God in prayer, seeking a blessing at his hand, and at the same time be so disrespectful as to take his name in vain. During the dark days of the Civil War, Lincoln issued an order to the Army and Navy that contained the following statement: "The discipline and character of the National Forces should not suffer, nor the cause they defend be imperiled by the profanation of the Sabbath Day or the name of the Most High."

We are told that he went "so far as to admonish a certain general, who was addicted to the habit of profanity, to abandon the habit himself and to use his authority to discourage it among the soldiers."

Profanity is incompatible with reverence. Surely at this critical time in our nation's history, when we need the sustaining help of God, we should see that we do not offend him by reason of our language. I appeal to our young people everywhere to hold in reverence the sacred name of Deity, so that they may walk acceptably before the Lord and so that should there come a time in their lives when they need his sustaining help they may go to him with good conscience and call upon him with faith that he will hear their plea.

I now pass to a second problem confronting our youth, and that is the indiscriminate and intemperate use of alcoholic beverages. A short time ago I was asked to speak to the inmates of a state penitentiary. At the close of the meeting quite a number remained to discuss their problems with me, and I was invited to return and talk to the Alcoholics Anonymous group. I listened to the stories of some of this group. The leader, a comparatively young man, said something like this: "I thank God for the privilege of being in this institution." I was surprised at what he said, but he went on to explain: "Before I came here I was no good to myself, to my family, or my country. I was just no good—period. But now I have hope that when I leave here I will be worth something to somebody."

Can you imagine a man having followed the "broad" road so far that he could thank God for the privilege of being behind prison bars in the hope that he might be able to extirpate himself, and again be able to plant his feet on the strait and narrow way "which leadeth unto life"?

One cannot go among such men without having his heart touched with great sympathy for them and their families. You think of all the factors that brought them to this status. You think of blighted hopes and aspirations. You wonder if perhaps their parents set them along this path by reason of a bad example. As you look at a man helpless, no longer master of himself, you think of the man who induced him to take his first drink.

The Lord has made it clear that our bodies are the tabernacles of our spirits. We cannot abuse and offend the body without offending our Creator. To our young people I should like to say that we live in a time when competition, whether in war or in peace, demands clear minds and steady hearts. It becomes each of us to refrain from those substances which in any way might impair our abilities or which might place us in a position where we no longer would feel that we were on the Lord's side.

I mention one other matter with concern in my heart for our young people. It is encouraging to find men and women in all walks of life who are seriously disturbed about our moral standards. I state my case with a quotation from the *Woman's Home Companion* of September 1949, under the heading "Is Chastity Outmoded?"

"Today we talk about sex with an unembarrassed frankness that would have filled our grandparents with amazement and horror. This new liberty of speech has its counterpart in behavior. In many circles the traditional restraints in sex conduct are considered stuffy and out of fashion. Chastity, say modern people, is outmoded."

People may have changed their thinking, but God has not changed. His laws are eternal. Truth is eternal. If we will save our civilization, it will be because we return to an observance of God's laws.

The Lord gave unto ancient Israel the commandment: "Thou shalt not commit adultery." (Exodus 20:14.) And the Savior put his stamp of approval upon this commandment and added:

"Ye have heard that it was said by them of old time, Thou shalt not commit adultery:

"But I say unto you, That whosoever looketh on a woman to lust after her hath committed adultery with her already in his heart." (Matthew 5:27-28.)

In the light of such a statement, surely no Christian can feel that chastity is outmoded.

An American prophet, Alma, taught his son Corianton that adultery was "most abominable above all sins save it be the shedding of innocent blood or denying the Holy Ghost," that "wickedness never was happiness," and that "no unclean thing can inherit the kingdom of God."

I am happy to represent a people who have taught

such from the beginning of our history. We are striving to teach our children, as our parents have taught us, that there is no double standard of morality and virtue in the sight of God; that he expects every man to protect his virtue and that of every woman, even though it might cost him his life to do so.

During World War II, a doctor who was returning from service in the islands of the Pacific said to me: "In the islands everyone lets his standards down." Then he added, "But there was a young nurse there from your community whom no man could touch. She said, 'I left my home clean, and I am going to return the way I left.'" It was her faith in God and her respect for the teachings of her parents and church that gave her the courage to choose the strait and narrow way, "which leadeth unto life."

Surely her children and her children's children unto the latest generation will call her blessed for the nobility of her soul. When I think of this girl, and thousands of others throughout the land like her, I compare them with Joseph who was sold into Egypt by his brothers and who later became the savior of his father's family. Potiphar's wife tried repeatedly to seduce him, but as he resisted her and fled from her he said: ". . . how then can I do this great wickedness, and sin against God?" (Genesis 39:9.)

"How glorious is he who lives the chaste life. He walks unfearful in the full glare of the noonday sun, for he is without moral infirmity. He can be reached by no shafts of base calumny, for his armour is without flaw. His virtue cannot be challenged by any just accuser, for he lives above reproach. His cheek is never blotched with shame, for he is without hidden sin. He is honored and respected by all mankind, for he is beyond their censure. He is loved by the Lord, for he stands without blemish. The exaltations of eternities await his coming." (Message of the First Presidency, October 1942.)

And so I plead with the youth, keep yourselves clean.

Virtue may be old-fashioned, but it is the foundation on which great characters, great families, and great nations are established; and without it decay is inevitable.

I have some fear that we, the spiritual leaders of the people, in our interpretation of the word of the Lord with respect to the great principles of repentance and forgiveness of sin, have so emphasized the principle of forgiveness that an attitude of complacency is growing among us based on the assumption that if we sin a little we may be forgiven to go on our way without loss. I am inclined to believe that we are in need of placing greater emphasis on abstinence from sin and less on forgiveness, for God has not abrogated the law that as ye sow, so shall ye reap.

And so, I should like to urge our youth to resist the temptation to profane the name of Deity, that they may be blameless before the Lord; to keep their bodies free from those substances which will impede their progress; and to live according to the laws of virtue, that generations to come may call them blessed.

Finally, a word to those who teach and lead the youth of the land: Our great responsibility is to teach the youth, with the full power of example and precept, that the Lord desires that his children should be happy, and that the way of happiness is righteousness. If we are remiss in this responsibility, God will not hold us guiltless.

The prophet Joshua, in speaking to the hosts of Israel, said: ". . . choose you this day whom ye will serve: . . . but as for me and my house, we will serve the Lord." (Joshua 24:15.)

God help us to choose the right and to assist others so to do.

3

Laying the Foundation for Eternal Marriage

Some time ago a young lady called and made an appointment with me. When she came in, she sat and wept a little and said, "I guess I am jittery."

"Well," I said, "I have seen young people jittery before; now do not let that worry you. I will wait until you get over it."

Then she said, "I do not believe there is much in this world for us young people these days. All the boys are going to war, and we stay around home. Just what is there to live for anyway?"

I said, "Well, have you ever stopped to look at the other side of the story? You remember the story of the two buckets in the well. As one came up, it said, 'This surely is a cold and dreary world. No matter how many times I come up full I always have to go down empty.' And the other bucket laughed and said, 'With me it is different; no matter how many times I go down empty, I always come up full.' " I said, "You have not looked at the other side of the story. If you actually knew as God knows, you would know that you are living in the most desirable period of all the world's history from the beginning of time up to the present."

The Lord said, in a revelation to the Prophet Joseph,

that many are called but few are chosen. And why are they not chosen? Because they walk in darkness in the light of the noonday sun. The noonday sun is the brightest period of the day. There has never been a time as far as we know when there has been as much revealed truth available to man upon the earth as there is at the present time. Nor has there been a time when there were such comforts to be enjoyed as we now enjoy. The average home, even out on the farms as you go through the country, enjoys comforts and blessings and privileges such as kings and queens did not enjoy only a hundred years ago. I think of the time when I went on my first mission to Holland. They were still cutting grain with a sickle and a scythe and riding in streetcars drawn by horses, and they had no electric lights. For the first year I was there I went to bed and shaved by candlelight. We had no central heating plant, practically no telephones, no radios, and no television. They then lived a simple life, and that was only a few years ago. Today we have everything.

Now, when we read the scriptures we understand why, because the Lord said to his prophet Isaiah that darkness would cover the earth, and gross darkness the people. It is not because men today are so much more intelligent in and of themselves that the world has changed so much; but the Lord said that in the last days he would pour out his spirit upon all flesh, and young men should dream dreams, and old men should see visions, and so forth. We live in the day when that period of darkness has been dispelled. The Lord revealed unto Paul the mysteries of his will, that in the dispensation of the fulness of time he would bring together in Christ all that is in heaven above and that is in the earth beneath. My interpretation of that is, all things that God created in the beginning for the use of man upon the earth should ultimately be brought forth for his use in this dispensation in which we live.

I pointed out some of these things to this little girl who was jittery and did not think there was anything worth living for. I told her that it was the greatest privilege that ever came to anyone to be able to come upon this earth in this day and time. I reminded her that when John the Revelator saw the angel flying in the midst of heaven with the everlasting gospel to be preached to all those who dwell upon the earth, he had another message, and that was, "Fear God, and give glory to him, for the hour of his judgment is come." So the two go hand in hand—the restoration of the truth and the hour of the Lord's judgment—and that is why we have wars and contentions. In the words of the Savior, there should be wars such as had not been known from the beginning and should not be known until the end, until, were it not for the elect's sake, no flesh should remain upon the earth.

Now the thing for us to do is to make sure that we understand these things and that we understand and appreciate the things that God has prepared for us so that we will be found walking in his ways and keeping his commandments.

If you stop to think about it, possibly the most important thing in the life of each member of the Church is whom he is going to marry, because eternity is a long time, and when we marry, if we do what the Lord wants us to do, we will remain married forever and that is a long time to live with one individual. Yes, eternity is a long time, but it is God's time, and this probation here upon this earth is a preparation for it.

I have observed a good many men and women. I know some men who have been very successful as young men, and then they marry someone who is beneath their standards spiritually and otherwise, and little by little they lose their interest in the Church because they did not marry their equals (in a religious way) who would uphold and sustain them and help them to achieve the things that they thought were worthwhile as young men in life. And I have seen men who were great leaders marry women who lacked the ability to organize a home and take care of their children and raise them the way they ought to be raised, so that today some of them have none or few of their children active in the Church. I have now come to feel that this matter of marriage is one of the most important things one will ever face. So I thought I would remind you tonight of the words of the apostle Paul when he said, "Be ye not unequally yoked together with unbelievers: for what fellowship hath righteousness with unrighteousness? and what communion hath light with darkness?" (2 Corinthians 6:14.) Be ye not unequally yoked together. We have too many divorces in the Church.

I remember as a boy when I used to take the girls out. I went with nice girls—at least I thought they were nice. They were good-looking, some of them, but on the way home I would say to myself, "Well, I had a good time, but I wonder why I can't feel like I would like to marry her." Now, I don't think we ought to have to force ourselves into feeling that we want to marry a girl. I don't think we ought to marry a girl just because she is pretty or because she can dance well. I think that there ought to be some equality in our lives and in our way of thinking and in our objectives and our ideals and our ambitions and the things that we want to make of ourselves so that there is cooperation in the home. When women marry without that, often they are very unhappy, and if men marry without it, they are also very unhappy. So I think it is important to find equality.

Do not be impressed just because a person is a good musician or has some special talent or because there is something about his or her makeup that seems to fit your makeup, so that you think somewhat in the same channels and you have somewhat the same ambitions.

Let's look at what Moses said on the subject of marriage. He said, speaking of the fact that the children of Israel should not marry the heathens, "Neither shalt thou make marriages with them; thy daughter thou shalt not give unto his son, nor his daughter shalt thou take unto thy son. For they will turn away thy son from following me that they may serve other gods: so will the anger of the Lord be kindled against you, and destroy thee suddenly." (Deuteronomy 7:3-4.)

That was the Lord speaking through Moses to the children of Israel, telling them that they should not marry out of their own groups. I have always said that good Methodists should marry good Methodists and good Baptists should marry good Baptists and good Catholics should marry good Catholics and good Mormons should marry good Mormons, because if you marry out of your own group, your companion may wean your heart away from following after God, and if so the Lord says that "the anger of the Lord" shall "be kindled against you." I will give you an illustration of that. I remember a little woman who used to be my Sunday School teacher. She married a member of another church, and he won her over and she became active in that church and raised her children in it. All my life, every time I have seen her, I have felt a hurt inside of me to think that my Sunday School teacher had been led away to worship another God. That is the spirit of this command that comes from Moses.

I want to refer to a few words of the Lord from the eighty-eighth section of the Doctrine and Covenants: "For intelligence cleaveth unto intelligence; wisdom receiveth wisdom; truth embraceth truth; virtue loveth virtue; light cleaveth unto light; mercy hath compassion on mercy and claimeth its own. . . ." (Verse 40.) If you get the meaning of this revelation, the Lord lets us know that like should seek like. It is just his way of saying "birds of a feather should flock together."

One good sister came to me once and said she wanted to divorce her husband. I said, "Why do you want to divorce him? You must love him. At least you loved him when you married him, or you would not have married him."

"Well," she said, "President Richards, I loved him for what I thought he was, and I loath him for what he is."

That is what I mean about "virtue loveth virtue" and "truth embraces truth; wisdom receiveth wisdom," and "light cleaveth unto light." You see how the Lord has tried to warn us against entanglement with associates and associations that have different standards than we have. And so my admonition is that you seek those of your kind, that you are not so anxious to get married that you will marry any young gentleman or lady who comes along, but that you will make sure that you are right.

I have a son-in-law who is an attorney in Salt Lake City and has had to get a good many divorces for people, including some for young people who have been married only a very short time and find they are mismated and don't want to live with each other any longer. He said he thought the greatest mistake that is made in marriage occurs because people act too hastily; they just see someone and they fall for them. But such short acquaintance doesn't wear; it doesn't last; it doesn't endure after they know each other a little better. In other words, just because a girl is pretty or the boy has a nice car and they can dance well together doesn't necessarily mean that, when they assume all the responsibilities of a home and children, and the children need attention, and trouble comes, those glittering things that appeal at first glance are going to be the things that will be lasting and bring eternal happiness.

Now, take your time when you are going to mate. When you are going to live together for all eternity, be sure that you have found someone who is your equal.

Another thing: When you have been raised entirely

differently, it is quite a gamble you take. In other words, when a boy who is poor financially, who has never enjoyed anything much of this world's goods, and has been raised in rather a humble home, marries a girl who has been raised in a home where she has known all the luxuries and the comforts of life, it is hard for her to settle down and be satisfied with what he can afford to give her. You have heard the story of the girl who said she would follow her husband anywhere he wanted to take her and the minister replied, "Well, that is all right, but will you be satisfied to settle down and live in a $10 flat and raise his children for him?" That was a different question.

We live in a day of luxuries. It is like they say, "It isn't so much the high cost of living as it is the cost of high living." We seem to want everything.

I married a young couple in the temple a year ago, or a little over, and six months later the boy came in to see me in a peck of trouble. He had tried to buy everything he could on time. He had borrowed from one loan agency and then another, and another, and then to try to get himself out of trouble he had borrowed again on the same furniture without telling the loan agency that he had already mortgaged it, so he was standing in line to be prosecuted and sent to the penitentiary. When I suggested that he sell his auto, he didn't think they could get along without it.

I used to advise the missionaries as I released them as a mission president not to get in debt like that. I said, "We read about the day when the Israelites were in bondage and captivity to the Egyptians, and some of our own people get in almost that same condition when they just borrow and borrow and buy and buy things that they can't afford to pay for." So my counsel is to try and live within your means so that you will not have such things to worry about. I think you can be happier if you live on love without debt.

I have talked to young people about being careful in selecting their companions. And do you know what they think? They always think I am talking to the other fellow. I had a girl come to see me at my office and she said, "Brother Richards, I heard you talk about not marrying out of the Church. The man I was in love with seemed to have interest in the Church. I just knew that what you said would not apply to me, and so I married him. We have been married six months and now it is all over. He has walked out on me, and I don't know where he has gone." We always think the preacher is talking to the other fellow.

I was attending a conference in Chicago a few years ago. There was a young woman sitting on about the third row back with a baby in her arms. She came up after the meeting and said, "Brother Richards, I would like to meet you." And I said, "I would like to meet you." Then she started to weep, and I said, "I'll bet you are a western girl, aren't you?" She couldn't talk; she just nodded. I said, "And you married out of the Church?" I got another nod. And I said, "And your husband doesn't like you to come to church?" I got another nod. And then I said, "And you are homesick—homesick for your church and for your people." With that she dropped down on the front bench and wept like her little heart would break.

You know, you can't run away from God. You can't run away from these things that are sacred and dear to you. And there are many, many unhappy girls in this world who have married under conditions like that, and they have not found the happiness they thought they would find.

In Mesa, Arizona, I spent a week between conferences and visited with the people at the temple. A group of Primary teachers from one of the neighboring towns brought in a group of children from the Primary to be baptized for the dead on Saturday afternoon. While the ordinances were being performed we had a testimony meeting with these Primary teachers, and almost every one of them as they responded said with tears in their eyes that the greatest desire of their hearts was for the day to come when their husbands would be worthy to take them to the temple and have them and their children sealed to them for eternity. Their husbands could buy them automobiles, they could take them on trips, they could buy them nice homes, they could buy them pretty dresses, but they could not buy their way into the kingdom of God. They could not buy their way into the holy temple, to receive the blessings the Lord has in store for the faithful that would make life and eternal life a lovely and a sweet thing for them. So it will pay for you to seek your own kind. Virtue loveth virtue. Wisdom receiveth wisdom. Find your equal, even if you have to wait a little longer to get married.

I would like to mention one other thing. I feel that in this day when young people prepare themselves so well educationally for the battle of life, there needs to be some way to get a little more training in home building. It just happens that I was raised in a good home. My mother and father never quarreled. I thought all I would have to do would be to find a pretty girl and marry her, and it would be heaven on earth. And then I went away from home to attend school. I boarded in different homes, and it certainly was an eye opener to me. I found that not all men and women live together as did my father and mother. Some of them fought like cats and dogs, and I could not imagine how they could still live with each other and carry on as they did. I left a number of boardinghouses just for that very reason.

I boarded in one home of a newly married couple, and I was at school and the husband was working. I would get home before he did in the evening. She would be perfectly lovely with me until she would hear his footsteps coming up the old board walk; then she would look at the clock, and if he were twenty minutes late, she would close up like a clam. She didn't have any greeting for him when he came. She didn't kiss him. She didn't put her arms around him. And one night when he didn't get home until around ten o'clock, she really got excited. They had a long way to go to learn how to enjoy and appreciate each other.

I came to feel from those experiences that an irritable man or an irritable woman is about as objectionable a creature as I know anything about. I feel that if a man or a woman has an irritable disposition, they ought to get down on their knees and ask the Lord to give them strength to overcome, just as much as they would ask for help of the Lord to overcome the habit of liquor or tobacco, so that the home can be a happy place in which to live, where the spirit of the Lord can be present, where there is no bickering, no quarreling, and no nagging.

I am going to suggest another thing to the girls. I used to be in the real estate business. We used to go around every Tuesday morning and inspect the houses that were listed during the week. We had quite a sales force, so we had quite a few houses to inspect. We had one man on our sales force who had worked for a furniture company. Every time we would come out of a house he could tell us just what the furniture was worth. We had one man who had formerly been a piano salesman. He could tell me what the musical instruments were worth. But this was the thing that impressed me most. We made our visits in the forenoon and when I came out of many of those homes I said to myself, "I thank the Lord I don't have to live there." Some of the women would go around like scrubwomen: hair not combed and dresses not clean or attractive. Girls, don't you ever do it. After you get married, your husband may work in an office, where the girls come all trimmed up every day. They haven't anything you haven't, if you will take care of what you have, but if you let yourselves degenerate to the point of a scrubwoman, he won't think very much of you, and his eyes will go out to other women. So you let him buy you the clothes to keep you looking decent, and have nice tidy dresses to wear around the home when you are doing your homework. And if you can't afford to buy them readymade, then learn how to make them yourselves.

Sister Richards and I happen to have a few apartments where we have had some lovely girls stay. You would be surprised with the difference in girls and how they keep up apartments. Some of them let them go so slovenly and so dirty. And then you think, "Boy, wait until a husband gets that girl—what is he going to do with her? How is he going to enjoy living in a home the way she keeps house?" And other girls keep their apartments spanking clean and lovely and you can never go in and find them untidy. I am telling you girls, if you learn how to be good housekeepers, it will count a lot and go far toward making happy homes.

Another thing: many of our girls have not taken time to learn from their mothers how to cook. The old saying that "the way to a man's heart is through his stomach" is just as true today as it ever was, and when you get a women who can't do anything but open a can, I feel sorry for the man who happens to marry her. If you happen to be a girl like that, learn how to cook so that when you get a husband you will really know how to take care of him. It is a marvelous thing to have a wife who knows how to organize a home and keep it clean, and keep herself clean, and is able to spread a nice table and cook a nice meal.

I would like to leave with you the thought that marriage in the Mormon Church is different than in any church in the world. All other churches give a bill of divorcement the day of your marriage. They marry you until death do you part, which means that when one of you dies you are released from each other. Would any man have the courage to ask a woman to marry him for that short period of time when there is an eternity ahead of him, and then turn his wife over to someone else? I am sure no woman would want to raise a family for a man and then walk out on him, or have him walk out on her when there is an eternity ahead of them. Just think, God has restored his holy priesthood with the power to bind on earth, and it shall be bound in heaven. And when a marriage is performed by the power of the priesthood for those who are worthy, they commence to lay the foundation of a kingdom that will project itself into the eternal worlds. It is a marvelous thought to contemplate. When boys and girls marry in our church, if they are prepared for it, and if they know why they are marrying, and if they are marrying their equals—then they lay a foundation in that marriage that is intended not only to stand through the millennium, but throughout all eternity.

When they start with their little family they start building a kingdom that they will add to and multiply until their posterity shall become as the sands of the seashore and the stars of heaven, and they shall ultimately become gods, even the sons of gods, over their own posterity. That is what the Lord meant when he said, "I will make thee ruler over many things." So God help you to realize the importance of this matter and to prepare yourselves and to know your companions well enough before marriage so that you will never have to fear divorce, and so that your companionship will be an equality all the way through and thus be projected into the eternal worlds.

4

To Those Called Into the Service

The Savior of the world indicated that if we would be his disciples, we must be willing to forsake all that we have in this world, even to fathers and mothers, lands and herds. I do not believe men and women will forsake all they have because of any reasoning power they possess. They will do it when their souls are touched by the inspiration and power of the Spirit of the living God, which is the testimony of the truth, and then it is that men can love God more than they love anything else in this world, and hence forsake all because of their love of him.

I wish we could send our boys into the service of their country with the faith and testimony the two thousand Lamanite boys had in the time of Helaman of old when they went forth to battle and came back every man because of his faith.

We have great promises resting upon us as a people and as individuals through obeying and keeping the commandments of God. We remember the promise of the Lord that, through our observance of the Word of Wisdom, not only will we run and not be weary, walk and not faint, and receive hidden treasures of knowledge, but the destroying angel will pass by us and not slay us, even as the children of Israel.

It has been said that man's extremities are God's opportunities. We have all known that in our day should come the judgments of God, the great and dreadful day of the Lord, when all the proud, yea, all who do wickedly, should be as stubble, and that day should burn them up that it should leave them neither root nor branch. We have reason, if we have faith in God and keep his commandments, to believe that the destroying angel might pass us by as a people, and individually, and not slay us; that we might stand as a light and an ensign to the world; and that God does not forget his promises.

The counselor of a stake president in Arizona once told me of an experience he had that typifies many similar experiences of the members of the Church. He said that during the World War he was drafted. He was a young man and did not want to go to war; he felt if he ever went into action he would never return alive. So he went to the patriarch, and the patriarch said to this good brother: "You sit down at the table and write as I dictate." He laid his hands upon the head of this young man and pronounced a blessing upon him. Here are a few words from that blessing:

"Inasmuch as ye have been called to go to the defense of your country, I promise you if you will be humble and faithful and prayerful, that if your life is ever brought into danger, the way will be opened for your escape, and you will yet be given in marriage and have sons and daughters of good repute and be the means of doing much missionary work in the world."

You see, all this is conditioned upon his being faithful and prayerful and humble. It is a grand and glorious thing to bind the God of Israel to us through obeying and keeping his commandments. You will remember that he said to the Prophet Joseph: "I give unto you a new commandment, that . . . I, the Lord, am bound when ye do what I say; but when ye do not what I say, ye have no promise." (D&C 82:8, 10.) This man had a promise from the Lord that was worth living for.

I would rather have the promise of God resting upon me than that of any mortal man, just as this brother who went forth to battle for his country. Within ninety days after he received his patriarchal blessing he was in France, and in his company were 250 men to which were added thirty replacements. On the day that the Armistice was signed, at ten o'clock in the morning, there were eighty men left out of the 280, and they were told they should cease firing. The men gathered around, three of them in one hold, including this brother. Two hundred yards away he saw the army kitchen, and he invited his companions to go with him to get something to eat. They had had no supper or breakfast and were sure they would get nothing if they went, so he went alone. Just as he was being handed a stack of hot cakes, a bomb fell in the midst of the little company of eighty he had left behind and thirty of them were killed and fifty were left. When he returned, he found that the two men who were in the hole with him had had the tops of their heads blown off. The patriarch had said: "If your life is ever brought into danger, the way will be opened for your escape, and you will yet be given in marriage and have sons and daughters of good repute." He now has six children.

The Lord made also this statement regarding the judgments that are to come in these latter days: "But my disciples shall stand in holy places, and shall not be moved; but among the wicked, men shall lift up their voices and curse God and die." (D&C 45:32.)

I do not know what you think about this promise. So far as I am concerned I think the Lord did not mean that we should stand on Temple Square or in Independence, Missouri. I think he meant that his children should live such lives that wherever they stand, the ground upon which they stand should be holy and sanctified because of their presence.

You will recall that in the early days of the gathering of the Saints it was considered as good as an insurance policy when a company of Latter-day Saints embarked on a vessel crossing the Atlantic. I recall reading in my grandfather's diary of a time when the boat upon which he was sailing was in great jeopardy, so much so that the captain of the boat came to him and pleaded with him to intercede with the Lord in behalf of the boat and her passengers. My grandfather, remembering that he had been promised that he should have power over the elements, walked out on the deck of the boat and raised his hands to high heaven and rebuked the sea and the waves, and they were immediately calmed. And the appreciation of the captain of the boat was so great that he offered Grandfather the use of his private quarters during the balance of the journey.

I believe that in the experiences that are ahead of us, through the judgments that are to befall the nations, God will stand by our side; he will stand by the side of our boys even though they go forth to battle, if they take with them a testimony of the truth and the kind of faith they ought to have in the living God and in this great latter-day work.

5

A Royal Priesthood

When a boy is honored with the priesthood, he has more authority than the President of the United States, for the President's authority is derived from the people and ends with the expiration of his term of office, while the priesthood is authority from God and will endure forever.

There are various groups and organizations with which boys and men may affiliate themselves, but these are all of a temporary nature directed by their associates. The Savior has said, "Every plant that my Father hath not planted shall be rooted up," but of the priesthood we are told that it is "without beginning of days or end of years," for it is the power by which the worlds were created and the power by which the worlds will be governed even after they put on their celestial glory. And at the head of this priesthood stands the Savior of the world. Hence, those who receive the priesthood become members of an organization of authority over which he presides.

When I think that the priesthood is so important in the eyes of the Lord that he sent first John the Baptist and then Peter, James, and John, glorified heavenly persons, to confer it upon Joseph Smith and Oliver Cowdery to prepare them for the restoration of the gospel in these latter days, I wonder if our boys and men would feel any more the importance of the priesthood if it were conferred upon them directly from these heavenly messengers; and yet the authority they hold when it is properly conferred upon them by their bishops or others holding the priesthood is just the same, and it is so recognized by our Heavenly Father.

Our boys, like Father Abraham, are born heirs to the priesthood. In Abraham 3:23 we read: "These I will make my rulers; for he stood among those that were spirits, and he saw that they were good; and he said unto me: Abraham, thou art one of them; thou wast chosen before thou wast born."

No doubt Abraham understood this calling in the spirit world before he was born and was prompted thereby to make the following statements: "I sought for the blessings of the fathers, and the right whereunto I should be ordained to administer the same; . . . and desiring to receive instructions, and to keep the commandments of God, I became a rightful heir, a High Priest, holding the right belonging to the fathers.

"It was conferred upon me from the fathers; it came down from the fathers, from the beginning of time. . . .

"I sought for mine appointment unto the Priesthood according to the appointment of God unto the fathers concerning the seed." (Abraham 1:2-4.)

Our boys, like Father Abraham, are born heirs to the blessings of the fathers, and may they all receive and appreciate the same.

It was Peter of old who, addressing the saints of his day, made a declaration something like this: ". . . ye are a chosen generation, a royal priesthood, a peculiar people, an holy nation, that ye should shew forth the praises of him who hath called you out of darkness into his marvellous light." (1 Peter 2:9.)

Brethren, we are just as much a royal priesthood

today as the priesthood was in the days of Peter, and the Lord has called us forth that we might show forth the praises of him who has called us out of darkness into his marvelous light, and there is scarcely a day of our lives that we do not have an opportunity to show forth his praises because the world looks upon us and expects more of us than they do those who are not members of our church, and we can hardly stoop to do the things that others do.

To illustrate what I mean, when I was attending a stake conference in San Diego during the war, we had about thirty-five boys in uniform present. We called some of them up to speak, and one lieutenant made a statement something like this. He said: "When I first entered the service I went back east to attend an officers' training school, and one day when we were sitting in the reception room the boys started telling dirty stories. When my turn came I told one too, and that night when I went to go to bed my companion, not a member of the Church, turned to me and said, 'I didn't think you would do it.' "

And that lieutenant, as he stood there in that stake conference, said, "That was the best sermon I had listened to for many a day, and it just keeps ringing in my ears until the present." The Lord has called us out of the world to be a light unto the world, and in all men's sight we cannot afford to let our light go out.

In a town in California, one of the ladies' clubs was giving a luncheon; the hostess had an extra plate placed at the table at the hotel, and she said, "We'll invite the first soldier who comes along to occupy this extra plate at the table."

Well, sure enough, it happened to be a Mormon boy. And thank the Lord he was a good one. The Lord had called him out of the world to be a light unto the world, and he did not hide his light under a bushel. When the women passed the coffee around, he would not touch the coffee. I do not think he thought of the harm a cup of coffee would do his body, just one cup; no one whom he knew was there to see what he was doing. But he knew that there was an all-seeing eye of God upon him. He knew that he bore the priesthood of God. And they offered to get him tea but he did not want any tea, and so they asked him all about how he was raised; and finally when they were through they passed the cigarettes around to the women, but this boy would not touch the cigarettes. And right there one of those women said: "I resolved that if a Mormon elder ever called at my door I would let him in. I wanted to know more about a people that could raise a boy like the young man who sat at our table."

In Miami, Florida, at the close of a meeting, a man came up and said: "My first experience with the Mormons came when I went out into Arizona and worked in an implement house, a cash store. We never gave time on anything. One day a man came in and wanted two hundred dollars credit for about sixty days and I said, 'Well, we don't do any credit business.' And this man said, 'Well, would you mind asking the boss?' He went to the owner of the store and the owner said: 'Who is this man?' When he was told the name, the boss said, 'He's a Mormon bishop. Let him have anything he wants.' After that," the man told me, "whenever a Mormon came in the store and wanted anything, I didn't even bother the boss about it."

Would it not be a marvelous thing if every Latter-day Saint could be trusted like that!

While I was president of the Southern States Mission, I was crossing the state of Florida one day with one of our brethren who went there from the West, and he said: "President Richards, there is a new convert living right over here. He would be thrilled if we would visit him."

"Well," I said, "let's call on him."

And we went over and this was his story: "I used to be a fruit merchant in these parts. I bought up the entire products of these fruit farms and sold them on the New York market." He said: "When I heard of Mormonism, met the elders, and joined the Church, I began to think of all the shrewd deals I had made as a fruit merchant. One day I left my home. I put my checkbook in my pocket and when I returned, I had spent three thousand dollars, just among my neighbors and my friends, to try to even up some of those shrewd deals that I had made. But," he added, "I felt like I could then look my neighbors in the face and tell them that I was a member of The Church of Jesus Christ of Latter-day Saints."

"Ye are a chosen generation, a royal priesthood," and may your light never go out in the presence of men, no matter where you go.

6

A Campus Built on Rock

President John Taylor, third president of the Church, once said: "We want to so educate children . . . in order that they may be men and women capable of coping intellectually with any persons that live on the earth. We are seeking after these things . . . that our children may grow up, not only in the fear of God, but possess intelligence of every kind. Now these are our feelings in regard to these matters, and by and by, if we do this and keep doing it, how will it be? It will not be long before we will be as far ahead of the world in regard to the arts, science, mechanisms and every principle of intelligence that exists upon the face of the earth as we are in religious matters today."

What vision he had! Today we recognize the fulfillment of this prediction, and it reminds us of that scripture in Proverbs 29:18: "Where there is no vision, the people perish."

In a revelation of the Lord to the Prophet Joseph Smith, the Lord said none of his commandments were temporal, they are all spiritual. In the sight of the Lord, the building and operation of our Church university—Brigham Young University—is spiritual. It is a part of building his kingdom upon the earth.

President McKay paid a tribute to the faculty of BYU in these words: "I am sure that all of us are grateful to this sincere and dedicated faculty. Nowhere else in all the world can such a faculty be found. It is thrilling to see scholarship, learning, and intelligence, coupled with faith, devotion, and spirituality. It is of the highest order to help mold character and instill in the hearts of the young a faith in God."

The fruits of the efforts and faith of such a faculty can best be found in the lives of its alumni, and many of the alumni of this university have achieved great prominence in their various fields.

James Fletcher, who served as president of the University of Utah and then was selected to head the National Aeronautics and Space Agency, graduated from the Brigham Young University and is one of more than 50 other alumni who have served as college and university presidents. University presidents can wield such an influence for good in the lives of so many of the youth of the land. In Tempe, Arizona, I was told that the former president of that university, Dr. G. Homer Durham, wielded such an influence in that community that it had helped the missionary work more than anything else that had happened there.

O. Leslie Stone, former president of the Salt Lake Temple, a former stake president, and a founder of a multimillion dollar business, is an alumnus of BYU.

David J. Wilson has served as senior judge of the U.S. Customs Court.

Philo Farnsworth was known as the inventor or father of television. He graduated from BYU along with many other distinguished leaders.

Now let us give consideration for a moment to what the students individually and collectively have done to bring great honor to this university and to the Church.

On December 8, 1967, Paul Harvey, nationally known broadcaster, originated a nationwide broadcast from Salt Lake City studios and paid a glowing tribute to the Brigham Young University. After telling how he was met at the airport in Salt Lake City by students of Brigham Young University and his impressions of them, he added:

> Each eager common handsome young face mirrored a sort of . . . a sort of sublime assurance. These days many young eyes are prematurely old . . . from continual compromise with conscience. But the young lads and ladies of Brigham Young University have that enviable head start which derives from discipline . . . dedication . . . consecration. For that campus . . . literally and figuratively . . . is built on rock.

After describing his impressions of the Brigham Young University, on the campus, he observed the following:

> Six students—students including myself . . . driving north again through the snowswept mountain pass approaching Salt Lake City . . . at midnight . . . singing "Jingle Bells" . . . and "Joy to the World" . . . and "Santa Claus Is Coming to Town" . . . and "God Rest Ye Merry, Gentlemen" . . . and "God Be With You Till We Meet Again."
>
> The songs are ended—the melody lingers . . . but it's the faces I will see in my mind's eye until I die. The beautiful faces . . . of young people who know where they are going . . . because they are following an example worth following . . . and along the way, day by day, renewing . . . reinforcing . . . revitalizing . . . their mother faith and their father land.

God bless the students for wielding such an influence and making such an impression upon the mind of a stranger who came among us.

Another complimentary article appeared in the *Viltis*, a folklore magazine, under the title "B.Y.U. Campus and the Mormons":

> The week of June 10-17, 1968, I spent at the Brigham Young University in Provo, Utah. I have been visiting that campus since the mid-1940's and I am becoming convinced that the only salvation for the United States is for all Christians converting to Mormonism. They are, indeed, latter-day saints. With Mormonism

as the general religion, there would be no saloons, no drunkenness, no pot-smoking, and no crime, certainly, not to such an extent. They are industrious and generous. The students come to B.Y.U. to learn, not to riot, and leave to serve (their motto). We saw no one on the campus who looked as if he were something which the rat dragged in from a garbage pile. The people are wholesome and their cities are clean. My admiration is tremendous for them.

Again our students are to be complimented for making such an impression.

And now a recent compliment to the conduct of the students that brought to the university the gift from Dr. and Mrs. Ray R. Reeves of their 1044-acre ranch in Southern California. I quote from the *Universe,* the student newspaper:

> Just how the Reeves, who are not members of the Church of Jesus Christ of Latter-day Saints, came to give B.Y.U. this valuable piece of land is a story which needs to be told. Dr. Reeves tells it thusly:
>
> "Some time ago, my wife Nellis and I read a syndicated newspaper article by Dr. Max Rafferty of California describing Brigham Young University as a place where youngsters still have ideals, still cut their hair, still believe in God. We had to see it, so we drove to Provo, Utah.
>
> "The young people at B.Y.U. were all clean-cut, good looking. We didn't see any mini-skirts. There was no beatnik atmosphere. Those students had their feet on the ground. Instead of finding fault, they were accepting leadership. In short, we liked the way the university was being run.
>
> "Our association with the people at B.Y.U. has been marvelous. To show our support, we've given the university our ranch."

Another compliment to the students came a few years ago from Dr. William E. Fort, Jr., president of Deep Springs College near Bishop, California, and member of the Episcopal Church; he taught at Brigham Young University in the summer school of 1959. In an interview with a newspaper reporter at the close of the summer school, he stated:

It may well be that the Mormons have the key that will eventually save this country. I am impressed with the extremely high level of intellect I encounter in the students here . . . and even more important, the character of the students.

Dr. Fort has since joined the Church. I received a letter from him from which I quote:

I really think I must have been born an unbaptized Mormon because when I taught at B.Y.U. in the summer of 1959, I felt that I had returned home. I have believed all of the basic principles of the Church as long as I can remember and it has been a tremendous experience to me to now be associated with the Church.

What more can one say to evidence that this great institution is accomplishing the destiny outlined when it was organized? Those of us who have been close to BYU through having children or grandchildren attending as students will ever be most grateful to the Lord for its influence upon their lives.

The primary mission of our educational programs in the Church is that we might know the truth, and that the truth might make us free, for we believe that only by knowing and living the truth can men become free. The schoolroom of the Lord is greater than any schoolroom within the walls of any institution. When the Lord had created the earth and placed man upon it, he said, "And we will prove them herewith to see if they will do all things whatsoever their God shall command them," for he was concerned with preparing men and women not only for mortality, but for eternal life, since it is the work and glory of our Father in heaven to bring to pass the immortality and the eternal life of man.

The achievement of this great objective requires the best efforts of all the agencies the Church possesses, for through them the Lord has called his people out of the world to become a light unto the world; and to the extent that we heed the call, we are made free, not only for mortality, but for the life to come.

To Parents, Teachers, and Leaders

7

The Worth of a Child

What do you think a child is worth? What would you take for one of yours?

In the teachings of the Master, there is not anything, it seems to me, that is more beautiful than the constant expressions of his love and regard for little children. You remember that even his apostles were steeped in some of the old traditions of the day, and when people brought their children, they were not going to let them get up near the Savior. Why, he was too important to have to spend his time with little children! And then the Master gave that saying that is so precious to Latter-day Saints: "Suffer little children to come unto me, and forbid them not: for of such is the kingdom of God." (Mark 10:14.) And then he went on to say that "except ye be converted, and become as little children, ye shall not enter into the kingdom of heaven." (Matthew 18:3.) And then he said that "whoso shall offend one of these little ones which believe in me, it were better for him that a millstone were hanged about his neck, and that he were drowned in the depth of the sea." (Matthew 18:6.) Now, conversely, if that kind of an end should come to one who would harm a child, what must the reward be for one who would bless a child and help him to achieve in life his destiny and his purpose?

53

I thank the Lord that every child born into the world has an individuality, a purpose.

When spirits are born into the world, we do not realize how great is their destiny; we do not realize what the Lord has intended shall be their mission in life and the things that they shall accomplish. But the Lord has things for them to do. He has a value that he places upon them, but the great achievement of their destiny depends largely upon the instruction and the direction and the leadership they receive, so that they will be able to achieve and accomplish that for which the Lord sent them into the world.

Now, you remember when Jesus appeared to the Nephites and how he ministered among them; how the Father introduced him and how his voice was heard; and how, when Jesus taught them and knelt down before them and prayed unto the Father for them, they shed tears of joy. And the historian in writing it said, ". . . no tongue can speak, neither can there be written by any man . . . the joy which filled our souls at the time we heard him pray for us unto the Father." But the climax of all that experience was when they brought their sick and their afflicted and he healed them, everyone. And then, when they brought their little children, he took them up in his arms and blessed them, and when he did that, the heavens were opened and the holy angels descended and ministered. The angels did not come when he healed the sick; the angels did not come when he prayed for the people; but when the little children were taken in his arms and blessed, the heavens opened and the angels of God descended and circled around them. (See 3 Nephi 17.) We have no conception of what the value of a soul is in the sight of the Lord.

Every child born in this world is a son or a daughter of God, the Eternal Father, and each one is born with the undeveloped attributes to become like unto him, to possess ultimately the powers that he possesses, just as our children are born to achieve the abilities and attributes that we, as earthly parents, possess. And so, if those children born into this world possess the possibilities ultimately, in the eons ahead, to become like unto their Father in heaven, they will create worlds. The Lord said that he had created worlds innumerable to man, but, he said, they are numbered unto him, for he created them by the power of his Only Begotten. (See Moses 1.)

And so, every child has the possibility to achieve something of the perfectness of his Father. As Paul said, "We have had the fathers of our bodies, and we yielded obedience unto them. Should we not be much more obedient unto the Father of spirits, and live?" If he is literally and actually—as the Church teaches—the Father of our spirits, what then are the limitations that can be placed upon children born into this world? Can we afford to lose any of them? We do not need to lose a child if we are willing to pay the price to save them. I believe that. I believe it with all my heart. I believe there is enough of godhood in every boy and in every girl that they can be saved if we are willing to pay the price.

I know some women who think their kids are "little devils." I said to a woman once, "I'll bet you are proud of your little girls." And she said, "Well, Mr. Richards, they are an awful burden now, but I guess they will be all right when they grow up." Well, now, maybe they will, but as long as she thinks they are an awful burden, I do not know whether they will be all right when they grow up or not.

But the Lord said: "In the beginning was the Word, and the Word was with God, and the Word was God . . . all things were made by him. In him was the life; and the life was the light . . . which lighteth every man that cometh into the world." (See John 1:1-9.) Just as God puts the germ of life into seeds, he has planted into every human soul born into this world that light which lighteth every man coming into the world. And when we do our part and we bring it under proper environment, it will be just like the seed.

The story is told that when they uncovered King Tut's tomb, they found a jar of wheat there that had been imprisoned over three thousand years. It never grew —not because God had not put into the kernels of that wheat the germ of life, but because the environment was wrong. And so they changed the environment and went out and prepared a plot of ground, sowed the seed, and watered it, and the sun shone upon it, and the report is that the seed grew. You see, the only reason that it did not grow sooner was because of the bad environment.

Well, in my way of thinking, that is true with every one of God's children born into this world. The light that lighteth every soul coming into the world is there, and we must all do our part—parents, of course, have the first responsibility and then we, as leaders, have the next responsibility.

I want to close with this one little story. I was up in Wyoming at a conference and I had been talking to the young people and telling the leaders that I did not think we needed to lose a boy if we were willing to pay the price. At the close of the afternoon meeting, a little Primary boy came up and he said, "Bishop, I would like to shake your hand." I said, "I cannot think of anything I would rather do than shake yours." And he looked up in my face and he said, "Bishop, the Rock Springs Ward will never need to worry about losing me." And I said, "God bless the Rock Springs Ward."

If we can plant that kind of faith and feeling in the hearts of these boys and girls, we are preparing them then for priesthood responsibilities and for all the developments, for without that priesthood they never can become gods and create worlds.

8

Instilling Faith in the Hearts of Youth

I believe that if there is one thing that we need in the Church today more than any other, it is increased faith in the hearts of our boys and our girls in the restoration of the gospel, in the divine mission of the Prophet Joseph Smith, and in the fact that God lives, that every boy and girl will answer to him for their lives. It was Paul who said: "But without faith it is impossible to please him: for he that cometh to God must believe that he is, and that he is a rewarder of them that diligently seek him." (Hebrews 11:6.)

I believe that unless this faith is planted in the hearts of our boys and girls, they will not be able to meet the temptations of the day and come out gloriously victorious, true to the faith, and true to the standards of the Church.

We have felt that education might achieve this end. We now have compulsory education of our youth, and yet today there seem to be more immorality, more use of liquor, more use of the things that God has forbidden than in any other day.

It seems to me that in our church we must be able to plant in the hearts of our boys and girls a faith in the promises of God that if they will shun these things, they will receive of his blessings. It would be a terrible thing if, as our boys and girls come out of Latter-day Saint homes, they come with their faith destroyed, with lack of confidence in the leaders of this great church, lack of faith in the divine and holy principles that God has established in the Church in these latter days; and it would be a great reproach upon us if our boys and girls were to come out of our auxiliary organizations, our priesthood quorums, our Church schools or seminaries, with lack of faith in these great eternal truths.

God has placed a great army of officers in the Church as watchmen upon the towers of Israel, and I believe the Lord expects the presidents of stakes and the bishops of wards to know that there is nothing being taught that will destroy the faith of their boys and their girls. I might be just a little specific. I met a young lady who told me of what she had been taught in one of our institutions. She was told that patriarchal blessings were not really to tell us what the Lord had in store for us, but they were beautiful thoughts that might encourage us to try to live better lives. Now, if that were true, it would be all right; but as far as I am concerned, it just isn't true. If it be true, then I think one of two things must be acknowledged: that God has withdrawn his spirit from this church or that we have no need of patriarchs in the Church.

I call your attention to the patriarchal blessings given upon the heads of the sons of Israel of old, when their father Jacob, the patriarch, said: "Gather yourselves together, that I may tell you that which shall befall you in the last days." (Genesis 49:1.) One of the great fundamental truths of Mormonism is based upon the promise made upon the head of Joseph, when he was promised a new land in the utmost bounds of the everlasting hills, for his blessings should exceed the blessings of his progenitors.

I was privileged to have been raised in the home of a patriarch. My father was the acting Presiding Patriarch of the Church. I received my first blessing at his hands when I was eight years old, and I want to say to you that all the philosophizing in this world could not make me believe that my father knew what he pronounced upon my head of his own knowledge and his own understanding. That blessing has been a guide to me all my life, and I thank God that I received it when I was a boy eight years of age.

While working in the field with my father when I was a mere lad, I received one of the greatest testimonies that ever came to me, and that through the giving of a patriarchal blessing. My father related to us three boys, who were engaged with him in filling up an old cellar, a visit he had made the night before to administer a patriarchal blessing. After he had taken his hands from the head of the brother blessed, some disappointment was expressed that Father had not promised the man, who was very sick, that he should get well and live. Father said that when he placed his hands upon the head of this brother, something seemed to say to him that he should not give him too good a blessing for this life, for his days were numbered; so he promised him the blessing of eternal life for his faithfulness. When disappointment was expressed, and the voice of inspiration came again, Father said: "If I am inspired by the Spirit of the Lord, Brother So-and-so will not live more than so many hours," and he told us the time.

While we were working together, a good brother passed along the old hedge fence. Father called to him and asked if he knew how Brother So-and-so was. He said he had passed away. Father asked the hour and he told us. Then Father looked at us, because it was the exact time he had told us.

When I was called on my first mission I walked on crutches, with my leg in a plaster cast, into the office of Brother George Reynolds. He said: "What are you here for?" I said: "I am here to answer a call for a mission."

He said: "It looks to me like you had better go home and take care of yourself." I said: "I will be ready to go at the appointed date." He said: "When do you want to go?" I said: "In April, with my other friends." That was February.

I went out to Tooele, where my father lived. I told him I wanted a blessing so I could go on that mission, and my father promised me that I should go and that I should not be handicapped because of lameness—and I never lost a day's work. I threw my crutches away a few days before it was time to leave, and I went on that mission.

Many years ago my wife and I laid away in the grave our oldest son, who was nearly sixteen years of age—the greatest sorrow that has ever come into our lives. We had four daughters before he was born. Less than a year prior to that we took him and his younger brother into the office of the Patriarch to the Church, Brother Hyrum G. Smith, and he gave them each a blessing.

Now, I ask you, suppose the Patriarch had known that one of these boys would die within a year, couldn't he promise him anything? What would it have meant to the oldest son, had he walked out of the Patriarch's office with no promise and no blessing, and the younger son had all the promises and the blessings, for the older boy truly loved God and kept his commandments? When that boy passed away, I wondered, if God could only give us to understand that boy's blessing, so that Sister Richards and I might be comforted.

In the oldest boy's blessing, the one who passed away, the Patriarch said: "For it will be thy privilege to bear the Holy Priesthood and to go even among strangers and in strange lands, in defense of truth and righteousness." And to the younger boy he said: "For thou shalt bear the Holy Priesthood in defense of righteousness and truth, both at home and abroad."

A few nights later I took Sister Richards for a ride. We asked the younger boy if he would like to go with us. He said, "No, I think I will stay home." The next morning he came in and, holding in his hand the two patriarchal blessings, said, "While you were out riding last night I read these blessings. You see, I am going to labor at home and abroad, but LeGrand was to go to strange lands and strange people. They are not on this earth. We know all the lands of this earth and we know all the people that are here."

To the oldest boy the Patriarch had said: "And in due time thy home shall be a fit abode for the spirits of thy loved ones," and to the younger boy he had said: "Thou shalt enjoy the comforts of a happy home and the blessings of honored fatherhood, for thou shalt see thy posterity grow up around thee, to honor thee in the same kind of way in which thou hast honored thy parents."

Now, reverse the blessings and give the younger boy's blessing to the older boy, and there would be no explanation. He said, "You see, LeGrand's home is to be the home of the spirits of his loved ones, and my home is to be here on this earth, where I will see my children grow up around me."

You can't tell me that God, the Eternal Father, didn't give that fourteen-year-old boy the inspiration and revelation to understand these blessings, and our hearts have been comforted.

My faith in God and his eternal purposes is such that I never doubt but that he has made adequate provision for the fulfillment of every promise, and to complete and perfect the work that he has here commenced. In a revelation to the Prophet Joseph, he said: "For his purposes fail not; neither are there any who can stay his hands." And again: "A new commandment I give unto you, that I, the Lord your God, am bound when ye do what I say, and when ye do not what I say, ye have no promise." And when we receive a promise from the Lord through his servants, it is my faith that that promise shall be realized if we keep his commandments, if not in this life, then after this life.

Do you understand all the things in the scriptures? Did not the Savior say, when he taught in parables and his disciples came to him and asked him why he spoke in parables, "Because it is given unto you to know the mysteries of the kingdom of heaven, but to them it is not given"? (Matthew 13:11.) Sometimes I wonder why we go to the world for explanation of the scriptures, when we have the revelations of God, the Eternal Father, to guide us.

I think that the thing we need more than any other thing today is to plant in the hearts of our boys and girls this living faith in God, that like David of old they may feel and know that there is no spot so dark and no place so far removed and remote that the all-seeing eye of God is not upon them, and that they shall be held accountable for their deeds.

I hope that in all Israel, both in the homes and in the institutions, and in the priesthood quorums and auxiliaries, we shall never be accused of destroying faith in the lives and in the hearts of our boys and girls.

9

"Feed My Lambs"

I am very grateful for my assignment to labor with the young men of the Aaronic Priesthood and for the fine work that is being done by the bishops and their associates in their behalf. I recall a statement of the Master, who, as he went along the Sea of Galilee and gathered to himself the fishermen, said, "Come, and I will make you fishers of men." All over the world there are literally thousands and tens of thousands of boys who are waiting to be caught, if we only use the right kind of bait.

There are some of us, I fear, who have the feeling that there are only a few that will be saved. I am not unmindful of the fact that the Savior said, "Strait is the gate, and narrow is the way"; but I also remember that in the seventy-sixth section of the Doctrine and Covenants, the Lord indicates that he will save all the works of his hands except the sons of perdition, and I have never been able to feel that the sons of Latter-day Saint fathers and mothers, born under the covenant, are likely to be so classified. They are born heirs of all the gifts and blessings of the gospel of Jesus Christ. So, as far as I am concerned, I believe that if we will do our duty, with the help of the Almighty, we need not fear that any of our boys will be lost.

Now, when we gather them in, it is very important that we have something for them. They want to be fed, and I think that besides teaching them their duties in the priesthood, one of the greatest things we ought to have in mind is to try to plant in their hearts a testimony of the gospel of the Lord Jesus Christ.

My experience in the Church has taught me that the most powerful motivating thing in the world is a testimony of the gospel. Men and women who possess it will do anything for the Church; they will make any sacrifice. I am reminded of when Peter and John went to the temple and at the gate thereof found a man who had been a cripple from his youth; and when he asked alms at their hands, Peter said: "Silver and gold have I none, but such as I have, give I thee. In the name of Jesus Christ of Nazareth, rise up and walk." And immediately the cripple's feet and ankle bones received strength, and he walked into the temple with Peter and John.

You do not buy gifts like that with money. They are the riches of heaven, riches that come through faith and a testimony of the gospel of the Lord Jesus Christ.

I remember the story of the life of President Daniel H. Wells. When he saw the Saints move toward the West, although he was not a member of the Church and at that time possessed much property, a wife who was opposed to the Church, and a son, he had to make a choice to cast his lot with the Saints or to remain with his wife and son and property. Leaving his property to her, he went on with the Saints, and the Lord multiplied unto him because of his sacrifice and his testimony of the gospel.

We witness on every side, particularly in our ministry in the Church, how marvelously people sacrifice and how willingly they do it when their souls are touched with a testimony of the gospel.

I think of a little woman in our ward. We as a bishopric approached her and her husband, who was not a member of the Church, and asked them if they were in a position to send their son on a mission. We said, "We don't know whether you have any rich relatives who can help you [we knew they were of meager circumstances] but the boy is worthy to go, and we would be proud to have him represent our ward."

By that time tears were trickling down the little mother's face, and she said, "Bishop, if you will send my boy on a mission, I'll see that he has the money if I have to work every day he is gone to keep him in the mission field."

When living in California, I passed a bakery night after night on my way home from work and saw one of our good sisters in her little bakery uniform clerking while she kept two of her sons in the mission field.

I would like to see this testimony planted in the hearts of our boys and our girls, and I want you to know that I know boys can have a testimony of the gospel, even in their youth.

After the Savior was resurrected, he commissioned his disciples to go into all the world and preach the gospel to every creature, and then he promised them spiritual gifts and blessings as a result of their faith. I find nowhere in all Holy Writ where the Savior ever rescinded the promises he made unto those who would accept his gospel.

On the day of Pentecost, the Spirit of God was poured out like cloven tongues of fire, and Peter, representing the apostles, spoke until men were moved upon and pricked in their hearts. They said to him: "Men and brethren, what shall we do?" And Peter, the mouthpiece of God upon the earth, replied:

"Repent, and be baptized every one of you in the name of Jesus Christ for the remission of sins, and ye shall receive the gift of the Holy Ghost.

"For the promise is unto you, and to your children, and to all that are afar off, even as many as the Lord our God shall call." (Acts 2:37-39.)

I want you to know that as far as I am concerned, that promise has been made good in my life, and I have faith it will be made good in the lives of my children and their children, unto the latest generation, if they have faith in God and are willing to keep his commandments.

In the last chapter of the Book of Mormon, Moroni writes at some length on this subject. He tells of the marvelous gifts of the Holy Ghost and says that by the power of the Holy Ghost we might know the truth of the words contained in that book, for "by the power of the Holy Ghost ye may know the truth of all things." (Moroni 10:5.) Then he warns us to deny not the gifts of God, for these gifts shall never be done away as long as the world shall stand, except according to the unbelief of the children of men.

It is my testimony that when you read the words of the Master that "this is life eternal, that they might know thee the only true God, and Jesus Christ, whom thou hast sent" (John 17:3), you are not going to know him just because you read about him in books; you are going to know him because you have partaken of his Spirit and of his power. And you will be lifted up until you know there is a power in this world so much greater than yours that it leaves no room for doubt.

We should remember the words of Paul when he said that the things of God are understood by the Spirit of God, the things of men are understood by the spirit of man, and the natural man understandeth not the things of God, for they are foolishness unto him. We do not want natural men teaching our boys in the Aaronic Priesthood; we want men of God, men who have faith in God, faith in his promises, and faith in spiritual gifts and spiritual power.

Those who exercise their priesthood need not be afraid to promise their children or the youth of Zion that the blessings and gifts of the Holy Ghost will be theirs if

they will live for them. God, the Eternal Father, will fulfill these promises to our youth. And when they have a
testimony and spiritual conviction in their souls, we do
not need to worry about them, no matter where they
go.

I referred earlier to the experience of the Master at
the Sea of Galilee. You will remember how he gathered
his followers from their nets and their fishes. Later,
after he was crucified, Peter said, "I go a fishing," and
you remember that others of the disciples followed him,
and then how Jesus came and found them when they
were not successful in their fishing and told them to cast
their nets on the other side, and you know the success
that followed.

And then Jesus said, directing himself to Peter,
"Simon, son of Jonas, lovest thou me more than these
[meaning the fishers]? He saith unto him, Yea, Lord; thou
knowest that I love thee. He saith unto him, Feed my
lambs.

"He saith to him again the second time, Simon, son
of Jonas, lovest thou me? He saith unto him, Yea, Lord;
thou knowest that I love thee. He saith unto him, Feed
my sheep.

"He saith unto him the third time, Simon, son of
Jonas, lovest thou me? Peter was grieved because he said
unto him the third time, lovest thou me? And he said
unto him, Lord, thou knowest all things; thou knowest
that I love thee. Jesus saith unto him, Feed my sheep."

Now, I do not know anything in the world that we
can do to more pleasingly demonstrate to our Father in
heaven our love of him than feeding the sheep and the
lambs of his fold. He has said that the good shepherd
leaves the ninety and nine to go out after the one strayed
away.

Home teachers and Relief Society teachers have the
responsibility to go into the homes of the Latter-day
Saints, taking with them the spirit of the gospel, the

spirit of Christ, and to look after the lost ones and gather in and help and encourage where encouragement is necessary.

If all members of the Church will unite in the spirit of the priesthood to try to awaken within the hearts of the Latter-day Saints, particularly those who have been inactive and indifferent, a love of the truth and a devotion to God and his great latter-day work, I am sure we will see the work of God going on as it has never done before, and the day will come when we will learn how to do our work for the salvation and exaltation of our Father's children in a far better manner than we have ever done before.

God bless each person who is in the service of the Lord, in the wards and stakes, and give you vision and power and inspiration, that you may touch the hearts of your people, that you may arise in your great assignment to heights you have never dreamed of before, to the honor and glory of God and the blessing and the salvation of his children.

10

Set the Example for Youth

A leader in the Aaronic Priesthood in one of our stakes once handed me a copy of an article that appeared in a magazine published by the Kiwanis Club. I want to refer to a few excerpts from it:

"There is a general opinion that children are bright. In my opinion there is no greater fallacy. They are so dumb that it is a wonder we ever make really useful citizens out of them." To illustrate, the article says, "I know a fellow, a Kiwanian by the way, with a lovely wife and a nice home. Those two boys have been reared with every advantage. This man takes his golf clubs and hikes out to the golf course every Sunday morning of his life, and can you imagine it, those two boys are so dumb that they can't understand why they should be made to go to Sunday School? They think they should be permitted to go fishing or swimming Sunday morning instead of going to church! Nothing their father says to them seems to convince the dumb little creatures that they should spend two hours in church on Sunday morning.

"A father and mother who always preface their meal with a cocktail have a son and daughter in high school who went to a dinner dance, and the father found out that the children each had a cocktail before dinner. Those two kids were so dumb that when they were called on the carpet by their dad, they couldn't understand why they shouldn't drink cocktails! I tell you, kids are dumb.

"A man who occupied a prominent position in his community, when he was out in the yard and would hit his finger with a hammer or run against a wire clothesline, would make the sky blue with his profanity, and yet when his six-year-old boy called the cat a damned cat because it ran across the table, the father promptly spanked him and washed his mouth out with soap, but he was never able to make that dumb kid understand that it was wrong to swear. And a mother did not like to entertain company when she wasn't in the mood, and so when someone would call and want to come over to visit her, she would immediately say she had house guests and couldn't receive them, or if they wanted to speak to her on the phone and she wasn't in the mood, she would turn to her little girl and say, 'Tell them I am not home.' Do you know, that dumb little girl lies like Ananias! The mother has done all she can to break her of it, but the child is just a natural-born liar."

If the fathers and mothers in Israel understood the importance of this, they would take their boys and girls with them to church. No father would ever let a boy of his grow up dishonoring the Sabbath day, working on the Sabbath day when it is work that does not absolutely have to be done. Brigham Young's statement to the Saints when they first entered the Salt Lake Valley was that if they worked on the Sabbath day, they would lose more during the week than they gained by so doing. And we can't get away from the command of the Lord when he said that we should honor the Sabbath day and keep it holy. If fathers think they can work on the Sabbath when they don't have to, they must not be surprised if their boys are just dumb enough to do the same thing when they grow to manhood.

On the other hand, what a marvelous thing if we set

out with the thought in our minds that no matter what the cost, we will say with the prophet of old: "As for me and my house, we will serve the Lord." (Joshua 24:15.)

Contrasted to this, let me tell about a convert to the Church who came to my office. She and her husband had come to the United States for the gospel's sake. They had misfortune after they arrived; through sickness and hospital bills they were brought down to where they had to move into a section that was not desirable. She said to me, "Bishop Richards, there are some wicked young people in the locality where I am, and unless something is done about it, they are going to destroy the virtue of my daughters. I have come here to see if something can't be done." We have heard the Saints bear testimony that they would give their lives for the testimony that is theirs, and that is marvelous, but I wonder if they would be just as willing to live for the testimony that is theirs as to die for it? When we find conditions that threaten the virtue and the honor and the integrity of our children, do we do something about it? This little mother did something about it. She said: "Bishop Richards, if I have to do it, I will protect the virtue of my daughters, even if it means purchasing a tent and going up on the foothills to live." We got the bishop and the stake presidency on the job. That is the kind of faith that will win and bring the parents out triumphant in watching over their children who have been entrusted to them.

I remember reading in the *Improvement Era* a statement about one of our good Latter-day Saint mothers over in Germany who, when the invading army came in, knowing how they ravished the women, took her two daughters up in the attic of a house almost destroyed by the bombs; and there, exposed to the weather, she and the daughters remained for several days. When she thought it was safe she came down, but she left the daughters there to protect their virtue. God bless that mother and every mother like her who is willing to do all in her power to protect her children against the wickedness of this world.

We have all heard the story about Sister Mary Fielding Smith, the mother of President Joseph F. Smith, who traveled to the tithing office from her home in East Millcreek with a load of produce. The good brother in charge, knowing she was a widow and how hard it was for her to get along, hardly had the courage to let her unload that wagon. He said, "Take it home. You need it as much as anyone in the Church." Sister Smith said, "I can't do it. My children must know that we pay our tithing." She knew that lesson must be taught to her children. Has she been rewarded? Her son and her grandson grew up to become prophets of the Lord to preside over this great church.

When I was the bishop of a ward and we were building a meetinghouse, a little German widow came to me one day and said, "Bishop, I haven't received my allotment for the meetinghouse."

I said, "No, Sister, and you aren't going to get one. If you will just care for those little children your husband left with you, we will build the meetinghouse."

"But, Bishop," she said, "I must be able to point to that meetinghouse and tell my children we have done our part."

So I said, "God bless you, Sister, but you will have to say what your part is, then," and she gave us a substantial contribution toward that meetinghouse. I have met her children as I have traveled about from place to place in this church and have found them active, and I want to tell you, she didn't cast her bread upon the water in vain, for as the prophet of old said, ". . . thou shalt find it after many days."

You remember what Alma did when his son Alma didn't walk in the ways of the Lord and went about trying to destroy the church. He just did not give the Lord any rest about it; he went to the Lord in mighty prayer until an angel of heaven appeared unto his son and the sons of Mosiah; and when the angel spake unto Alma and his brethren, the earth shook. They all engaged in the ministry and labored as missionaries unto the Lamanites, and one by one the sons of Mosiah refused to serve as king over the people, desiring rather that they might continue their ministry among the Lamanites.

And this is Alma's statement after his conversion:

"O that I were an angel, and could have the wish of mine heart, that I might go forth and speak with the trump of God, with a voice to shake the earth, and cry repentance to every people.

"Yea, I would declare unto every soul, as with the voice of thunder, repentance and the plan of redemption, that they should repent and come unto our God, that there might not be more sorrow upon the face of the earth." (Alma 29:1-2.)

The greatest sorrow upon the face of this earth is when men and women depart from the ways of the Lord, for truly the prophet hath said: ". . . but the way of transgressors is hard." (Proverbs 13:15.)

Now I want to admonish you to pray for your children, to work for your children, to do all within your power to help save them. God may not always send an angel from heaven, as he did in answer to Alma's prayer, but there are men and women in this church by the thousands and tens of thousands who are as angels of heaven in the hands of God in helping to show the youth of Zion the way to eternal life. God help all of us to use all our power for the salvation of our boys and our girls.

11

"Remember the Worth of Souls"

We hear a great deal about how the bishops are overloaded, have too much to do, how many of them are wanting to be released because of the great responsibility they are carrying. I have taken occasion to inquire of many of them, "Bishop, how are you enjoying your work?" And each has replied in about these words, "Very much—it is the grandest opportunity I have ever had."

When I was on my first mission, I received a letter from my father in which he said, in words to this effect, "My son, I would like to say to you that there is no organization, corporation, or society in the world that will pay as great dividends on your time, your means invested, and your talents as the Church and kingdom of God."

Jeremiah saw the gathering of the Latter-day Saints in our day and described it as plainly as we can read it in Church history, even to the long trek along the Platte River in order to reach these valleys of the mountains:

"For there shall be a day, that the watchmen upon the mount Ephraim shall cry, Arise ye, and let us go up to Zion unto the Lord our God. . . .

"Therefore they shall come and sing in the height

of Zion, and shall flow together to the goodness of the Lord, for wheat, and for wine, and for oil, and for the young of the flock and of the herd: and their soul shall be as a watered garden; and they shall not sorrow any more at all. . . .

"And I will satiate the soul of the priests with fatness, and my people shall be satisfied with my goodness, saith the Lord." (Jeremiah 31:6, 12, 14.)

I do not believe we could go anywhere in the world and find men engaged in the ministry, I care not how great their salaries are, who would testify that the Lord has satiated their souls with fatness and that they are satisfied with the Lord's goodness to them, as are those brethren who bear the priesthood of God and are privileged to feed the flock under his divine leadership and inspiration.

We are dealing with the most precious things in all the world, the souls of men. The Lord declared to the Prophet Joseph Smith:

"Remember the worth of souls is great in the sight of God;

"For, behold, the Lord your Redeemer suffered death in the flesh; wherefore he suffered the pain of all men, that all men might repent and come unto him.

"And he hath risen again from the dead, that he might bring all men unto him, on conditions of repentance.

"And how great is his joy in the soul that repenteth!

"Wherefore, you are called to cry repentance unto this people."

"And if it so be that you should labor all your days in crying repentance unto this people, and bring, save it be one soul unto me, how great shall be your joy with him in the kingdom of my Father!" (D&C 18:10-15.)

These souls who are so precious in the sight of God are not only those who live out among the Gentiles, but many of them are also the sons and daughters of Israel.

In the veins of some of them flows the very best blood of this generation, and many of them are inactive, waiting to be called into service.

President Rudger Clawson once described at some length the marvelous creations of the Lord. Then he said, "But, brethren, I say unto you that the soul of one of his children is more precious in his sight than all the earth and the things he has created."

How precious are the souls of the sheep of the flock among whom we are called to labor! Those who have had the privilege of laboring in the mission field have seen men arrive, some of whom had never prayed in public in their lives, never done anything in the Church in a public way, and have seen what these young men have become in a year or two under the inspiration of the Lord. I have come to feel that there is no man in Israel who is without potential power for good in the midst of the people, if he is only given opportunity to render some service.

In the twelfth chapter of First Corinthians, Paul talks about the gifts of the Spirit:

"Now there are diversities of gifts, but the same Spirit.

"And there are differences of administrations, but the same Lord.

"And there are diversities of operations, but it is the same God which worketh all in all. . . .

"But the manifestation of the Spirit is given to every man to profit withal." (1 Corinthians 12:4-7.)

The Lord has not left any without some gift. He never did give all his gifts to any one individual. Even in the great work the Prophet Joseph accomplished, the Lord told him that his gifts were limited in some respects. You remember how Alma of old said he would that he had the voice of an angel, that he might cry repentance to all the world, but the Lord did not grant his desire, even though he was a prophet. Paul carried a thorn in his flesh all his days, but the Lord did not see fit to remove it; and the Book of Mormon says thereto are we given weaknesses, that we might remain humble.

Is there anyone who does not feel his weakness and would that he had greater power than he possesses for achievement in this great and mighty latter-day work? And yet we have to satisfy ourselves to do the things that are within our own reach and with the gifts that the Lord has seen fit to bestow upon us. "The manifestation of the Spirit is given to every man to profit withal." That is why the Lord gave the parable of the talents. To one he gave five talents; to another, two; and to another, one. And remember, the Lord will return and expect an accounting according to the talents given.

I am grateful for the great Welfare Program of the Church. I see in it a marvelous opportunity to use some of the men who have not applied themselves in more spiritual activities. A man sat in my office not long ago who had only recently become active in the Church. He had been very successful in his own business affairs, but apparently the bishop had never asked him to do anything. Then they had to build a chapel; the bishop selected him to head the finance committee, and he did a marvelous job.

This man said, "Why couldn't my bishop have given me something to do twenty-five years ago so I could have known the joy of service all these years?" Then he told about having a son who had married in the temple and was not doing anything in the Church. He said, "Why cannot the bishop give him something to do so he will not remain inactive as I have been?"

I plead for every person whom the Lord has endowed with his gifts through the power of his Spirit, that we find a way whereby they can fit in and do something for the building up of the kingdom. We have the opportunity of home teaching, of doing missionary work, and of serving as stake, ward, and auxiliary officers and

teachers. We can go even further, for there is so much to
be done in a temporal way, in beautification, in the Welfare Program, in the building of storehouses, in the
acquiring of land, in the production of the things not
yet being produced that are needed for the storehouses.
Some of the finest leadership in the Church is available,
but as yet inactive. There are marvelous possibilities
within the priesthood quorums to lift men, to rehabili-
tate them, and to cause Zion to put on her beautiful garments, as the Lord declared to the Prophet Joseph two
years after this church was organized that she should do,
because, he said, "Zion must increase in beauty and in
holiness; her stakes must be strengthened; her borders
must be extended; yea, Zion must arise and put on her
beautiful garments."

It is my feeling that we can be, as Latter-day Saints,
free and independent from every power beneath the
celestial kingdom and become so united that we will
literally become a light upon a hill, an ensign unto the
nations.

God help us that we may all be worthy shepherds of
the flock, and that we may bring into activity in our wards
and stakes of Zion every person who is a member of this
church.

12

Leadership That Saves

The philosophy of the Church is that we learn to do by doing, and we don't learn any other way. We may study a bit, but you could study until doom's day out of all the books that have ever been written on how to play golf and you would still never be able to knock that ball straight down the fairway until you got hold of the clubs and learned the little quirk necessary to keep it straight. You could listen to all the musicians who have ever lived and you would still never be able to play a tune on the piano until you got your fingers on the keys and used them yourself. And that is how one learns in this church. I think that half, or better, of the manpower of this church is going to waste today because we haven't yet learned how to harness it and put it to work.

This has been one of my hobbies all of my life. When I went to preside over the Southern States Mission and found 18,000 members on the records, I wasn't half as much concerned about adding another thousand names to the list as I was about what was going to become of the 18,000 we already had on record.

We only had one full-time missionary from our mission in the mission field when we arrived, and I told the Saints they were being cheated; they ought to have at least one missionary from the South for each one from the West, and so we started calling their local young people. I told them that if they would live for it, and pray for it, and work for it, and save for it, their boys and girls could go on missions just as well as the boys and girls from the West, and it was only a short time until we had fifty-six full-time missionaries from the South serving in that mission.

You have to have objectives and set your mark high.

We had district presidents' conventions for three days—three meetings a day, three hours a meeting—and outlined every objective we wanted to achieve and how we expected to achieve it. When the district presidents returned to their districts, I thought they were prepared to turn the whole world upside down. Later I went to visit one of these district presidents and I said, "Do you feel that I give you as much help as I should?"

He said, "Sometimes I don't."

"Well," I said, "be a little more specific."

He said, "Well, you send me all of these missionaries for my district and you don't tell me where to put them. You leave the responsibility up to me."

"Oh, I see," I said. "You want me to be the mission president and the district president too. Fine. From now on every missionary will be tagged when he comes to you. But when you are through, you won't be worth much as an executive in this church."

And he said, "President Richards, please don't tag them. Send them out just the way you have been doing."

We started a youth program in the mission, and at the first program we held in one particular district, we let each branch present a number, and each one of them presented a number that wasn't too appropriate. At the close of the entertainment, the district president said, "President Richards, I dare not ask you what you thought of the program."

"Oh," I said, "I think it was wonderful."

He said, "You don't mean that, do you?"

And I said, "Yes, I do, because it shows us where our starting point is. But," I added, "if you ever have another one like it, it will not be wonderful." So we had to learn where our starting point was, and then we had to set our mark high. We had to teach the people to raise their standards.

I learned a statement when I was a young man that has been worth a great deal to me. It goes like this. There are three requisites to successful leadership in the church, in business, or in anything else: first, the planning of your work; second, the assignment of your work; and third, the checking up on the assignments.

This checking up is especially important. In one stake one night I talked the whole evening on these three points, and afterward a new bishop came up and said, "I certainly got a lot out of that." The next day we called him to talk in the conference. The blackboard was still on the stand with those three requirements—the planning of your work, the assigning of your work, and the checking up on your assignments—and he said: "Last night I heard Bishop Richards talk on the importance of checking up on assignments. I thought about it all night and this morning I got in touch with every boy of the Aaronic Priesthood in my ward and they are all here but three." You see what checking up does.

We had a slogan in our stake when I was president: "Not failure but low aim is often our greatest sin." It isn't always that we have tried and failed as much as it is that we haven't tried.

And that brings me to the necessity of holding council meetings. I feel that there is nothing more important than council meetings, where we meet together and plan our work and make our assignments, and then check up and follow through on assignments made.

Bishop Marvin O. Ashton used to say that the only difference between a grave and a rut is that one is a little deeper than the other. Too much of our leadership today is in a rut or the ditch.

The Lord said: "Wherefore, now let every man learn his duty, and to act in the office in which he is appointed, in all diligence. He that is slothful shall not be counted worthy to stand, and he that learns not his duty and shows himself not approved shall not be counted worthy to stand. Even so. Amen." (D&C 107:99-100.)

To illustrate: In Idaho we had a man talk on his duty as a coordinator in the Aaronic Priesthood, and he said something like this: "Well, I don't know what my duty is, but this is what I think it is," and then he went on to say what he thought it was. When my turn came to speak I said, "Brother, why don't you know what your duty is? Don't you have a handbook?" He replied that he did not. I then turned to the stake president and said, "Couldn't you get him a handbook?" There was a man trying to do a job without knowing what his duty was. I tell you, every person needs to know what his duty is and then see that he does it.

Have you ever been in an automobile assembling plant? Well, I have. They start the conveyor going and it runs probably for two blocks and never stops. The rough chassis is dropped on the conveyor and while it is traveling, the entire automobile is assembled, ready to go off at the end of the assembly line under its own power. This thought came to me as I watched every man do the little intricate job that was assigned to him. What if, when that great army of men rushed into the plant at the change of shifts, they did not know what their duty was? Wouldn't it be a wonderful-looking jalopy by the time it ran off the assembly line at the other end?

If it is good for every man in that plant to know his duty so that when the gates swing open he knows where he belongs, he knows exactly what he is going to use, he knows exactly what is expected of him, he knows that if he fails that automobile will not be ready when it goes off the assembly line, why can't we become just as efficient in doing the work of the Lord? This we can do if every man will learn his duty and act in the office in which he is appointed, in all diligence, as the Lord has commanded.

It has been my experience, as I have labored in the Church, that the Lord can make mighty men out of humble people, and he can make them great workers, capable workers. I have seen men join this church who could not read or write, and I have later heard them deliver sermons that I would have been proud to have heard delivered in the Salt Lake Tabernacle. I think every one of us ought to remember that each one of us is a son or daughter of God, and that we have within us some of his attributes.

I have heard President Heber J. Grant say many times that the greatest testimony to him of the divinity of this work is what God does with the material he has to do with. I have seen the Lord accomplish so much by bringing inexperienced men and women into activity that I plead with you, as leaders, that you try and bring every man and woman into activity in the Church, "for this is my work and my glory, to bring to pass the immortality and eternal life of man." And that is the kind of leadership that saves.

13

A Round Man in a Round Hole

The Lord said: "For this is my work and my glory, to bring to pass the immortality and the eternal life of man." And he was speaking about all men.

Rodger Babson made a statement to the effect that our greatest wealth is not our mines, nor our waterways, nor our forests, but the undeveloped souls of our citizens. The Lord said, in a revelation to the Prophet Joseph, "Remember the worth of souls is great in the sight of God."

I believe that the science and the mission of Mormonism is to develop and to utilize the gifts and talents with which God has endowed men for the building of the kingdom of God and for the blessing and betterment of humanity.

I think that is what Jesus had in mind in the Parable of the Talents, when one servant received five talents, another two, and another one. And then the ruler came and held an accounting with them. The one who had had five talents brought back another five; and the ruler's statement was, "Well done, thou good and faithful servant: thou hast been faithful over a few things, I will make thee ruler over many things: enter thou into the joy of thy lord."

But the one who had had the one talent went and hid it in the earth; and when the master came to hold accounting with him, the servant said:

"Lord, I knew thee that thou art an hard man, reaping where thou hast not sown, and gathering where thou hast not strawed:

"And I was afraid, and went and hid thy talent in the earth: lo, there thou hast that is thine."

And what did the Lord say?

"Take therefore the talent from him, and give it unto him which hath ten talents.

"For unto every one that hath shall be given, and he shall have abundance: but from him that hath not shall be taken away even that which he hath.

"And cast ye the unprofitable servant into outer darkness: there shall be weeping and gnashing of teeth." (See Matthew 25:14-30.)

Now we believe that every man born into this world is accountable to God for the way he uses the gifts and the talents with which the Lord has endowed him, and there are none of us who come without that endowment. I realize that it was because God so loved the world that he sent us his Only Begotten Son. And so the development of the souls of men, to me, is one of the greatest responsibilities of leadership in this great church.

An article on the Mormons as empire builders appeared a few years ago from the pen of Thomas Dixon Carver, who was then the professor of political economy at Harvard University. He said how he liked to study the Mormons and went on to say that Mormon leaders had an uncanny ability of discovering hidden talent and of putting it to useful service. And then he said:

The Mormons did not even start with a mass of educated or skilled manpower. They started, as a general rule, with very commonplace people, from the backwoods, the prairies, and the mountains of this country. From overseas they came, from peasant farms, from coal mines, and from workshops, and out of these they built a great and glorious commonwealth.

Plutarch tells us that Themistocles was once twitted in a polite gathering because he could not play any musical instrument. He replied that "although he could not fiddle, he could make a small city into a great and glorious one." The Mormon leaders did even better than that. They did not have even a small city to start with. They started with nothing and built a great and glorious commonwealth. They found a desert and made it bloom and blossom as the rose.

To discover hidden genius is better than to discover a hidden gold mine. . . . The power to save skill, talent and genius from going to waste, is as near to divine wisdom as anything we are very likely to know in this world.

Joseph Smith taught that the one thing of supreme importance in the Universe was human personality. To perfect this personality—that is to make it like God—everything else must become contributory thereto. And so, in the religion established by him, the motivating power of it was the gradual unfolding of the human personality—not that of one man, or a few men only, but of all men.

The Prophet Joseph said, "I was a rough stone until the Lord took me in hand to polish me." And he saw this power transform his disciples from men and women dominated by self-interest to men and women dominated by group interest. We have no leader in the Church who has not been polished by experience and by training.

We had a man in the South, when I was president of the mission there, who could neither read nor write when he joined the Church. And one day his daughter saw him looking in a geography book, and she said, "What are you looking for, Father?" And he answered, "I am looking for the meaning of the word *utmost.*" She said, "You have the wrong book," and got him the dictionary. Now, I heard that man deliver a sermon on the "Utmost Bounds of the Everlasting Hills" in the courthouse in Douglas, Georgia, that I would have been proud to have heard anywhere. He had everybody in tears. He had the spirit of God. And you remember in the scriptures where Paul tells us that God has chosen the weak things of this world to confound the mighty and the strong. That man became a great leader.

In Mississippi, while I was there, I heard a man give a magnificent address—a man who could not read and write when he joined the Church. And when he was through, I said, "Brother Wainwright, I would have been proud to have heard that sermon delivered in the Salt Lake Tabernacle."

We had a man who wanted to join the Church in Holland when I was there on a mission. He looked more like an escaped convict than a Mormon, and I hardly had the nerve to let him into the Church. I said, "You wait a little while and study the gospel a little more." Then, finally, a few weeks later, he said, "Now Brother Richards, what am I waiting for anyway? I have quit my tobacco, and I have quit my liquor, and my tea and coffee, and I have quit my profanity except when a word slips out before I can grab it, but I get most of them. I am willing to attend church and to pay my tithing and my fast offerings. Now, what else do you want?" I said, "Well, I guess we had better baptize you."

As impossible as he seemed to me at that time, I lived to see him immigrate to America with his family and learn the English language well enough to fill a full-term mission in the United States and then go back to Holland with his wife, where both of them filled a mission.

We read in the first chapter of John the following:

"In the beginning was the Word, and the Word was with God, and the Word was God.

"The same was in the beginning with God.

"All things were made by him; and without him was not any thing made that was made.

"In him was life; and the life was the light of men.

"And the light shineth in darkness; and the darkness comprehended it not.

"That was the true Light, which lighteth every man that cometh into the world." (John 1:2-5, 9.)

From this we learn that that light "lighteth *every*

man coming into the world," not just one or two. And we
believe that with all our hearts. We believe that every
man and woman with a normal mind is a potential
worker for the kingdom of God. And our greatest responsibility is to develop the gifts and the talents with
which we are endowed—not only for service in this world,
but also for the eternities that are to follow.

We realize that there are the good and the bad. Take
music, for instance. Music is the song of the angels, and
we are told that the song of the righteous is a prayer unto
the Lord. And yet in the greatest dens of vice, one finds
music. We have to learn to discriminate between the good
and the bad. And the same with the voice. The voice
can praise God, but it can also curse him. And we have
to learn to choose the good from the bad. That's what
leadership is for.

A few years ago we held what we called a bishop's
workshop at Brigham Young University. I talked at this
workshop on the delegation of authority, and I used this
illustration: "Now when you bishops divide your responsibility with your counselors, if you give your first counselor the Sunday School to look after, and your second
counselor the Mutual Improvement Association, and then
the superintendent of the Sunday School comes to you
and wants to know whether he can have Brother or Sister So-and-so to teach in the Sunday School, if you
answer him, you immediately release your first counselor
from the assignment you gave him to look after the Sunday School. But if you say to him, 'In the division of
responsibility we have asked the first counselor to take
care of the Sunday School. You take up your needs
with him. He will bring his recommendations to our
bishop's meeting, and we will let you know,' then you are
through with the Sunday School as long as that man is
superintendent. And the same with the Mutual. If the
Mutual superintendent comes to you and wants Brother
So-and-so as a Scout leader, if you answer him, you will

immediately release your second counselor from looking after the Mutual. But if you tell him to take it up with the second counselor, that he will bring his recommendations to the bishop's meeting, and you will let him know, then you are through with MIA as long as that man is the superintendent."

When I was through, there was a bishop sitting on about the third row back, rocking his head in his hands. And he said, "Bishop, why didn't somebody tell me that eight years ago?" You see, for eight years he had been the bishop, and the first counselor, and the second counselor. And I think we still have many bishops like that in the Church, and not only bishops, but also leaders in our auxiliary organizations. I believe in letting the other man grow and develop by taking part.

I am a great believer in mass participation, and still, notwithstanding that belief, I think it is a good thing to put a round man in a round hole and a square man in a square hole. To illustrate that point: When I was bishop of a ward, we had a chorister who would, I think, have given his life for his choir; he would have gone out and hauled them all in to practice. But we never got invited to sing anywhere, neither in stake conference nor in any public gathering. That man's brother, who was a chorister in a ward adjoining ours, sang with his choir in the Salt Lake Tabernacle, in the Assembly Hall, in stake conferences, etc. So I said to my counselors, "Let's see if our chorister will let us transfer him to some other job." One counselor said, "You will break his heart," and I said, "Oh, no; let's try it."

So we called him in, and I said, "Do you have enough confidence in the judgment of the bishopric of this ward that, if you knew we felt that the ward would be blessed by changing you to another assignment, you would be willing to give up the choir?"

He thought a few minutes and said, "Yes, I do."

This incident occurred in the time before the Mutual

had the activity program of the Church, and we turned the activity program over to him. He did a grand job with his new assignment, and we called another man to lead the choir. And it was only a few weeks until the new man had a waiting list of people wanting to join the choir. They sang at the next stake conference, and the people said, "What in the world has happened to such-and-such ward?" We got invited to sing all over. You see, we put a round man in a round hole and we put a square man in a square hole.

Sometimes I feel that we need to do a little shuffling within, because some of our ward organizations grow up like patchwork quilts. We add a little here; someone else moves in and we put him there. And they are not always fitted to give the best of leadership.

Counsel to Missionaries

14

That Others Might Share the Gospel

The Lord indicated, when he gave the signs of his second coming, that this gospel of the kingdom—the gospel that he preached, the gospel that he left with his Twelve—would be preached in all the world for a witness unto all nations and then should the end come.

It is not that we expect everybody will accept the truth, because the minds of many are blinded, but if they would, it would greatly enrich their lives. If I could have the desire of my heart above all other things, it would be that all men everywhere, our Father's sons and daughters might share with us the glorious truths of the restored gospel of the Lord Jesus Christ.

One of our noted commentators is reported to have said that he was once asked what message could be broadcast to the world that would be considered more important than any other, and he replied, after giving it consideration, that the greatest message that could be broadcast to the world would be that a man who had lived upon this earth and had died had returned again with a message from God.

That being true, the Latter-day Saints have the greatest message. We testify that the Father and the Son appeared to the boy, Joseph Smith. There was doubt in the hearts of even the followers and the apostles of Jesus when the report came to them that he was not in the tomb but was risen, and they thought it was an idle tale. When we talk today of God the Father and his Son Jesus Christ coming back to this earth and of holy messengers visiting this earth in our day, the world thinks that these are idle tales, and yet they profess to believe in the Bible; that the Lord appeared to the prophets of old; that the Bible bears witness that he is the same yesterday, today, and forever without shadow of changing. How can they believe in that kind of God and then believe that the heavens are sealed so that he cannot talk to us today as he did in days of old?

I have thought that it would not be necessary to study everything and read all the scriptures if one really wanted to know if our message is true; there is no other message like it in all the world. No other people profess an opening of the heavens and the visitation to this earth of holy messengers in our day, for the most tangible evidence of the truth of the story of the Prophet Joseph Smith is the Book of Mormon. The Book of Mormon has been distributed by millions of copies all over the world, and there are even many who are not members of the Church who believe that the Book of Mormon is true.

Just read the testimony of the Three Witnesses in the front of every book, where they testify that an angel of God came down from heaven, and he brought and laid before their eyes the plates and the engravings thereon and declared unto them that they were translated by the gift and the power of God. Why cannot the world believe such a testimony as that? There is also the testimony of the eight witnesses to whom the Prophet was privileged to show the plates, and there is the testimony that comes from those who accept the gospel.

I attended a conference once where a young woman, a convert and the mother of two little children, was asked to bear her testimony. She said something like this:

"When the elders came into my home, they read to me the promise in the Book of Mormon that when that book came to us, if we would read it, asking God the Eternal Father in sincerity, then the Lord would manifest the truth of it unto us by the power of the Holy Ghost."

She said, "I believed that promise, and I went into my bedroom and got down on my knees and asked God the Eternal Father to let me know whether that book was true or not. I read it, and my whole soul was illumined, and I knew that it was divine."

A man visited Temple Square a few years ago, a minister from Texas, and after returning home he wrote a letter back saying that he had purchased a copy of the Book of Mormon. He said, "I have a library of important books that cost me over $12,000, but I have one book that is more valuable than them all because it is the Word of God, and it is the Book of Mormon."

A letter came in to the headquarters of the Church from a minister back in the East. He said he bought a copy of the Book of Mormon years ago from a Mormon elder who called at his home. He said, "I put it in my library. I never read it until recently, and now I have been reading it, and I have been quoting from it in my sermons." In his letter he mentioned the words of Alma and the words of Nephi that he had used in the preparation of his sermons.

Why cannot the world believe? Why cannot they accept it?

I love the Book of Mormon. I know that no honest soul searching after God can study that book without knowing that it is divine and that it was not written by Joseph Smith. It is what it purports to be: a volume of scripture that the Bible promised should come forth in our day. If people will open their hearts and their minds to the messages of Moroni, John the Baptist, Peter, James, and John, Moses, Elijah, Elias, the prophets who have visited this earth in the restitution of all things spoken by the mouths of all the holy prophets since the world began, things that Peter declared and promised would transpire in this world before the coming of Christ, they will know that the message of the Prophet Joseph Smith is true.

The Book of Mormon was preserved to be a witness that Jesus is the Christ, the eternal God, manifesting himself unto all nations.

Some years ago a questionnaire was sent out to 500 Protestant ministers by Northwestern University, and out of 500, 130 persons denied the Deity of Jesus. When the blind lead the blind, Jesus said, "they fall in the ditch together."

We invite all men everywhere to make an investigation, and we promise them as servants of the living God that they can know that this work is divine.

15

"How Great Shall Be Your Joy"

I have had the privilege of filling four missions for the Church away from home, and I tell the missionaries they cannot get any sympathy from me. The more missionary work I do the better I like it. There has been no sweeter story told in this world since the shepherds were guarding their flocks by night than the story we have to tell, and no man needs sympathy who has been called to tell this story to those who know it not. When we read the words of the prophet Jeremiah, regarding the gathering of latter-day Israel, that many fishers would be sent to fish them, and many hunters would be sent to hunt them from every mountain, and from every hill, and out of the holes of the rocks, we need not tell men and women they are favored of the Lord when they are called to do this fishing and hunting. When they are set apart by those having authority to labor in the ministry either at home or abroad, they receive something that ordinary men know nothing about.

It is customary when we engage in any particular line of church activity to feel that this particular activity is the most important work in the Church. Whether it be Sunday School, MIA work, or quorum work, it is the same in each activity; but as far as I personally am con-

cerned I haven't been able to find anything in the scriptures that would indicate that there is anything more
important for this church to do than to preach the gospel
of the Lord Jesus Christ to those who know it not.

I recall that the apostle Peter was somewhat disturbed in his feeling that John might be favored, and the
Lord said unto Peter: "If I will that he tarry till I come,
what is that to thee?" (John 21:22.) In modern revelation
(D&C 7) we find that John expressed the desire to the
Savior to be permitted to tarry and bring souls unto Christ,
while Peter had desired to speedily rejoin Christ in his
kingdom. John had in his heart a love for missionary
work. He wanted to bring men to a knowledge of the
truth, even to the extent that he be permitted to tarry until Christ should come again, and this desire was granted
by the Lord.

When the Savior was administering among the
Nephites, three of his disciples there were sorrowing in
their hearts, for they dared not speak to him the thing
that they desired, and the Savior said unto them:

"Behold, I know your thoughts, and ye have desired
the thing which John, my beloved, who was with me in
my ministry, before that I was lifted up by the Jews,
desired of me.

"Therefore more blessed are ye, for ye shall never
taste of death; but ye shall live to behold all the doings
of the Father unto the children of men, even until all
things shall be fulfilled according to the will of the Father,
when I shall come in my glory with the powers of
heaven;

"And ye shall never endure the pains of death; but
when I shall come in my glory ye shall be changed in the
twinkling of an eye from mortality to immortality; and
then shall ye be blessed in the kingdom of my Father.

"And again, ye shall not have pain while ye shall
dwell in the flesh, neither sorrow save it be for the sins
of the world; and all this will I do because of the thing

which ye have desired of me, for ye have desired that ye might bring the souls of men unto me, while the world shall stand." (3 Nephi 28:6-9.)

I know of no other desire that seems to have been more pleasing unto the Master than that of "bringing souls unto him."

After the crucifixion and resurrection of the Savior, when he appeared to his disciples and commissioned them to go into all the world and preach the gospel to every creature, you will remember the promises made concerning those who believed in their words and were baptized, and then he ended his remarks by saying: ". . . and, lo, I am with you alway, even unto the end of the world." (Matt. 28:20.) There is not a missionary in the Church who has gone out, having responded to the divine call, devoted himself honestly and earnestly to his work, and remained prayerful before the Lord, who will not testify that the Lord has truly been with him.

When the Master sent out his disciples of old, upon their return he asked if they had wanted for anything, and they responded that even the devils were subject unto them in his name. I have had such experiences, and I testify that what the missionary accomplishes is not done by his own power, but by the power of the Lord that is given him because of his holy calling.

When the seventy were sent out in times of old, two by two, into every land, they were told by the Lord that they who received them received him, and they who rejected them rejected him. It is really a marvelous thing to be sent out to represent the Lord, knowing yourself that if people receive you as his representative they are receiving the Son of God.

I was impressed, while reading the Church history sometime ago, with an experience the Prophet Joseph had in the Kirtland Temple the day his father was made the first Presiding Patriarch of the Church. He received the marvelous vision wherein he saw his brother Alvin in the celestial kingdom, Alvin having died without baptism, and it was then revealed to the Prophet that those who have died who would have received the gospel had they lived were candidates for celestial glory. He saw also the apostles of the Lamb in this dispensation in foreign lands; their clothes were worn and tattered and Jesus was standing in their midst but they did not see him, and Jesus looked upon them and wept. He also saw Brother M'Lellin in the South preaching the gospel, and a lame man standing before him threw his crutches down and leaped by the mighty power of God. He saw Brigham Young preaching to a group of hostile Indians in their own tongue, and an angel of God standing over his head with a drawn sword in his hand protecting him. ". . . and lo, I am with you alway, even unto the end of the world."

I could tell you many experiences of how the Lord has opened the way for his servants.

While in the South I received a letter from a member of the Church in South Carolina, which said, "I understand there is an Elder Shurtleff in our mission, and if he is the son of Elder Arthur T. Shurtleff, please let him come to Carolina to attend our conference. I would like him to visit in our home and spend a few days with us. I would like to put my arms around that boy whose father the Lord had used as an instrument to give me a testimony of this great and mighty latter-day work. I would like to explain in detail how his father was shown to me, not in a dream, for I was wide awake, a year before he called at my home."

". . . and lo, I am with you alway, even unto the end of the world."

Sister Richards and I visited a woman from Tampa, Florida, whose son, twenty-two years of age, had died without baptism. She had formerly been a Baptist, and it was her understanding there was no chance for her son since he had passed away without having been baptized. She went into her bedroom one morning, and while

kneeling, seeking the Lord, wondering if there was anything she could do for her son and if so, if He would
make it known to her, a knock came at the door. There
stood two lady missionaries, and one held in her hand
the tract "Baptism for the Dead." "I looked at the girls
and then the tract," she said, "and then I said, 'Come in.
Tell me all about that—that is just what I want to know.' "
After a few visits of the missionaries, she was baptized
a member of the Church. ". . . and, lo, I am with you
alway, even unto the end of the world."

We were preaching on the street corner in New Bed-
ford one evening during my short-term mission. A lady
who was listening to us seemed very interested, and after
meeting and talking to her, I invited myself to her home,
as was my habit, since I was afraid she might be afraid
to invite me, and I didn't want to miss the opportunity of
delivering my message. I found this woman had been in-
vestigating the various churches in her search for the
truth, and she told me she had just about decided there
was no truth, but that she had had a dream in which
she saw a man coming to her and offering her a new book.
We left her a copy of the Book of Mormon. We met with
no opposition in her home. We taught her the truth.
The Lord had indicated in her dream that she would be
the means of bringing salvation to many of her people,
and many have joined the Church.

The opportunity is ours here for every one of us to
be a missionary. Sometimes the opportunity is so close
that we do not realize it. We send missionaries far away
from home, traveling by land and sea to hunt people
from the mountains and from the hills and from the holes
in the rocks, but sometimes those who would accept our
message are so close to us that we cannot see them.
The story is told of a good brother who lived in Davis
County north of Salt Lake City, and an Englishman who
purchased the farm adjoining his. The English neighbor
was not a member of the Church. Of course, our dear

brother didn't want to force his religion upon the Englishman, so when they met they merely passed the time of
day. Finally the member of the Church received a missionary call to England, and not long after he had arrived in his field of labor his English neighbor decided to
visit his relatives in England. While in England one day,
he read a newspaper announcement of a Mormon conference. He said: "I have lived among the Mormons. I
had better go and see what they believe." To his surprise the principal speaker at this conference was his
neighbor from Davis County. He had to go to England to
hear the gospel message from his neighbor next door.

In one of the stakes of Zion the stake president told
this story:

"When I was a bishop I was called on the phone,
and the person said to me: 'I wonder if you think I am
good enough to join your church.' I then began to realize
that I had permitted this neighbor to live in my ward
all these years without extending to him an invitation
to join our church. The appointment for his baptism was
made for Friday evening. In the meantime I called another good neighbor lady and told her that on Friday
Brother So-and-so was going to be baptized, and asked
her how she would like to come along. She replied:
'Bishop, I have been wondering how long I would have
to live in your ward before you would invite me to join
your church.' "

While traveling in New Mexico I met a fine-appear-
ing man. He had previously lived in Salt Lake City for
years. His wife and children had belonged to the church,
but no one had invited *him* to join; however, when he
moved to New Mexico the missionaries got hold of him
and now he is working in the Church himself.

In another stake, in a meeting with a bishopric, I
was told that the bishop was a convert and that he had
been on a mission. "How did it happen?" I asked.

"Well, I was working in the railroad shops and my

companion straightened up and said, 'Say, where did you live before you were born?' 'I didn't live anywhere.' 'If not, the Bible isn't true.' We spent the noon hour discussing from the Bible about where I lived before I was born, and later I became a member of the Church."

I know another brother whom I respect and had known in a business way, long before he became a member of the Church. The home teachers called on him one evening. He invited them in and was anxious to talk to them. He told them that the only thing the matter with our church was that we believe that everyone must be baptized or they cannot enter heaven. The teachers replied to the effect that we don't just believe so, but that the Lord had said so. "Show me where the Lord says so," he said, and they started off. The result is that he is now a member of the stake high council and is a fine, useful man in the Church. What if someone hadn't taken the time?

While on my first mission in Holland, I spent eighteen months in the Rotterdam office and then was made president of the branch. One of the first things I did was to check the names of all Saints of record. I couldn't find the names of one good sister and her grown daughters who frequently came to our meetings. One day I said to her: "You know, Sister, I have been all through our records, but do not find your name."

She replied, "I am not a member of the Church."

"You aren't? Well, you ought to be. Just what is the matter?"

"There are some things I don't understand."

"Let me come to your home and explain these things to you."

Just one visit cleared up all her troubles, and she and her two daughters were baptized.

We baptized a woman in the South and asked her how it was she finally decided to join the Church. "Well, you made so much better man of my husband, I thought if it would do him that much good, it would surely help me."

There are hundreds and thousands in this world converted to Mormonism who have not the courage to accept it. I have found them everywhere. There are many who know it is true. I have a letter from a treasurer in the Presbyterian Church in the East, thanking me for bringing him the truth but admitting that he is too big a coward to accept it until his family and friends feel more favorably disposed toward it.

I entered another home in the East and the lady of the house showed me a copy of the Book of Mormon in her library. She told me that her minister had asked her what she was doing with it, to which she responded that it was the word of God. The minister stated that he wouldn't call it that, but she said that is what she considered it to be. "Why don't you join the Church?" I asked. "Well, you see, we are in business here, and must maintain a high social standing; we haven't the faith, but we know it is true."

I had a gentleman tell me not to call again. "Every time you ring the bell," he said, "it doesn't matter what hour of the day or night, something goes through me, and I know you are there."

"All right, I will not ask to come again. I have finished my work. You wouldn't get that thrill if I were not sent of God. The responsibility is yours from now on," I told him.

An investigator in Holland turned the missionaries away many times. Finally I succeeded in winning his friendship and got to talk with him about the gospel. He would invite us to his home and also any minister who was not afraid to meet a Mormon elder. One night he said to me: "I would give all I own if I could prove you were wrong."

I told him that if he would do that, I would not ask to come again. I told him that he didn't want to prove we were right, but if in trying to prove that we were wrong he proved that we were right, then he had one of two choices: either join the Church and help build the kingdom of God in the earth and have honor and endless happiness, or to have to "kick against the pricks." I reminded him of the words of the Lord to Saul of Tarsus: "It is hard for thee to kick against the pricks." He told me that he had all the religion he needed, and that no one could add to it.

A few weeks later he joined the Church. The next time I saw him he said: "I didn't realize anyone could be so happy. How could I have been so blind to it all?"

After having called several times at a home while tracting, the lady said: "What are you trying to do, Mr. Richards, make Mormons of all of us?"

I replied: "I can promise you one thing, and that is that I will never ask you to join the Mormon Church. But if I could show you where you could trade a one dollar bill for a five dollar bill, I wouldn't have to ask you to do it, would I?"

She answered, "I get you."

Later I received a letter from her, addressing me as "Brother Richards" and advising that she had decided to trade the one dollar for five, that she had joined the Church. I have often said to my missionaries: "If you cannot make Mormonism look better than five to one as against any other religion or philosophy I have ever heard of, I think you are poor missionaries."

I spent from Thursday night to Saturday evening once with a man from Birmingham, Alabama. A deacon in the Baptist Church, he was an older man than I, and better educated. He had heard me preach Thursday night and invited me to stop at his home. We talked until two o'clock in the morning and began again early the next morning. Then he offered to take me thirty miles to fill an evening appointment I had, and I am the kind of person who knows that if you want to convert a person, you must let him do something for you. We filled this appointment and then I spent another night at his home. He offered to drive me to Montgomery, a distance of 125 miles, and I accepted his invitation. That evening, unsolicited, he made this statement to a group we were with: "I have learned more religion since last Thursday evening than in all the rest of my life put together." This wasn't because of my knowledge, but because we have something bigger, better, and more beautiful than anything he had ever heard of.

I spent an evening with a group of Bible students in The Hague. The man in whose home we met owned a large furniture store. That night we talked about work for the dead, universal salvation, opportunity hereafter, and so forth. The daughter turned to her father and said: "I don't understand it. In any gospel conversation or discussion of the scriptures you have always had the last word, but tonight you haven't said a thing." The father said: "There isn't anything to say. This man is teaching us things I have never heard before."

I had a similar experience in Massachusetts. I went into a home, and after I had explained our message, the man said, "I guess I have been a Mormon all my life and haven't known it." His wife would not come into the room but was quietly busy in the kitchen with her ironing while I was talking with her husband, and you can readily understand that I saw to it she heard what I had to say. When I was there for the last visit I asked her if she would not honor me with her presence, telling her that she may never see me again and that I would like her to do me the favor of listening to what I had to say, to which she consented. Just as we commenced the discussion, her son, who was attending Harvard University, came in and she said to him, "My boy, you take this Bible and follow this man. You have a fine education and you will be able to show us how he is trying to lead us astray."

They followed me for an hour and a half, and when I closed my Bible I said to the young man, "Will you kindly tell your mother and father how I am trying to lead you astray?"

He replied, "Mother, this man isn't trying to lead you astray. He is teaching you the truth."

Then she said to me, "Even though I don't believe all you say, there is something about you that I cannot help but like. Won't you pray with us before you leave?"

I think of the promises of the Lord to the early elders of this church who made inquiry of the Lord through the Prophet Joseph as to what they could do that would be most acceptable to the Lord. They were commanded to thrust in their sickles with their might and reap while the day lasts (D&C 6:3), and were then told that if they labored all their days in crying repentance unto the people and brought save it be one soul unto him, how great should be their joy with that soul in the kingdom of God (D&C 18:15).

I never fully realized what this meant until I had a letter from a brother in Arizona while I was president of the Southern States Mission. He told me that his father was one of the first converts to the Church in the state of Mississippi, back in 1840, and that since then his father's descendants had given over one hundred years of missionary service to the Church, and that at that time ten were in the mission field. Add to this the number of years of service of their converts and their converts' converts, and you have literally a nation of men and women in the Church today because of one missionary's going into Mississippi and bringing one man into the Church. This missionary may have felt that he hadn't accomplished much, but he will have joy untold in the eternal worlds seeing that man at the head of his posterity in the kingdom of God.

I have an idea that most missionaries often run *from* rather than *to* their work. That may sound foolish, but it seems we are sometimes afraid of people and do not remain with them long enough to tell our story. How can a man judge the beauty of a building if all he ever sees is the plan or foundation of it, not seeing the final structure with its decorations and adornments? He cannot know much about what it is to be. We sometimes go into a home, say a few words, and bear our testimonies, and think we have fully warned that house and that it will stand condemned in the day of judgment if they receive not the gospel. I tell you, I believe there are thousands upon thousands of men and women who love the Lord enough that they would join the Church and bear his name if they could only see the picture as we see it, and we simply don't take the time to tell them of it.

I had one experience I will never forget. I called at a home one day while tracting and spent about an hour with a Catholic lady discussing the principle of baptism, and whether it should be by pouring, sprinkling, or immersion. Finally the lady said to me: "What difference does it make anyway?" I excused myself. I knew I had failed, and I kept saying on my way home: "What difference *does* it make? If Joseph Smith wasn't chosen of God, if the heavens have not been opened, if God the Eternal Father and Jesus Christ, his Son, have not appeared in this day, if the priesthood of God has not been restored through the Prophet Joseph Smith, and if the commitments foretold by ancient prophets have not been made to the Church in this day, what right have I to be out as a missionary anyway?"

I then resolved that as far as I had missionary work to do, I was going to start at the beginning and follow through to the end. I have told the missionaries that if they would learn how to tell our story, they would never have to feel they were going out to battle. They should invite their hearers to listen to them and to be the judge and jury, but they should withhold judgment until they have heard all the story and then make an analysis of all the evidence, as a jury would do.

We are not going to convert the world by merely telling them a little about our Welfare Plan, the Relief Society, or MIA. We must take the word of God, which is sharper than a two-edge sword, and show how the plan has been contemplated and unfolded through the years, and that the Church as it is today was seen by the prophets of old. We should point out that the revelations to Joseph Smith brought truth and knowledge to earth that could not have been known without divine revelation; that the organization of this church is patterned after the organization of the primitive church. The missionary has an inexhaustible amount of material. If he will leave his message with the people, he will experience joy such as he has never before known. As for myself, I would rather have such an opportunity than to sit down to the finest dinner ever served.

When I went on my first mission, President Anthony H. Lund told our group of missionaries: "Wherever you go the people will love you. Don't be lifted up in the pride of your hearts and think you are better than other men. They will love you because of your influence, and because of the power and spirit of your calling which you take with you." I did not know then what he meant, but when I saw a man in Rotterdam, who for years had been in the service of his government, get down on his knees and kiss my hand when I left him, and when a mother said, "It is harder to see you go than it was to see my own daughter leave a few weeks ago because you brought me the gospel," I began to realize what President Lund had meant. As I left for home, all the way from Amsterdam to Rotterdam my eyes were filled with tears of joy for the privilege that had been mine of proclaiming the gospel message to the people of that land.

President Lund said, "If you ever run out of something to say when called upon to speak, I promise you if you will bear your testimony to the effect that Jesus Christ lives and that Joseph Smith was a true prophet of God, the Lord will give you something to say."

God bless our missionaries with the spirit of their calling. May they find great joy in his service. May they enjoy the sweet spirit of the Lord, and as his servant, I promise them if they will go to with their might, the promise he made long ago will also be theirs: "Behold, I will be with you alway, even unto the end of the world."

16

Who Is to Do This Preaching?

As descendants of Abraham, Isaac, and Jacob, we are a chosen people with a great responsibility and a wonderful opportunity for service.

Before Abraham was born the Lord showed unto him the intelligences that were organized before the world was, and among them were many of the noble and great ones. And the Lord said unto Abraham, "These I will make my rulers; for he stood among those that were spirits, and he saw that they were good; and he said unto me: Abraham, thou art one of them; thou wast chosen before thou wast born." (Abraham 3:23.)

Thus Abraham was chosen before he was born to be a ruler among men, and because of his faithfulness, he was called a friend of God. The Lord made mighty promises unto him and his seed, and we are his seed. Hear the word of the Lord unto Abraham:

"And I will make of thee a great nation, and I will bless thee above measure, and make thy name great among all nations, and thou shalt be a blessing unto thy seed after thee, that in their hands they shall bear this ministry and Priesthood unto all nations.

". . . for I give unto thee a promise that this right shall continue in thee, and in thy seed after thee . . . shall

111

all the families of the earth be blessed, even with the blessings of the Gospel, which are the blessings of salvation, even of life eternal." (Abraham 2:9, 11.)

This promise the Lord renewed upon the head of Isaac, the son of Abraham, and upon Isaac's son Jacob, whose name was changed to Israel; and this promise with its responsibilities therefore is unto all the descendants of Abraham, Isaac, and Jacob. Since we are their descendants, it becomes our responsibility to help the Lord to fulfill his promise, for he has to have instruments for the fulfillment of his promises.

It will be noted that the Lord promised Abraham that through his seed, "They shall bear this ministry and Priesthood unto all nations," that thereby "shall all the families of the earth be blessed, even with the blessings of the Gospel, which are the blessings of salvation, even of life eternal."

The spiritual leadership of the world thus rests upon the shoulders of the descendants of these great patriarchs and has done so from their day unto the present.

We can only refer briefly to a few of these great spiritual leaders; of them, Moses was probably the greatest, for we read: "And there arose not a prophet since in Israel like unto Moses, whom the Lord knew face to face." (Deuteronomy 34:10.) Probably the works of no other prophet of ancient time are as well known as are those of Moses: how the Lord showed forth his mighty power through Moses to free the children of Israel from bondage and captivity of the Egyptians; how they passed through the Red Sea on dry land; how Moses smote the rock and water gushed forth to quench the thirst of the Israelites; and above all, how, amid the thunder and lightning of Sinai the Lord gave unto him the Ten Commandments, which has been the foundation of the spiritual leadership of the world from that day unto the present.

We mention Joseph, who was sold into Egypt by

his brethren and who during the famine saved his father's family from starvation by feeding them from the granaries of Pharaoh. There were the prophets Micah, Jeremiah, Ezekiel, and Daniel; and there was Isaiah, unto whom the Lord gave such wonderful revelations pertaining to the work of the latter days, the dispensation in which we now live. It has always seemed to me that the prophet Isaiah lived almost more in our day than when he was actually upon the earth because of the wonderful things he was permitted to see through the revelations of the Lord to him pertaining to the latter days. The prophets of the Book of Mormon seem to share this concept. In Mormon we read: "For the eternal purposes of the Lord shall roll on, until all his promises shall be fulfilled. Search the prophecies of Isaiah. . . ." (Mormon 8:22-23.)

Of course the greatest of all the prophets through the seed of Abraham, Isaac, and Jacob was Jesus the Christ, who atoned for the sins of the world and thus redeemed all mankind from the fall: "For as in Adam all die, even so in Christ shall all be made alive." (1 Corinthians 15:22.) He took upon himself the sins of the world, as he said, "For behold, I, God, have suffered these things for all, that they might not suffer if they would repent." (D&C 19:16.) And he became the first fruits of the resurrection. Through his great atoning sacrifice all men will be resurrected from the dead.

Thus more than any other prophet he fulfilled the promise made to Abraham that through him and his seed "shall all the families of the earth be blessed, even with the blessings of the Gospel, which are the blessings of salvation, even of life eternal." (Abraham 2:11.) It should be remembered that Jesus came through the loins of Judah, and that during his ministry and that of his apostles, the gospel was preached first to the Jews and later to the Gentiles with the promise that in the latter days the gospel would be preached first to the Gentiles and then to the Jews. (1 Nephi 13:42.)

Great were the promises of the Lord to the descendants of Abraham through Isaac and Jacob and their seed, all of whom were known as the children of Israel, of whom the Lord said: "For thou art an holy people unto the Lord thy God: the Lord thy God hath chosen thee to be a special people unto himself, above all people that are upon the face of the earth." (Deuteronomy 7:6.)

The House of Israel was divided into two great kingdoms, the kingdom of Judah and the kingdom of Israel, with the latter under the leadership of Joseph and his sons Ephraim and Manasseh. (See 1 Kings 11:31-32 and 2 Samuel 2:4, 8:11.) Reuben, the firstborn of the twelve sons of Jacob, lost his birthright through transgression; it was taken from him by his father, Jacob, and given to Joseph and his sons Ephraim and Manasseh with the promise that his name should be named upon them, and his name was Israel. (See 1 Chronicles 5:1-2; Genesis 48: 4, 9, 16.)

The kingdom of Israel under leadership of Joseph and his sons was sifted among the Gentile nations and thus became known as the Gentiles. (See Amos 9:8-9.) But technically they are the House of Israel through whom the gospel was to be established in the earth in the latter days and by whom it was to be taken to all nations, including the House of Judah. We are the kingdom of Israel or the Gentiles, and great are the responsibilities that rest upon us in this dispensation.

When Joseph received the blessing at the hands of Jacob and from Moses (see Genesis 49:22-26; Deuteronomy 33:13-17), he was promised a new land in the utmost bounds of the everlasting hills; and foreseeing the gathering of the latter days, he was told that his seed should "push the people together to the ends of the earth; and they are the ten thousands of Ephraim, and they are the thousands of Manasseh." (Deuteronomy 33:17.)

We should remember that through the seed of Joseph

came Lehi and Nephi and other Book of Mormon prophets. Through the prophet Nephi we learn of the promise made to Joseph that in the latter days the Lord would raise up from his loins a "choice seer" who would "be great like unto Moses," and unto him, the Lord promised, "will I give power to bring forth my word . . . and not to the bringing forth my word only, saith the Lord, but to the convincing them of my word which shall have already gone forth among them. . . . for the thing, which the Lord shall bring forth by his hand, by the power of the Lord shall bring my people unto salvation." And then the Lord said: "And I will make him great in mine eyes; for he shall do my work." (2 Nephi 3:7, 9, 15, 8.)

This "choice seer . . . like unto Moses" was, of course, Joseph Smith, who brought forth the word of the Lord: the Book of Mormon, the Pearl of Great Price, the Doctrine and Covenants, and other writings, and through the revelations of the Lord unto him, he has been able to make plain many wonderful teachings of the Bible which had "already gone forth among them," which the world did not understand.

The calling of this prophet from the loins of Joseph in the latter days was the first step in the establishment of a "marvellous work and a wonder" that the Lord promised through his servant Isaiah he would proceed to do in the latter days. (Isaiah 29:13-14.) We will therefore consider a few of the important events foretold by the prophets that should transpire in the latter days under the leadership of this "choice seer" and prophet "like unto Moses."

In Moroni's statement to Joseph Smith when he visited him three times during the night when Joseph was but eighteen, he quoted from the eleventh chapter of Isaiah and indicated that this prophecy was about to be fulfilled in which the prophet said that the Lord would "set his hand again the second time to recover the remnant of his people. . . . And he shall set up an ensign for the nations, and shall assemble the outcasts of Israel, and gather together the dispersed of Judah from the four corners of the earth." (Isaiah 11:11-12.) Joseph was told that the Lord would call him to do this work. How could the Prophet accomplish this great task without helpers?

When Jesus gave his apostles the signs of his second coming and the end of the world, he said: "And this gospel of the kingdom shall be preached in all the world for a witness unto all nations; and then shall the end come." (Matthew 24:14.) Who is to do this preaching?

Before the gospel could be preached in all the world, it had to be brought back to the earth; hence the declaration of the apostle John: "And I saw another angel fly in the midst of heaven, having the everlasting gospel to preach unto them that dwell on the earth, and to every nation, and kindred, and tongue, and people." (Revelation 14:6.) Who then should preach this everlasting gospel unto every nation, kindred, tongue, and people?

To Daniel, the God of heaven made known King Nebuchadnezzar's dream and the interpretation thereof, and after describing the destruction of the nations of the earth, he declared that "in the latter days" the God of heaven would set up a kingdom that would never be destroyed nor left to other people, but it would break in pieces and consume all these kingdoms and stand forever. (Daniel 2:27-28, 44-45.) How could the God of heaven set up such a kingdom in the earth without the help of his servants?

Isaiah declared that it would come to pass in the "last days" that "the mountain of the Lord's house shall be established in the top of the mountains, and shall be exalted above the hills, and all nations shall flow unto it; . . . many people shall go and say, Come ye, and let us go up to the mountain of the Lord, to the house of the God of Jacob; and he will teach us of his ways, and we will walk in his paths. . . ." (Isaiah 2:2-3.) Who do you suppose was to build this house unto the God of Jacob in the last days?

In the preface to the Book of Mormon we read the purpose for which it was preserved: "Which is to show unto the remnant of the House of Israel what great things the Lord hath done for their fathers; and that they may know the covenants of the Lord, that they are not cast off forever—And also to the convincing of the Jew and Gentile that JESUS is the CHRIST, the ETERNAL GOD, manifesting himself unto all nations."

Who is to take the Book of Mormon to the Jew and Gentile that it may convince them that Jesus is the Christ, the Eternal God, manifesting himself unto all nations?

The prophet Jeremiah declared, "Therefore, behold, the days come, saith the Lord, that it shall no more be said, the Lord liveth, that brought up the children of Israel out of the land of Egypt;

"But the Lord liveth, that brought up the children of Israel from the land of the north, and from all the lands whither he had driven them: and I will bring them again into their land that I gave unto their fathers.

"Behold, I will send for many fishers, saith the Lord, and they shall fish them; and after will I send for many hunters, and they shall hunt them from every mountain, and from every hill, and out of the holes of the rocks." (Jeremiah 16:14-16.)

Now if the children of Israel were to be gathered from every land, who are the fishers and hunters who are to do this great work?

There are many other important prophecies pertaining to the "marvellous work and a wonder" that the Lord promised to bring forth in the latter days.

In the song "O My Father" we sing: "For a wise and glorious purpose/Thou hast placed me here on earth." Each man should desire to learn what that purpose is. We should not want to see the kingdom of God established in power in the earth according to his promises without an assurance that we have done our full part in helping to accomplish this great objective.

President Brigham Young once said that if we walk on streets paved with gold, we will pave them. I like that thinking. I like to feel that the Lord needs us to help him to achieve his purposes in the earth.

The little poem by Mary Ann Evans regarding Antonius Stradivarius, whose violins two hundred years old are worth their weight in gold, has always appealed to me:

> If my hand slackened, I should rob God
> Since He is fullest good
> Leaving a blank instead of violins.
> He could not make Antonio Stradivarius violins
> Without Antonio.

And so when the kingdom of God is finally established in its perfection in the earth, preparatory to the coming of the Son of Man, each of us should want to feel that the Lord has needed us to help bring about his decreed purposes in the earth.

17

A Marvelous Work and a Wonder

I have been informed that the book I wrote to assist the missionaries in presenting the message of the restored gospel, *A Marvelous Work and a Wonder,* has been translated into several languages. I am grateful for this widespread use of my book.

I have a firm testimony that there isn't an honest person in this world who really loves the Lord who would not join this church, The Church of Jesus Christ of Latter-day Saints, if he really knew and understood what the Church is and how it came into existence. But so many false stories have been told about it that the eyes of the people have been blinded so that they have not been willing to listen and to judge for themselves of its truth.

It is my feeling that one cannot judge what a house is to be by looking at a hole in the ground. He must wait until the house is completed and decorated before he can know what it actually is going to be like.

So it is with the gospel. One must hear the whole story before judging. If one were sitting in the jury box, he would not think of reaching a verdict without first analyzing all the evidence.

I like to compare the gospel to a jigsaw or picture puzzle. If you dump all the pieces on the table and pick

119

them up one at a time, they do not mean anything. You may have a giraffe's neck or an elephant's trunk, and after examining each piece you will not know what the picture is supposed to be; but when all the pieces are properly fitted together you have a perfect picture, and not one piece could be taken away without doing injury thereto.

It is my feeling and testimony that if one will analyze the message of the restored gospel as given to us through the Prophet Joseph Smith, taking into consideration the promises of the prophets of old as to what must come in the latter days before Christ can make his second appearance, he will come to the conclusion that the story of Mormonism, so called, must be true or that the Lord must yet do a work that will be an exact duplicate of what he has already done through the instrumentality of the Prophet Joseph Smith and as taught by The Church of Jesus Christ of Latter-day Saints.

In preparing my book it was my thought to so fit the pieces together that one could not possibly make a mistake in judgment if he would but read the book carefully and prayerfully.

Hardly a week passes that someone does not write, or that I do not meet them as I visit the stakes and missions of the Church, telling me that the reading of this book has been the means of bringing them to a knowledge of the truth.

Only this morning I received a letter from a mission president in Hong Kong enclosing a copy of a letter from a man in South India, advising him that through reading the book *A Marvelous Work and a Wonder* and the Book of Mormon he had obtained a testimony that we have the truth, and he has taught this to his family and friends until there are forty-four now holding regular meetings and studying the book who are ready to join the Church as soon as missionaries can be sent to them to perform the ordinance of baptism. Among the number are his father and mother, five sisters and their husbands and children, and other friends coming from various churches, such as the London Mission, the Lutheran Mission, the Seventh-Day Adventists, the Catholic Church, and from Hinduism. The man who wrote the letter was employed by the London Mission but was forced to leave because of his interest in our message.

Recently I met a man and his wife in California who had joined the Church through reading this book. He had served for years as a Presbyterian minister.

I met a man in Idaho who joined the Church through the book. He gave a copy to his mother and she joined the Church. He gave a copy to his best friend and he and his wife joined the Church. And I met them all while visiting in that stake.

Letters have come from many lands, particularly from the boys in the armed forces of the United States, indicating that they have joined the Church largely through reading this book.

Many people here at home who have been exposed to the Church and its teachings for years, but who have not had our message presented to them in a manner that they have been convinced, have joined the Church after reading this book.

A good sister came to my office sorrowing because her husband was not a member of the Church and she had to raise the children herself. I asked her if her husband did much reading. She said he did. I gave her a copy of the book and asked her to get her husband to read it and then to write and let me know what he had to say about it. In a few weeks she wrote me saying, "He read your book. He did not say much. Then he read the Book of Mormon. Then he read your book again, and then he said, 'Now I am ready for baptism.' " After he was baptized, he immediately went to work as a stake missionary. A year later he and his wife went to the Manti Temple together. And now he is the stake mission president. He was a good enough man all the time, but no one had presented the gospel to him in such a manner that he could understand its truth and importance. So this good wife had lived with him as a nonmember of the Church for nearly twenty years.

These illustrations are given in the spirit of humility, for no credit is due me for writing the book; its contents are all truths I have learned as a member and missionary in the Church. I take no royalty for writing the book, my only purpose being to help honest seekers after righteousness to find the truth.

Jesus said, "For blessed are they which do hunger and thirst after righteousness, for they shall be filled." I know that he is the author of this work just as much as he was the head of the church that he established while upon the earth. And I know that anyone who is truly seeking after righteousness may know this beyond any shadow of a doubt, for the promise of the Lord is as true today as it was when he uttered the same.

My hope and prayer is that the book may continue a great service in uniting homes that are divided on religious matters and in bringing many to a knowledge of the truth who really love the Lord and desire to serve him as he would be served.

The Message of
the Restoration

18

The Mormons and the Jewish People

If the Jewish people really understood, they would realize that no other people, organization, or church has as much in common with them as do the Mormons, as members of The Church of Jesus Christ of Latter-day Saints.

You have been driven, robbed, and ravished—so have we. You have been persecuted, mistreated, misunderstood—so have we. Why? We were driven from our homes to desolation beyond the boundaries of the United States. You, too, have been driven. Why? There may be other reasons, but it can scarcely be denied that conflicting religious opinions have played a major role in such unfortunate and related experiences.

There is possibly no other question upon which the children of God are as seriously divided as upon religious matters. Some of the greatest recorded persecutions have been instigated by religious leaders of men. This is very displeasing to our Heavenly Father. What a power we could be in the world if we were united.

The Jewish people will find our message most fascinating. The complete accomplishment of our mutual and heaven-assigned responsibilities involves our becoming united (as the descendants of Joseph) with the descendants of Judah (the Jewish people) in the fulfillment of the promises given by the Lord to Abraham and renewed upon the heads of Isaac and Jacob, that through them and their seed all nations of the earth would be blessed.

Therefore, we as descendants of Joseph, a part of the great family of Israel, invite the House of Judah to consider with us some very important matters that affect both of us and our future as promised by the Lord and proclaimed by his holy prophets. In the words of the prophet Isaiah, we say: "Come now, and let us reason together. . . ." (Isaiah 1:18.)

Today the Jews, descendants of Judah, are often looked upon as the only Israelites. Because Jacob wrestled with an angel at Peniel and prevailed, the angel said: "Thy name shall be called no more Jacob, but Israel for as a prince hast thou power with God and with men, and hast prevailed." (Genesis 32:28.) Jacob's new name, Israel, therefore, became the family name, and all of his descendants, his twelve sons, were known variously as Israelites, children of Israel, House of Israel, tribes of Israel.

Ultimately, the descendants of Jacob or Israel were divided into two kingdoms, known as the kingdom of Judah and the kingdom of Israel—the kingdom of Israel under the leadership of Joseph and his sons, Ephraim and Manasseh. The kingdom under the leadership of Joseph and his sons was called the kingdom of Israel in keeping with the blessing given the two sons of Joseph by Jacob (Israel) when he said: "Let my name be named on them, and the name of my fathers Abraham and Isaac." (Genesis 48:16.) This is further sustained by the fact that the birthright was taken from Reuben because of his transgression and was given to the sons of Joseph. (1 Chronicles 5:1-2.)

The Lord, "the God of Israel," inspired the prophet Ahijah to predict the division of Israel into two kingdoms. (See 1 Kings 11:31-32.) Of this division we read:

"And the men of Judah came, and there they anointed David king over the house of Judah. . . .

"But Abner the son of Ner, captain of Saul's host, took Ishbosheth, the son of Saul, and brought him over to Mahanaim;

"And made him king over Gilead, and over the Ashurites, and over Jazreel, and over Ephraim, and over Benjamin, and over all Israel.

"Ishbosheth, Saul's son, was forty years old when he began to reign over Israel, and reigned two years. But the house of Judah followed David." (2 Samuel 2:4, 8:10.)

"And Joab gave up the sum of the number of the people unto the king; and there were in Israel eight hundred thousand valiant men that drew the sword; and the men of Judah were five hundred thousand men." (2 Samuel 24:9.)

From this it would appear the kingdom of Israel was greater in numbers than the kingdom of Judah. To this day, these kingdoms have never been reunited, although the prophets have foretold their ultimate reunion. But together they embrace all the descendants of Abraham through the loins of Isaac and Jacob. Therefore, in looking for the fulfillment of the promises of the Lord to the Fathers Abraham, Isaac, and Jacob and their descendants, we must not look to the Jews alone as the decendants of Judah. We must realize that great were the promises of the Lord to Joseph and his descendants. Of this fact, our brothers, the Jews, should be fully informed, because they without us, the descendants of Joseph, cannot accomplish what the Lord expects at their hands as foretold by his holy prophets.

BLESSING OF THE SONS OF JACOB

In this brief study, it will not be possible to consider the blessings and promises of the Lord made to the . twelve sons of Jacob. However, since they were divided into two kingdoms under the leadership of Judah and of Joseph, we will, of necessity, consider the promises made to them.

"And Jacob called into his sons, and said, Gather yourselves together, that I may tell you that which shall befall you in the last days.

"Gather yourselves together, and hear, ye sons of Jacob; and hearken unto Israel your father. . . ." (Genesis 49:1-2.)

"Judah is a lion's whelp: from the prey, my son, thou art gone up: he stooped down, he couched as a lion, and as an old lion; who shall rouse him up?

"The sceptre shall not depart from Judah, nor a law-giver from between his feet, until Shiloh come; and unto him shall the gathering of the people be.

"Binding his foal unto the vine, and his ass's colt unto the choice vine; he washed his garments in wine, and his clothes in the blood of grapes:

"His eyes shall be red with wine, and his teeth white with milk." (Genesis 49:9-12.)

"Joseph is a fruitful bough, even a fruitful bough by a well; whose branches run over the wall:

"The archers have sorely grieved him, and shot at him, and hated him:

"But his bow abode in strength, and the arms of his hands were made strong by the hands of the mighty God of Jacob; (from thence is the shepherd, the stone of Israel:)

"Even by the God of thy father, who shall help thee; and by the Almighty, who shall bless thee with blessings of heaven above, blessings of the deep that lieth under, blessings of the breasts, and of the womb:

"The blessings of thy father have prevailed above the blessings of my progenitors unto the utmost bound of the everlasting hills: they shall be on the head of Joseph, and on the crown of the head of him that was separate from his brethren." (Genesis 49:22-26.)

Jacob's blessings upon his sons, therefore, were to tell them "that which shall befall you in the last days." It would appear that the blessing given to Judah contemplated the coming of Shiloh, or the Redeemer, who would gather his people unto him.

Joseph's blessing seems to contain a promise that his seed would go into a new land in the "utmost bound of the everlasting hills," where they could be blessed "with blessings of heaven above, blessings of the deep that lieth under, blessings of the breasts, and of the womb," even with blessings greater than those of his progenitors. Joseph's blessing also foreshadows his separation from his brethren. This thought is made even more plain by the great prophet Moses:

"And this is the blessing, wherewith Moses the man of God blessed the children of Israel before his death. . . .

"And of Joseph he said, Blessed of the Lord be his land, for the precious things of heaven, for the dew, and for the deep that croucheth beneath,

"And for the precious fruits brought forth by the sun, and for the precious things put forth by the moon,

"And for the chief things of the ancient mountains, and for the precious things of the lasting hills,

"And for the precious things of the earth and fulness thereof, and for the good will of him that dwelt in the bush: let the blessing come upon the head of Joseph, and upon the top of the head of him that was separated from his brethren.

"His glory is like the firstling of his bullock, and his horns are like the horns of unicorns: with them he shall push the people together to the ends of the earth: and they are the ten thousands of Ephraim, and they are the thousands of Manasseh." (Deuteronomy 33:1, 13-17.)

Moses' description of Joseph's land is most impressive. Note the number of times he uses the word "precious." His blessing goes a little farther than that of

Jacob, by foretelling the day when the Lord would gather together unto this new land of Joseph his descendants through Ephraim and Manasseh, from "the ends of the earth." The reader might like to compare this blessing with that given to Judah by Moses as recorded in Deuteronomy 33:7.

Joseph's Dream

Consider Joseph's dreams, which were given him of the Lord and which caused his brothers to hate him and to sell him to the Ishmaelites of Egypt:

"And Joseph dreamed a dream, and he told it his brethren: and they hated him yet the more.

"And he said unto them, Hear, I pray you, this dream which I have dreamed:

"For, behold, we were binding sheaves in the field, and, lo, my sheaf arose, and also stood upright; and, behold, your sheaves stood round about, and made obeisance to my sheaf.

"And his brethren said to him, Shalt thou indeed reign over us? or shalt thou indeed have dominion over us? And they hated him yet the more for his dreams, and for his words.

"And he dreamed yet another dream, and told it his brethren, and said, Behold, I have dreamed a dream more; and, behold, the sun and the moon and the eleven stars made obeisance to me.

"And he told it to his father, and to his brethren: and his father rebuked him, and said unto him, What is this dream that thou hast dreamed? Shall I and thy mother and thy brethren indeed come to bow down ourselves to thee to the earth?

"And his brethren envied him; but his father observed the saying." (Genesis 37:5-11.)

When all the facts are known and fully understood, the descendants of Judah (the Jews) will realize that when Joseph fed his father Jacob and his eleven brothers and their families from the granaries of Egypt, during the period of famine, and thus saved their lives, that that gift was not to be compared with what the descendants of Joseph have to offer the descendants of Judah at this time.

Notwithstanding the fact that the descendants of Jacob, all of whom were called Israelites, were divided into two kingdoms, nevertheless, the title "Israel" is often used in the Bible to refer to the whole House of Israel, or all of the descendants of Jacob. By keeping this in mind, we shall be less confused in our further consideration of the words and predictions of the prophets. In our day, the term "Israel" often refers to the descendants of Judah only, since they have maintained their identity as a race, while the descendants of Joseph and the other sons of Jacob, who constituted the kingdom of Israel, were sifted among the Gentile nations, as the prophet Amos declared: ". . . I will not utterly destroy the house of Jacob, saith the Lord.

"For, lo, I will command, and I will sift the house of Israel among all nations, like as corn is sifted in a sieve, yet shall not the least grain fall upon the earth." (Amos 9:8-9.)

Not only did the prophets foretell the scattering of the House of Israel among the nations, but the House of Judah was to be scattered also: "And the Lord said, I will remove Judah also out of my sight, as I have removed Israel, and will cast off this city Jerusalem which I have chosen, and the house of which I said, My name shall be there." (2 Kings 23:37.)

TWO RECORDS TO BE KEPT

Because Israel was to be divided and scattered, the Lord made provision that two records should be kept: one for Judah and one for Joseph. This command was given by the Lord to Ezekiel, a prophet of Judah. The Lord further promised through his prophet that he would

132 LE GRAND RICHARDS SPEAKS

join these two records together and make them one in his hands:

"The word of the Lord came again unto me, saying,

"Moreover, thou son of man, take thee one stick, and write upon it, For Judah, and for the children of Israel his companions: then take another stick, and write upon it, For Joseph, the stick of Ephraim, and for all the house of Israel his companions:

"And join them one to another into one stick; and they shall become one in thine hand.

"And when the children of thy people shall speak unto thee, saying, Wilt thou not shew us what thou meanest by these?

"Say unto them, Thus saith the Lord God, Behold, I will take the stick of Joseph, which is in the hand of Ephraim, and the tribes of Israel his fellows, and will put them with him, even with the stick of Judah, and make them one stick, and they shall be one in mind hand.

"And the sticks whereon thou writest shall be in thine hand before their eyes." (Ezekiel 37:15-20.)

The Bible as used by the Jewish people contains no history of the House of Joseph after approximately 721 B.C. Since we have considered the wonderful promises of the Lord to Joseph and his descendants, even that of a new land in "the utmost bounds of the everlasting hills," we respectfully inquire—"Where is the record of the fulfillment of these promises? Is it possible that the Lord would have given Joseph such outstanding promises, even above those given to any of his eleven brothers, and then have made no provision for a record of their fulfillment?" The prophet Ezekiel answers this question by telling us that the Lord commanded him that one record should be kept of Judah and his companions, which is the Bible that has remained with the House of Judah through the years, and that another record should be kept of Joseph and his companions, which record he indicates would be in the hand of Ephraim—implying that Judah would know nothing of this record. Then Ezekiel prophesied that the Lord would bring forth this record of Joseph and join it with the record of Judah and make them one in his hand.

RECORD OF JOSEPH BROUGHT FORTH

This command that two records be kept was obeyed, and part of Joseph's message to Judah today is that this record of Joseph has been brought forth by the Lord and has been joined to the record of Judah. In the eyes of the Lord they constitute one record, even as the Lord promised.

This new record of Joseph and his companions is a book of over 500 pages, and is known as the Book of Mormon, thus named after a prophet of the seed of Joseph who made an abridgment of many records that had been kept by descendants of Joseph who were led to the land of America about 600 years B.C., and covers a period of approximately 1,000 years. It also contains a record of the people of Jared who were scattered at the time the Lord confounded the language of the people when they were building a tower to get to heaven. They also were led, by the Lord, to the land of America. This abridgment was made by the prophet Mormon on plates of gold in the language of the Egyptians. The metal plates on which the record was inscribed were delivered to the Prophet Joseph Smith by the Angel Moroni, a resurrected being and a son of Mormon. At the same time, Moroni delivered to Joseph Smith the Urim and Thummim through which he was able to translate the engravings on the plates into the English language. The book (the Book of Mormon) was published in the year 1830.

No other people has attempted to offer to the world the record of Joseph which the Lord commanded should be kept and which he promised to bring forth and join to the record of Judah, to make them one in his hands.

Many of the prophets of Joseph, as recorded in the

Book of Mormon, spoke with great plainness pertaining to the latter days. They spoke of the destiny of the House of Judah and also of the House of Joseph. From them we learn that the land of America is the new land the Lord promised to give to Joseph and his descendants, and that it is a choice land, choice above all other lands. We learn that in the latter days the Lord would establish his Zion upon this land as a gathering place for the seed of Joseph which had been "sifted among the nations." We learn that the descendants of Judah (the Jews) would be gathered back to Jerusalem and its environs; that Jerusalem would be rebuilt with its temple. All of these predictions were made in great plainness long before there was any modern movement looking to this accomplishment in this generation.

The bringing forth of this record was to be such an important event in the sight of the Lord that he permitted his prophet Isaiah to behold its coming, together with other important events in connection therewith:

"Wherefore the Lord said, Forasmuch as this people draw near me with their mouth, and with their lips do honour me, but have removed their heart far from me, and their fear toward me is taught by the precept of men:

"Therefore, behold, I will proceed to do a marvellous work among this people, even a marvellous work and a wonder: for the wisdom of their wise men shall perish, and the understanding of their prudent men shall be hid." (Isaiah 29:13-14.)

The prophet Isaiah makes it clear that the coming of this "marvellous work and a wonder" would put at nought the "wisdom of their wise men" and would confound "the understanding of their prudent men." He makes it clear that it would come at a time when men would worship the Lord with their lips, but that their hearts would be far removed from him. Isaiah stated that their worship of the Lord would be through the precepts of men. The lack of unity among the Jews and in the

Christian world is evidence enough that men everywhere, of all races, are worshiping God through the precepts of men, else they would be happily united instead of so unfortunately divided.

It is evident that the "marvellous work and a wonder" which the prophet Isaiah predicted the Lord would bring forth would include a record of a people who had been destroyed and who would "speak out of the ground" and "whisper out of the dust":

"Woe to Ariel, to Ariel, the city where David dwelt! add ye year to year, let them kill sacrifices.

"Yet I will distress Ariel, and there shall be heaviness and sorrow: and it shall be unto me as Ariel.

"And I will camp against thee round about, and will lay siege against thee with a mount, and I will raise forts against thee.

"And thou shalt be brought down, and shall speak out of the ground, and thy speech shall be low out of the dust, and thy voice shall be, as of one that hath a familiar spirit, out of the ground, and thy speech shall whisper out of the dust." (Isaiah 29:1-4.)

It would appear from these words that Isaiah looked far into the future, "add ye year to year," and beheld the destruction of a people like unto the people of Jerusalem, and that after their destruction, they would "speak out of the ground." Obviously this could only be possible through a written record. The prophecy stated that the voice of this people would have "a familiar spirit." When prophets of the Lord speak, they always have "a familiar spirit." This prophecy will be better understood when it is known that the plates from which the Book of Mormon was translated were deposited in a stone box in the Hill Cumorah in the State of New York by the same Moroni who, 1400 years later, as a resurrected being, delivered them to Joseph Smith for translation.

In the same chapter, Isaiah further states:

"For the Lord hath poured out upon you the spirit

of deep sleep, and hath closed your eyes: the prophets and your rulers, the seers hath he covered.

"And the vision of all is become unto you as the words of a book that is sealed, which men deliver to one that is learned, saying, Read this, I pray thee: and he saith, I cannot; for it is sealed:

"And the book is delivered to him that is not learned, saying, Read this, I pray thee: and he saith, I am not learned." (Isaiah 29:10-12.)

The "book" could have been nothing other than the Book of Mormon, the record of Joseph, which the Lord commanded Ezekiel should be kept. In its coming forth, every detail of this prophecy of Isaiah was fulfilled. Therefore, as we have stated, the coming forth of this record was at least part of the marvellous work and a wonder the Lord promised to bring about as foretold by Isaiah.

In this brief discussion we cannot mention all of the important things the descendants of Joseph have to offer the descendants of Judah as part of this marvellous work and a wonder. No one else has announced or proclaimed the fulfillment of this promise. No one else has offered to Judah the record of Joseph. Prophets are prophets, when sent and inspired by the Lord, whether they be descendants of Judah or Joseph. Surely Judah will want to know what the prophets of Joseph have to say as affecting them and their future destiny and responsibility in the world.

The "marvellous work and a wonder" described by Isaiah was nothing more or less than the establishment of the kingdom of God upon the earth.

The prophet Daniel foretold the rise and fall of the kingdoms of this world and the ultimate establishment of the kingdom of God "in the latter days":

"But there is a God in heaven that revealeth secrets, and maketh known to the king Nebuchadnezzar what shall be in the latter days. Thy dream, and the visions of thy head upon thy bed are these. . . .

"Thou sawest till that a stone was cut out without hands, which smote the image upon his feet that were of iron and clay, and brake them to pieces.

". . . and the stone that smote the image became a great mountain, and filled the whole earth. . . .

"And in the days of these kings shall the God of heaven set up a kingdom, which shall never be destroyed: and the kingdom shall not be left to other people, but it shall break in pieces and consume all these kingdoms, and it shall stand forever." (Daniel 2:28, 34-35, 44.)

The establishment of this kingdom by "the God of heaven" was to be the greatest event "in the latter days." Though small as its beginning would be, its ultimate destiny would be to "fill the whole earth."

We live in "the latter days." It is Joseph's privilege to announce to Judah that "the God of heaven" has set up his kingdom upon the earth, according to his promise. He has accomplished this by raising up a prophet from the loins of Joseph, according to his promise. There was no prophet upon the earth, neither in the House of Judah nor in the House of Joseph. Prophets are never self-sent. They must be called and sent of God: "Surely the Lord God will do nothing, but he revealeth his secret unto his servants the prophets." (Amos 3:7.)

It would require many books to tell all that the Lord has done in these "latter days," in the establishment of his kingdom in the earth for the last time, which kingdom the prophet Daniel declared "shall never be destroyed . . . and it shall stand forever."

When Judah comes to understand that this promised "latter day" kingdom has been established in the earth through a prophet of Joseph, they may then grasp and comprehend more fully the meaning of the dreams the Lord gave Joseph. We, the descendants of Joseph, invite the descendants of Judah to share with us every gift and blessing and opportunity and responsibility this "latter day" kingdom has to offer.

"CHOICE SEER . . . LIKE UNTO MOSES"

The prophet Lehi, who was a descendant of Joseph who was carried captive into Egypt, was led to the land of America by the Lord through a dream which warned him of the approaching destruction of Jerusalem about 600 B.C. In talking to his son Joseph in the wilderness during their travels, he told him of a promise the Lord made to Joseph, the son of Jacob and brother of Judah, that in the latter days the Lord would raise up from his loins a "choice seer . . . and he shall be great like unto Moses . . . and I will make him great in mine eyes, for he shall do my work." (See 2 Nephi 3:3-16.) This is a great promise, for we read in Deuteronomy: "And there arose not a prophet since in Israel like unto Moses, whom the Lord knew face to face." (Deuteronomy 34:10.) When one familiarizes himself with all the promises of the Lord through his holy prophets, he can easily understand how it would require a prophet of the stature of Moses to accomplish all these things in "the latter days."

The latter-day prophet "like unto Moses," the Lord also knew "face to face." In the spring of 1820, in the state of New York, God the Father and his Son Jesus Christ talked with Joseph Smith, face to face, as they instructed him pertaining to the establishment of the kingdom of God in the earth in "the latter days." Joseph Smith was subsequently visited by many heavenly messengers sent to prepare and instruct him in the establishment of the kingdom and to bestow upon him the necessary priesthood authority.

In addition to the visit of the Angel Moroni, Joseph Smith was also visited by Elijah, according to the promise of Malachi:

"Behold, I will send you Elijah the prophet before the coming of the great and dreadful day of the Lord:

"And he shall turn the heart of the fathers to the children, and the heart of the children to their fathers, lest I come and smite the earth with a curse." (Malachi 4:5-6.)

Because Elijah came, we build temples to the Most High in which we perform holy ordinances not only for the living, but vicariously for our dead, thus fulfilling the promise made by Malachi. When Malachi refers to the coming of Elijah, he indicates that were it not for his coming, the Lord would come "and smite the earth with a curse." What an important event!

When Moroni appeared to Joseph Smith in "the latter days," he quoted many passages of scripture, which he declared were about to be fulfilled. Among others, he quoted these words from the prophet Isaiah:

"And it shall come to pass in that day, that the Lord shall set his hand again the second time to recover the remnant of his people, which shall be left, from Assyria, and from Egypt, and from Pathros, and from Cush, and from Elam, and from Shinar, and from Hamath, and from the islands of the sea.

"And he shall set up an ensign for the nations, and shall assemble the outcasts of Israel, and gather together the dispersed of Judah from the four corners of the earth.

"The envy also of Ephraim shall depart, and the adversaries of Judah shall be cut off: Ephraim shall not envy Judah, and Judah shall not vex Ephraim." (Isaiah 11:11-13.)

This is but one of the many prophecies indicating a separate gathering of Israel and of Judah, and that they would finally be united.

Following these visits of Moroni and of Elijah, Moses appeared to Joseph Smith in the Kirtland (Ohio) Temple and bestowed upon him the keys of the latter-day gathering of Israel and of Judah. Because of this, and many other prophecies bearing on this subject, the Prophet Joseph Smith sent Apostle Orson Hyde to the Holy Land in 1841, where he dedicated the land for the return of the children of Judah. We quote briefly from his dedicatory prayer:

"Grant, therefore, O Lord, . . . to remove the barrenness and sterility of this land, and let springs of living water break forth to water its thirsty soil. Let the vine and olive produce in their strength, and the fig-tree bloom and flourish. Let the land become abundantly fruitful . . .; let it again flow with plenty to feed the returning prodigals who come home with a spirit of grace and supplication; upon it let the clouds distil virtue and richness, and let the fields smile with plenty. Let the flocks and the herds greatly increase and multiply upon the mountains and the hills; and let Thy great kindness conquer and subdue the unbelief of Thy people. Do Thou take from them their stony heart, and give them a heart of flesh; and may the sun of Thy favor dispel the cold mists of darkness which have beclouded their atmosphere." (*Documentary History of the Church,* vol. 4, p. 456.)

This prayer seems to be prophetic, for while sterility and barrenness had existed in that land for nearly two thousand years, it is now becoming as a "watered garden." Flocks and herds are increasing with great rapidity.

The prophets of Judah were no less positive in their pronouncements of the redemption of that land from its barren and sterile condition under the blessing of the God of their fathers. The prophet Jeremiah had a very clear understanding of that which would befall Judah "in the latter days":

"Thus saith the Lord; Behold, I will bring again the captivity of Jacob's tent, and have mercy on his dwelling places; and the city shall be builded upon her own heap, and the palace shall remain after the manner thereof. . . .

"The fierce anger of the Lord shall not return, until he have done it, and until he have performed the intents of his heart: in the latter days ye shall consider it." (Jeremiah 30:18, 24.)

The words of the prophet Ezekiel specifically describe this rebuilding.

"Thus saith the Lord God; In the day that I shall have cleansed you from all your iniquities I will also cause you to dwell in the cities, and the wastes shall be builded.

"And the desolate land shall be tilled, whereas it lay desolate in the sight of all that passed by.

"And they shall say, This land that was desolate is become like the garden of Eden: and the waste and desolate and ruined cities are become fenced, and are inhabited." (Ezekiel 36:33-35.)

There are many other equally important prophecies that have been fulfilled, and many that await fulfillment. Only by the bringing together, in these latter days, of the kingdoms of Israel and of Judah, and their becoming united in the building of the kingdom of God on the earth, can these prophecies find their fulfillment. Only in such unity of purpose and effort can the promises of the Lord to the Fathers—Abraham, Isaac, and Jacob— and their descendants be fulfilled.

Both Judah and Joseph are in the divine plan together by God's decree. The God of Abraham, Isaac, and Jacob hath spoken it and so it shall be. "For thou art an holy people unto the Lord thy God: the Lord thy God hath chosen thee to be a special people unto himself, above all people that are upon the face of the earth." (Deuteronomy 7:6.)

The Lord does not choose a people to be "a special people unto himself" without a purpose. Judah will not be able completely to understand the full purpose of this statement without the knowledge which the seed and the record of Joseph can give them.

Therefore, we say unto Judah, our brethren, "Come, let us reason together" and happily discover our common objectives—discover that neither Judah nor Joseph can say, one to the other, "I have no need of thee."

19

"The Hope That Is in You"

". . . be ready always to give an answer to every man that asketh you a reason of the hope that is in you with meekness and fear." (1 Peter 3:15.)

If someone were to ask just why you believe that this is the only true church in the world, what would your answer be?

Sometime back one of our Mormon girls was married and went East to live. When her neighbors found that she was a member of the Mormon Church, they all wanted to know what the Mormons believe. She wrote home to an editor of the *Deseret News* and said, "Please write and tell me what we believe. I know that the first two principles are that we should not use tea or coffee and play cards." I cannot quite imagine how anybody could expect to convert a neighbor or a friend to the truth of the gospel if that were all that we stand for. We have to have something more than that to offer if we expect to convert them.

The Lord said to the Prophet Joseph, ". . . it becometh every man who hath been warned to warn his neighbor." (D&C 88:81.) Every Latter-day Saint ought to aspire to be able to give a reason for the hope that is in him, just as the apostle Peter has indicated, so that we

142

can intelligently tell why we are members of the Church and not just that we do not use tea or coffee or play cards.

When I was on my first mission in Holland, my cousin went on a mission to Norway. One day I received a letter from him that read like this: "LeGrand, I met a man the other day who knows more about religion than I have ever dreamed of. I told him that if he had something better than I had, I would join his church."

I wrote him back and said:

You told him just the right thing. If he has something better than you have, you ought to join his church. But *does* he have something better than a personal visitation of God the Father and his Son Jesus Christ to this earth, to open the dispensation of the fulness of times? Does he have something better than the personal visitation of Moroni with the plates from which the Book of Mormon was translated?

Does he have something better than the coming of John the Baptist, who was the forerunner of Christ, beheaded for his testimony, and who returned as a resurrected being with the Aaronic Priesthood? Does he have something better than the coming of Peter, James, and John with the Melchizedek Priesthood? Does he have something better than the coming of Moses and Elijah and Elias, with the keys of their dispensations?

If he has something better than that, you join his church!

To me, that *is* Mormonism. As far as I am concerned those things absolutely are true and that is the foundation upon which this church is built. If you could recite all the scriptures by heart and you did not know these things to be true, it would not do you a bit of good.

That is why I say that testimony is the mortar that holds the building together. It is the mortar that holds this church together. It is the power by which it is growing. That is why we can ask men in any station in life to serve in the Church and they do so.

My testimony is such that I say that if the veil were parted and we could understand why this world has made such great progress since the gospel was restored as compared with all the history of the past, we would know that it was because the Father and the Son had come and broken the darkness, just as the scriptures say. Isaiah said, ". . . the darkness shall cover the earth, and gross darkness the people." (Isaiah 60:2.) During that time the world made no progress. Year after year, century after century, people lived in the same kind of houses and traveled in the same crude manner and lived in the same crude homes with no modern conveniences. Then all at once light broke forth. The Lord said: ". . . I will pour out my spirit upon all flesh; and . . . your old men shall dream dreams, your young men shall see visions." (Joel 2:28.)

When the Lord poured out his spirit, things began to happen, until we can hardly keep track of them. I recall an article from Ripley's "Believe It or Not" in which he indicates that back in 1830 the head of the United States Patent Office suggested his office be closed because there was so little use made of it. It had only had a few applications up to that time. Since then more than three million patents have been issued because the Lord has been pouring out his spirit upon all flesh.

Again, speaking of a testimony, we could approach that from so many different angles as to *why* we know that this is the work of God, the Eternal Father. To get to the bottom of things, let's look at Isaiah, the prophet. In the Book of Mormon we have many statements regarding the work of Isaiah. Consider the words of Moroni: "For the eternal purposes of the Lord shall roll on, until all his promises shall be fulfilled.

"Search the prophecies of Isaiah. . . ." (Mormon 8:22-23.)

As I search the prophecies of Isaiah, it seems to me that he almost lived in *our* day, because the Lord, through holy vision, permitted him to see our day and what should transpire here in this, the last dispensation.

I read to you from Second Nephi the words of Nephi

regarding Isaiah: "But behold, I proceed with mine own prophecy, according to my plainness; in the which I know that no man can err; nevertheless, in the days that the prophecies of Isaiah shall be fulfilled men shall know of a surety, at the time when they shall come to pass." (2 Nephi 25:7.)

We live in the day that the prophecies of Isaiah are being fulfilled, and we know that he spoke under the power of the Holy Ghost. Where did we get this? Out of the Book of Mormon. The Book of Mormon was published long before Joseph Smith ever had any vision of the fulfillment of the prophecies of Isaiah in the latter days, so he did not write these. This was his translation of the plates. Then he goes on to say: ". . . for I know that they shall be of great worth unto them in the last days; for in that day shall they understand them; wherefore, for their good have I written them." (2 Nephi 25:8.)

Could you write anything plainer than that—that we would be able to understand the prophecies of Isaiah in this day because they were written for our benefit?

When he appeared to the Nephites, the Savior said this about the writings of Isaiah:

"Ye remember that I spake unto you, and said that when the words of Isaiah should be fulfilled—behold they are written, ye have them before you, therefore search them—

"And verily, verily, I say unto you, that when they shall be fulfilled then is the fulfilling of the covenant which the Father hath made unto his people, O house of Israel.

"And then shall the remnants, which shall be scattered abroad upon the face of the earth, be gathered in from the east and from the west, and from the south and from the north; and they shall be brought to the knowledge of the Lord their God, who hath redeemed them." (3 Nephi 20:11-13.)

Do you suppose Joseph Smith could have written anything like that about Isaiah if he had not been translating the records that had already been written? Where could such things come from if the Book of Mormon is not true?

The following prophecy is recorded in Isaiah and was quoted by Moroni when he visited the Prophet Joseph three times during the night and again the next morning and told him the things that were about to come to pass. Just remember that at that time there was no Church of Jesus Christ of Latter-day Saints on this earth. The Book of Mormon had not been given or translated, and the priesthood had not been restored, and yet the Angel Moroni quoted these words from Isaiah:

"And in that day there shall be a root of Jesse, which shall stand for an ensign of the people; to it shall the Gentiles seek; and his rest shall be glorious.

"And it shall come to pass in that day, that the Lord shall set his hand again the second time to recover the remnant of his people. . . ." (Isaiah 11:10-11.)

Can you tell me any place in all the histories of this world where God has set his hand again the second time to recover his people except through the restoration of the gospel and the coming of Moses with the keys of the gathering of latter-day Israel? These are the things that we ought to get out of the teachings of Isaiah, to show us that he *saw* our day and that we live in its fulfillment.

He said that he would "set his hand again the second time to recover the remnant of his people." You know what the first time was, when he led Israel up out of Egypt, out of bondage and captivity. Then he goes on:

"And he shall set up an ensign for the nations, and shall assemble the outcasts of Israel, and gather together the dispersed of Judah from the four corners of the earth." (Isaiah 11:12.)

The Latter-day Saints are in the valleys of the mountains in literal fulfillment of that promise of Isaiah, and now we are living to see the seed of Judah being gathered back to their land, according to the promise. They waited two thousand years for that because it was one of the great events of the last dispensation, as Isaiah has indicated.

Let me give you one more:

"Wherefore the Lord said, Forasmuch as this people draw near me with their mouth, and with their lips do honour me, but have removed their heart from me, and their fear toward me is taught by the precept of men:

"Therefore, behold, I will proceed to do a marvellous work among this people, even a marvellous work and a wonder: for the wisdom of their wise men shall perish, and the understanding of their prudent men shall be hid." (Isaiah 29:13-14.)

Could you imagine living upon the earth when the God of heaven fulfills that promise made by the prophet Isaiah and not wanting to know what that "marvellous work and a wonder" is all about? No boy or girl or man or woman in this world, if they understood fully what God has done in restoring his truth to the earth in our day, could call it anything but "a marvellous work and a wonder." When the God of heaven says that it will be a "marvellous work and a wonder" in *his* eyes, then what ought it to be to those of us who are privileged to be partakers of it? Then he said, "For the wisdom of their wise men shall perish, and the understanding of their prudent men shall be hid." Can any man account for what the Lord has done in restoring his truth here in our day?

In the Book of Mormon we are told that the Lord would bring forth a prophet in the latter days like unto Moses. We are told in holy writ that there was no prophet in all Israel like unto Moses, because he talked with God face to face, and that is the kind of prophet God promised to send in the latter days from the loins of Joseph. (See 2 Nephi 3:11.) The Lord said this prophet should bring forth his, the Lord's, word, and he would bring men to a conviction of the Lord's word that had already gone forth among them. The Prophet Joseph Smith did bring forth the Book of Mormon, Doctrine and Covenants, and Pearl of Great Price, and the Lord gave him the key to the Bible, to understand the Bible and the teachings of the prophets.

Dr. Hugh Nibley's mother told me that he read the Book of Mormon eleven times by the time he was twelve years old. Then he started studying it, and he said it was the greatest book in the world. When he was writing the course of study for the Melchizedek Priesthood he wrote his mother a Christmas letter, and she let me copy this one paragraph from it.

> This is a strange state of things . . . always thinking of you but never writing. The same things happen day after day and the same thought night after night. It has been a steady diet of Book of Mormon and no other food is so invigorating. It is the bread of life in the most digestible form.

That was his appraisal to his mother, not to be printed, but just as he was studying in connection with his writing about the Book of Mormon.

On September 5, 1954, he gave a radio address in which he talked about the philosophers of the world and how they could lead you to the grave and then you have to turn to the prophets, and that is where you have to go if you want to know what the purposes of life are. And then he added:

> This is not the case with the Book of Mormon. What do we find in it—a wealth of doctrine embedded in large amounts of what is put forth as genuine historical material, not devotional or speculative or interpretive or creative writing, but genuine historical facts, stuff that touches upon reality, geographical, ethnological, linguistic, cultural, etc., at a thousand places. On all these points the book could sooner or later be tested, as Joseph Smith knew. We cannot possibly deny his good faith in placing it before the whole world without any reservation. Aside from all other con-

siderations, it is a staggering work. Its mass and complexity alone would defy the talent of any living man or body of men to duplicate today. Its histories are full and circumstantial, yet sober, simple, straightforward. There is nothing contrived, nothing exaggerated, nothing clever in the whole book. For a century and a quarter it has undergone the closest scrutiny at the hands of its friends and enemies, and today it stands up better than ever.

I do not think any of you would question Dr. Nibley's ability to analyze a situation. He knew what he was talking about. He realized that the coming forth of the Book of Mormon, as Isaiah said, would cause the wisdom of their wise men to perish. Do you realize that there are over twenty thousand volumes written about Joseph Smith, trying to discover what kind of man he really was and accounting for him and his writings? Yet in the Library of Congress at Washington there are only some twenty-six hundred books and pamphlets about the life of the great father of our country, George Washington. I just give you that as an evidence that he would bring forth a "marvellous work and a wonder."

In 1959 it was my privilege to meet in their convention with the ministers and leaders of two of the prominent churches of the western part of America. My assignment came from President David O. McKay. They had asked that one of the General Authorities be sent to take two hours in the morning session, then to have lunch with them as their guest, and then to remain in the afternoon for an hour and a half and let them ask questions.

They wanted to know the philosophy and teachings of the Church. They changed their program a little because some of the men wanted to get away earlier by plane, so they gave me two hours and a half, uninterrupted.

After I had laid the whole structure of what our church is, how we got it, and what our teachings are, I took a lot of prophecies from the prophets. Then I said,

"Now what would you do with them?" And I used this illustration:

"When we prepared the plans for the Los Angeles Temple and I was the Presiding Bishop, we showed those plans to the First Presidency. There were eighty-five pages, about four feet long and two and a half feet wide, and we did not have the plans for the electrical or the plumbing work.

"You could take those plans and you could go all over this world and try to fit them to any other building in the world, and you could not do it. There is only one building that they will fit, and that is the Los Angeles Temple.

"In that same sense, you can take the Bible and go all over this world, and you cannot fit it to any other church except the Mormon Church."

I took scripture after scripture, and I asked, "What would you do with that?"

At the close of the meeting, one of the ministers said, "Now, Mr. Richards, you've told us that you believe in a personal God."

I said, "That is right."

He said, "We've heard it said that you believe that God has a wife in heaven. Would you explain that?"

I said, rather facetiously, "Well, I don't see how in the world he could have a son without a wife, do you?"

I just might tell you that when I left that group that day, the man in charge said, "Mr. Richards, this has been one of the most interesting experiences of my entire life."

The Lord himself said, when he visited the people, that we were to study his words, because in the day in which they would be fulfilled, it would be given us to understand them. God help us to understand that this work really is "a marvellous work and a wonder."

20

America, a Land of Promise

"And it came to pass that the Lord spake unto me, saying: Blessed art thou, Nephi, because of thy faith, for thou hast sought me diligently, with lowliness of heart.

"And inasmuch as ye shall keep my commandments, ye shall prosper, and shall be led to a land of promise; yea, even a land . . . which is choice above all other lands." (1 Nephi 2:19-20.)

America has never ceased to be choice above all other lands, because it is the land of promise that the Lord has saved from dispensation to dispensation for his chosen people.

In Second Nephi, we read further the words of Nephi:

"But, said he, notwithstanding our afflictions, we have obtained a land of promise, a land which is choice above all other lands; a land which the Lord God hath covenanted with me should be a land for the inheritance of my seed. Yea, the Lord hath covenanted this land unto me, and unto my children forever, and also all those who would be led out of other countries by the hand of the Lord.

"Wherefore, this land is consecrated unto him whom he shall bring. And if it so be that they shall serve him

151

according to the commandments which he hath given, it shall be a land of liberty unto them; wherefore, they shall never be brought down into captivity; if so, it shall be because of iniquity; for if iniquity shall abound cursed shall be the land for their sakes, but unto the righteous it shall be blessed forever.

"And behold, it is wisdom that this land should be kept as yet from the knowledge of other nations; for behold, many nations would overrun the land, that there would be no place for an inheritance." (2 Nephi 1:5, 7-8.)

So you see, the Lord hid this land from the eyes of the world, and only those were brought here whom God led here. Jared and his people, because they did not abide in righteousness, were destroyed from off the face of the land. And Mulek and his colony and the Nephites were finally destroyed because of their unrighteousness. The Lord made it very plain that even the land would be cursed because of their unrighteousness. But for those who would serve the Lord, it should be a land of promise. The responsibility rests upon the shoulders of each of us to help to make it a land of promise by the way that we live and honor that we give to our Father in heaven. Just as he said that he would not hold guiltless those who taketh his name in vain, because he has sanctified and consecrated this great land, if we desecrate it, cursed shall be the land for our sakes.

It will be a land of liberty unto us if we serve the God of this land. We know it has been a land of liberty.

I want you to have this next reference because it has a marvelous promise in it.

"But behold, this land, said God, shall be a land of thine inheritance, and the Gentiles shall be blessed upon the land.

"And this land shall be a land of liberty unto the Gentiles, and there shall be no kings upon the land, who shall raise up unto the Gentiles.

"And I will fortify this land against all other nations.

"And he that fighteth against Zion shall perish, saith God.

"For he that raiseth up a king against me shall perish, for I, the Lord, the king of heaven, will be their king, and I will be a light unto them forever, that hear my words." (2 Nephi 10:10-14.)

Now we read about kings and potentates in other lands, and we see their kingdoms crumble and fall, but if we have the faith to believe and to understand the decrees of heaven, we know that there is but one king of this land, and that is the God of heaven, Christ our Lord, and he has indicated that he would fight the battles of this land and that he would protect it against all other nations. Aren't we a blessed and a privileged people to be permitted to live in a land with such God-given decrees resting upon it as to our future and our continued liberty and our prosperity?

"Wherefore, I will consecrate this land unto thy seed, and them who shall be numbered among thy seed, forever, for the land of their inheritance; for it is a choice land, saith God unto me, above all other lands, wherefore I will have all men that dwell thereon that they shall worship me, saith God." (2 Nephi 10:19.)

Let me now refer to a few words from Moroni with respect to America.

"For behold, this is a land which is choice above all other lands; wherefore, he that doth possess it shall serve God or shall be swept off; for it is the everlasting decree of God. And it is not until the fulness of iniquity among the children of the land that they are swept off.

"Behold, this is a choice land, and whatsoever nation shall possess it shall be free from bondage, and from captivity, and from all other nations under heaven, if they will but serve the God of the land, who is Jesus Christ, who hath been manifested by the things which we have written." (Ether 2:10, 12.)

What a promise! And it should be hoped that the
Lord will never see fit to destroy us because of our lack
of faith in him and obedience to his laws.

God has sanctified the land of America; it is a choice
land unto him, and it was preserved from the eyes of the
world until he permitted Columbus to come here under
the leadership of the Holy Spirit to give this land a new
birth, to prepare it for the day of the restoration of all
things and the establishment of the government under
which we live, which we have been told was inspired by
the Lord. It had to be an inspired government and constitution in order to prepare the land for all that God had
decreed should rest upon it by way of promised blessings
in the latter days.

Just as in a nation there is a capital, so in these
Americas, according to God's decree, there is a capital or
a headquarters, and the valleys of the mountains have
been preserved as the headquarters and the capital of
this choice land above all other lands. It was to be there
that the kingdom of God should be established—the
house of the Lord to be established in the tops of mountains, that all nations would flow unto it and say: "Come
ye, and let us go up to the mountain of the Lord, to the
house of the God of Jacob; and he will teach us of his
ways, and we will walk in his paths; for out of Zion shall
go forth the law, and the word of the Lord from Jerusalem." (Isaiah 2:3.)

Now we live in that day. Holy prophets beheld our
time thousands of years ago and proclaimed it, and the
prophets of the Book of Mormon have made it plain
that the prophecies of Isaiah and the other prophets
would be fulfilled to the very letter.

In 1849, two years after the Saints arrived in the
Salt Lake Valley, Brigham Young said, "Here is the
place that God appointed for this people. We have been
kicked out of the frying pan into the fire, and out of the
fire into the middle of the floor, and here we are, and

here we will stay." There was no equivocation in that declaration. Then he added, "This is the place that God has appointed for his people. God will temper the climate, and the land will become fruitful."

Shortly after that the commissioners of agriculture of the United States offered a prize for the land that could produce the greatest yield of potatoes and wheat, and both prizes came to Utah because of the fruitfulness of this land. So the Lord has been vindicating the truth of the things the prophets have said about the land of America.

I thought you might enjoy an oration on "I Speak for Democracy," by a sixteen-year-old girl, Elizabeth Ellen Evans. This was reproduced on a bronze plaque and given to the President of the United States. And this is what she said:

Listen to my words, Fascist, Communist. Listen well, for my country is a strong country, and my message is a strong message.

I am an American, and I speak for democracy. My ancestors have left their blood on the green at Lexington and the snow at Valley Forge—on the walls of Fort Sumter and the fields at Gettysburg—on the waters of the River Marne and in the shadows of the Argonne Forest—on the beachheads of Salerno and Normandy and the sands of Okinawa—on the bare, bleak hills called Pork Chop and Old Baldy and Heartbreak Ridge. A million and more of my countrymen have died for freedom.

My country is their eternal monument.

They live on in the laughter of a small boy as he watches a circus clown's antics—and in the sweet, delicious coldness of the first bit of peppermint ice cream on the Fourth of July—in the little tenseness of a baseball crowd as the umpire calls "Batter up!"— and in the high school band's rendition of "Stars and Stripes Forever" in the Memorial Day parade—in the clear, sharp ring of a school bell on a fall morning—and in the triumph of a six-year-old as he reads aloud for the first time.

They live on in the eyes of an Ohio farmer surveying his acres of corn and potatoes and pasture—and in the brilliant gold of hundreds of acres of wheat stretching across the flat miles of Kansas—in the milling of cattle in the stockyards of Chicago—the precision of an assembly line in an automobile factory in Detroit—and the perpetual red glow of the nocturnal skylines of Pittsburgh and Birmingham and Gary.

They live on in the voice of a young Jewish boy saying the sacred words from the Torah: "Hear O Israel: the Lord our God, the Lord is One. Thou shalt love the Lord thy God with all thy heart and with all thy soul and with all thy might"—and in the voice of a Catholic girl praying: "Hail, Mary, full of grace, the Lord is with thee . . ."—and in the voice of a Protestant boy singing: "A mighty Fortress is our God, a Bulwark never failing. . . ."

An American named Carl Sandburg wrote these words: "I know a Jew fishcrier down on Maxwell Street with a voice like a north wind blowing over corn stubble in January. He dangles herring before prospective customers evincing a joy identical with that of Pavlova dancing. His face is that of a man terribly glad to be selling fish, terribly glad that God made fish, and customers to whom he may call his wares from a pushcart."

There is a voice in the soul of every human being that cries out to be free. America has answered that voice.

America has offered freedom and opportunity such as no land before her has ever known, to a Jew fishcrier down on Maxwell Street with the face of a man terribly glad to be selling fish. She has given him the right to own his pushcart, to sell his herring on Maxwell Street—she has given him an education for his children, and a tremendous faith in the nation that has made these things his.

Multiply that fishcrier by a hundred sixty million—mechanics and farmers and housewives and coal miners and truck drivers and chemists and lawyers and plumbers and priests—all glad, terribly glad to be what they are, terribly glad to be free to work and eat and sleep and speak and love and pray and live as they desire, as they believe!

And those one hundred sixty million Americans—those free Americans—have more roast beef and mashed potatoes, the yield of American labor and land—more automobiles and telephones— more safety razors and bathrubs—more Orlon sweaters and aureomycin—the fruits of American initiative and enterprise—more public schools and life insurance policies, the symbols of American security and faith in the future—more laughter and song—than any other people on earth!

This is my answer, Fascist, Communist!

Show me a country greater than our country, show me a people more energetic, creative, progressive, bigger-hearted and happier than our people; not until then will I consider your way of life. For I am an American, and I speak for democracy.

When you read an oration like that and also think of what God said about this land and what he would do here, you can't help being grateful for the blessings of the Lord that have fulfilled the promises he made through the prophets. I bear you my witness that I know that the God of heaven is with this land and that his decrees will be fulfilled.

The Fruits of Mormonism

21

The Fruits of Mormonism

Visitors to the West enjoy visiting Salt Lake City and especially Temple Square, where they enjoy attending the free organ recitals and seeing the interesting Tabernacle, which was erected during the early days of the Church. It was built without the use of nails and provides seating capacity for nearly 10,000. Its acoustics are so good that a pin dropped on the stand at one end of the building can readily be heard at the other. On this block stands also the great Salt Lake Temple, which the Saints were forty years in completing, at a cost of over four million dollars.

One of the visitors to Temple Square was Carveth Wells, a nationally known authority on tourist travel and scenic wonders of America. After visiting this interesting block, he made this statement: "Temple Square is the most fascinating spot in all America."

In inviting people to visit this interesting and historic spot, there may be something of selfishness on our part, not that we desire their money, but we desire their friendship and good will; and in the face of the reputation our people have at times in the past had throughout the nation and the world, it is not to be wondered that we should desire to counteract that impression by seeking

161

an opportunity to have people learn the true facts about us, for to be unknown is to be unloved.

Among the tourists who have visited the Temple Square was Dr. Fredrick C. Waite of Cleveland, Ohio, professor of histology and embryology at Western Reserve University, who said while there: "Any antipathy toward the Mormon Church is due to a failure to understand the Church and its principles."

We entertained Dr. Charles E. Barker, well-known lecturer, who made this statement: "Two years ago in the East, I was asked by an audience to tell them which group of citizens were making the greatest contributions to civilization as I had witnessed them in my travels about the country. I told them it was a difficult question to answer. I said that if they had asked me twenty-one years ago, when I had not traveled about at all and my mind was very provincial and biased, who are the most undesirable class, I would have unhesitatingly said, 'The Mormons.' But having traveled about almost every year for sixteen years, and having learned to know these people, I have come to feel that the most desirable people, having the highest standards of morality and virtue, are the Mormon people."

A similar compliment or recognition came to us when the University of Southern California at Los Angeles decided to introduce the teaching of religion in their school, for which they would give college credits. Accordingly, an invitation was extended to five churches to present their history, philosophy, and literature, and to our great delight, the invitation was extended to our people. Dr. John A. Widtsoe, who was one of the Twelve Apostles of the Church and formerly president of both Utah State Agricultural College (now Utah State University) and the University of Utah, was sent to Los Angeles to conduct this course of study. While conversing with Dr. Kleinsmith, the president of USC, Dr. Widtsoe asked why it was that the Mormon Church had received such recognition, to which Dr. Kleinsmith replied: "Because we recognize your church as one of the outstanding leaders of advanced civilization in the world."

One of the most important undertakings of the Church is its Welfare Program, a program to take from the government relief rolls all its members. The newspapers and other media throughout the land have commented favorably about it. The New York *Herald-Tribune* carried an editorial entitled "Mormons to Lead the Way" and called upon other churches to follow their example.

M. J. Beherrell of London, England, visited Salt Lake City and Utah during which time he made a study of the Welfare Program. In a newspaper article he stated: "The action of the Mormon Church in establishing its social security program provides a lesson which might be copied with advantage by every country in the world."

We also have a great program for youth. We are eager to see our young people enjoying themselves everywhere, especially when that enjoyment can be accompanied by activities that will give them grace and culture of body, of mind, and of spirit. Ours is a joyous gospel, a social gospel. Ever since the days of Brigham Young, the Church has maintained two auxiliaries, the Young Men's and the Young Women's Mutual Improvement Associations, whose special assignment is the supervision of youth. In carrying out this assignment, they have prepared some wonderful manuals, some of which are used as reference books in some of the leading colleges of the land. Young people are taught to develop their personalities by improving their talents, and the program provides experiences in drama, speech, music, dance, sports, and athletics. The YMMIA fathers Scouting; the chief Scout executive of America once said: "It is interesting to note that The Church of Jesus Christ of Latter-day Saints leads all other churches in the high percentage of its boys who are registered with the Boy Scouts of America."

Dr. E. A. Ross, sociologist of the University of Wisconsin, said: "I want to give you some of my impressions of Utah as a sociologist. I am, first of all, very favorably impressed with the Mormon Church. I don't know any other place where the young people are so well provided for. . . . I don't understand how the Mormon people got the idea of providing for the recreational and social needs of people so much earlier than we sociologists got the idea. The Church was way head of us in making this discovery. I have never met so many fine young people as I met in Utah. The Mormon people have been decidedly misunderstood in the East."

Some years ago the agent of the Holland-America Steamship line from Rotterdam, Mr. Herschfeld, came to Salt Lake City on a visit. I had met him in Holland. He had a letter of introduction to President Heber J. Grant, and President Grant turned him over to me because I could talk Dutch with him. When evening came I said, "Now, Mr. Herschfeld, where would you like to go? I can take you to a show, or I will take you for a ride around the valley, but if you would like to see Mormonism in action, I will take you to a Mormon bazaar."

He said, "I would really like to see Mormonism in action."

So we went down to the old Granite Stake Tabernacle, on State Street and Thirty-third South. I introduced him to many of the Hollanders who were there, and he was thrilled with what he saw. We went upstairs to an operetta that was being presented, and then I said, as they announced the dance downstairs, "Probably you have had enough. I shall be glad to take you back to the hotel."

He said, "Mr. Richards, couldn't I see the dance?"

"Well," I said, "yes, if you would like to."

We went down to the dance hall and on our way back to the hotel he said, "You could not have made me believe that I could ever have seen a group of hundreds of young people like I have seen here tonight, dancing together with no evidence of any evil thought or anything of that kind. Mr. Richards, if I were a young man, I surely would cast my lot with the Mormon people."

Nearly all of our young men and many of our young women fill missions for the Church, spending an average of two years each. The expense is borne by themselves or their parents. The youth program is a great preparation for this missionary work.

I thank the Lord for the leadership of the Church in this youth program! I would like to admonish the bishops not to be too stingy with the Mutual officers whom they expect to carry on this activity program. Don't tell them there is no money in the budget. Go out and get the money, if necessary. These boys and girls of ours are worth more than our money, and they are entitled to the kind of leadership this church is prepared to give. You can requisition the finest talent living within your wards and stakes, and you don't have to pay for it. No one else can do that, so there is no excuse for not having the finest parties possible.

Our young people don't smoke. They don't drink. They use no tea or coffee. They don't swear. They are not taught so much the principle of forgiveness of sin, but of abstinence from sin, making forgiveness unnecessary. There is no double moral standard among our young people. Boys and girls alike are taught that in the sight of the Lord transgression of the moral law is next in grievousness to the shedding of innocent blood. They love education. They honor and respect their parents. They are good sports, and they are happy.

22

An Uncommon Church and an Uncommon People

Former President Herbert Hoover once made the following statement:

In my opinion, we are in danger of developing a cult of the common man, which means a cult of mediocrity. But there is at least one hopeful sign: I have never been able to find out just who this common man is. In fact, most Americans—especially women— will get mad and fight if you try calling them common.

This is hopeful because it shows that most people are holding fast to an essential fact in American life. We believe in equal opportunity for all, but we know that this includes the opportunity to rise to leadership. In other words—*to be uncommon!*

Let us remember that the great human advances have not been brought about by mediocre men and women. They were brought about by distinctly uncommon people with vital sparks of leadership. Many great leaders were of humble origin, but that alone was not their greatness.

It is a curious fact that when you get sick you want an uncommon doctor; if your car breaks down you want an uncommonly good mechanic; when we get into war we want dreadfully an uncommon admiral and an uncommon general.

I have never met a father and mother who did not want their children to grow up to be uncommon men and women. May it always be so. For the future of America rests not in mediocrity, but in the constant renewal of leadership in every phase of our national life. (Quoted by Utah State Management Institute.)

That made a great impression on me when I first read it, and I thought that it would be wonderful if everybody wanted to be uncommon and then tried to make their lives such that they could be uncommon.

I think that the Church, with its institutions, is the greatest influence in the world today to make really uncommon people who can touch the lives of others. To illustrate what I am trying to tell you, some years ago I was on a mission back in the Eastern States and we had a lady missionary there. She had to go to the hospital for an operation, and her mother came out to be with her. Her mother told me this experience.

She said she was riding on the train from Salt Lake to Los Angeles, and she was reading the Book of Mormon. A young man came walking through the train and noticed it, and he said, "Pardon me, lady, are you a Mormon?"

She said, "Yes."

He said, "Could I visit with you a few moments?"

He sat down, and this is his story. He said he was a graduate from Harvard College. He said, "When I graduated from there I thought I was able and capable to associate with any man or woman anywhere and feel at ease. Then I was drafted, and I went overseas [this was during World War I], and I was thrown right in with two Mormon boys. I hadn't been in their company long until I felt myself inferior in their company. I didn't know what it was that made them different than I was.

"After I was released and returned home, I got a contract to do some engineering work down in Arizona. I routed myself via Salt Lake City and stopped over a day." He opened his briefcase and showed her the Church works he had picked up. He said, "I am going down to Arizona now, and I am going to see if I can find in these books what made those two Mormon boys different than I was, and made me feel inferior in their presence."

We live in an uncommon day. There is more re-

vealed truth upon the earth today than there has been
in all the history of the world. These are the last days
when the Lord is to complete his work. The apostle Paul
said that the Lord had revealed unto him the mystery of
his will, that in the dispensation of the fulness of times—
and we live in that dispensation—the Lord would bring
together in one, in Christ, all that is in heaven above,
and that is in the earth beneath. We live in the dispensation of the fulness of times; we have the only program
in all this world to unite that which is in heaven above
and that which is upon the earth. That is another evidence that this work that we are engaged in is an uncommon work.

In the fiftieth Psalm we read:

"The mighty God, even the Lord hath spoken [that's
the message of every Mormon missionary], and called the
earth from the rising of the sun unto the going down
thereof.

"Out of Zion, the perfection of beauty, God hath
shined." (Psalm 50:1-2.)

When I think of what this church is doing and what
its organizations and institutions have to offer to the
world, surely God is shining out of Zion, the perfection
of beauty, unto all the world.

One of the greatest evidences of that is in the great
missionary program of the Church. Our boys go out with
little training to prepare them for missionary work,
and they meet the learned and the educated of the land.
Yet they are able to show them things that they have
never dreamed of. Yes, this work is not a common work.
It is the most wonderful thing in all this world.

President Wilford Woodruff, in a general conference
of the Church in 1898, told about when he first met the
Prophet Joseph Smith. He said he met the Prophet for
the first time when he attended a meeting where many
of the brethren bore testimony of the restoration. When
they got through, the Prophet said:

Brethren, I have been very much edified and instructed in your testimonies here tonight; but I want to say to you before the Lord, that you know no more concerning the destiny of this Church and kingdom than a babe upon his mother's lap. You don't comprehend it.

It is only a little handful of priesthood you see here tonight, but this Church will fill North and South America. It will fill the world. It will fill the Rocky Mountains [and this was thirteen years before the Saints came west to the Rocky Mountains]. There will be tens of thousands of Latter-day Saints who will be gathered to the Rocky Mountains, and there they will open the door for the establishment of the gospel among the Lamanites. (*Conference Report,* April 1898, p. 57.)

How could Joseph Smith, as the lad that he was, have made a statement like that, had he not been a prophet of God? He saw us driven to the Rocky Mountains; he saw us become a mighty people here. He said it should be the means of opening the door for the preaching of the gospel to the Lamanites. We do live in an uncommon day. This church isn't just another church— this is God's church, and he has established it. His priesthood is in it. It is the only organization in this world that can bind the heavens. This church that we belong to, with all its institutions and its accomplishments, is God-decreed, and it will stand forever until it shall fill the whole earth.

So I say, with all of these uncommon things that God is doing in our day and time, when we reach the end of our lives here upon this earth, if we have spent all our time in earning a living and in taking care of temporal affairs, we will know the meaning of the words of the poet when he said:

Of all sad words of tongue and pen
The saddest are these: It might have been.

Then we would wish we could just go back and live our lives again.

That is what our great educational institutions are for—to train our young people to be leaders of men in spiritual things as well as educational and temporal things. If it were only the temporal things, we would have no business in being in the educational field. We could get that from our tax money. But when we are spending the tithes of the widows and the orphans and the Latter-day Saint people the world over to maintain our institutions, it is because we want to train every boy and girl to be uncommon, to be a leader among their fellows, no matter where their lot is cast, and to take upon them the armor of righteousness to help build the kingdom of God in the earth and prepare for his glorious coming when he shall come as King of kings and Lord of lords.

We had a man come to us in Salt Lake a few years back and he was entertained at the Hotel Utah by one of our banker friends. This man was one of the greatest economists of the world, not just of America. There were twenty-five of us present at the banquet. After we were through eating, the governor was asked to say a few words (at that time, he was not a member of the Church). He stood up and said, "The finest men I know in this world are the leaders of the Mormon Church."

Then the President of the Church said a few words. Then they asked this great economist if he would like to speak. He stood up and his jaw began to quiver and the tears began rolling down his cheeks and he said something like this: "I have never stood in such presence in my life. I had to come out here to these valleys of the mountains to find the kind of Christianity I think can save the world."

We didn't ask him for that, but he felt it, because the Lord's work is an uncommon work, and it is making uncommon men and uncommon women.

We had a Dr. Polian in our midst a couple of years ago or more, from Iran. He was sent here by his government to study the American people. After spending two days in Salt Lake, he said to the receptionist in the Church Office Building, "I have obtained a more favorable impression of the American people in the two days I have spent here in Salt Lake than all the rest of my travels for the last eleven months." Isn't that what we are talking about? Uncommon people and uncommon institutions.

A few years ago, just before Sister Bertha Reeder was released as general president of the YWMIA, a woman came out from New York as the head of one of the national music organizations to attend one of our June Conferences. I had met her a number of times during the conference. Sister Reeder took her in tow and had her on the stand with her. After the morning session in the Tabernacle, as we walked off into the little anteroom where the General Authorities go, I walked up to her and said, "Mrs. Spofford, before you leave, there is one thing I would like to say to you, and I hope you will never forget it."

She said, "What's that, Mr. Richards?"

I said, "Someday you will know that the spiritual capital of the world is Salt Lake City."

She replied, "Mr. Richards, I know that already!"

We don't have to leave it to everybody else. Each one of us can wield an influence and touch the lives of others as they come among us. For instance, years ago as I completed a mission back in the Eastern States (I had been released as a bishop to go there), one of my friends came back with his wife and my wife. He bought an automobile (he was in the automobile business) in Detroit, and we traveled through the East. As we drove into the great city of New York—we had a Utah license plate on our car—a man honked us off to the side of the road. At first we thought it might be a policeman or somebody wanting to hold us up, but when we saw an elderly woman in the car, we didn't worry. This man said, "I see you have a Utah license plate."

"Yes, sir."

"Are you from Utah?"

"Yes, sir."

"Do you know where you want to go?"

We said, "We'd like to go to the Roosevelt Hotel."

"Do you know where it is?"

"No, we've never been here."

He said, "You follow me! I was out in Utah a few years ago, and everybody did everything they could to make me happy out there. I have just been waiting for a chance to get even with them."

We went through that big city all the way up to the Roosevelt Hotel. He waved good-bye, and away he went. I don't know who he was, but you see what a person can do in helping to show that this is an uncommon community that the Lord has established among his people. You see, we have to be a different people. We have to let our lights shine, and we have to be uncommon, just as President Hoover said.

I invite you to appreciate what you have and appreciate your membership in this church, to believe with all your heart and your soul that this work will achieve its God-decreed destiny. Brigham Young said that he had studied the gospel for twenty-one years as he had traveled by day and by night, by land and by sea, as religiously as any man ever studied any branch of science. Yet he said he had only gotten to the ABC's. If it took Brother Brigham twenty-one years to get to the ABC's, maybe we could be excused if we don't understand it all!

I think of the words of the apostle Paul, who was caught up into the third heaven and the paradise of God. He must have seen something marvelous by the time he got into the third heaven. He wasn't permitted to write what he saw, but he did say: ". . . Eye hath not seen, nor ear heard, neither have entered into the heart of man, the things which God hath prepared for them that love him." (1 Corinthians 2:9.)

We can conjure up in our own minds what we think would pay for a life of devotion, but we just don't have the capacity here in mortality to comprehend the glories that are to be revealed through our faith and our faithfulness. This is my testimony and my witness to you. I thank God, above all other things, for the privilege of living upon the earth at this time when his work, this uncommon work, is here. I pray that God will help us all to be uncommon men and women, that we will be his helpers to build his kingdom.

23

Giving of Ourselves

I should like to call to your attention one principle that the Latter-day Saints have learned to understand. They have learned to know the meaning of the word *give*. We give of our time; we give of our talents; we give of our means. Our fathers and mothers give their boys and girls to the missionary service of the Church, and wives give their husbands. As I have often said, if one is looking for an easy religion he had better not bother with Mormonism. Most of us know that we are at the call of the Church all the time.

We know the history of the Saints; we know the great sacrifices that have been made. Those of us who have filled missions in foreign lands have seen the Saints leave all that was dear to them. We know the history of the pioneers as they left their homes behind and came to the valleys of the mountains.

While traveling throughout the Church, my heart has been moved because of the faith of the Latter-day Saints. It seems to make no difference whether they are to travel ten miles, a hundred miles, or two hundred miles, they are always there when the call comes. They do not ask for compensation; they do not ask for expense money. They know that they are to bear the burden—

174

and the expense—of their missionary boys and girls. They have learned how to give, and as I study the scriptures and read the words of the prophets and of the Master himself, it seems to me that the one thing above all others in the gospel of Jesus Christ is that men should be willing to give their all.

We are commanded to love God first above all other things, and our fellowmen like unto ourselves. One good man who came to the Master said: "Lord, I will follow thee withersoever thou goest." As though he were saying to all coming generations, *"If ye follow me, ye need expect no compensation,"* the Savior replied: "Foxes have holes, and birds of the air have nests; but the Son of man hath not where to lay his head."

And to another he said: "Follow me." The man said: "Lord, suffer me first to go and bury my father." There are very few obligations in life more important than burying one's father, but the Lord wanted to impress upon his servants the importance of a call from him, and so he said: "Let the dead bury their dead: but go thou and preach the kingdom of God."

And another said: "Lord, I will follow thee; but let me first go bid them farewell, which are at home at my house." Jesus answered: "No man, having put his hand to the plough, and looking back, is fit for the kingdom of God." (Luke 9:57-62.) He expects real service but offers no monetary compensation.

Then he sent the seventy out. He gave them nothing, but he gave them of his power and said: "He that heareth you heareth me; and he that despiseth you despiseth me." And they returned again with joy, saying: "Lord, even the devils are subject unto us through thy name." (Luke 10:16-17.)

Speaking again of service, he said: "He that loveth father or mother more than me is not worthy of me: and he that loveth son or daughter more than me is not worthy of me. And he that taketh not his cross, and followeth after me, is not worthy of me. He that findeth his life shall lose it: and he that loseth his life for my sake shall find it." (Matthew 10:37-39.)

In addition to giving ourselves, and giving our services, the Lord has asked us to give of our means and our substance. We have men in the Church who give their time, who will go when they are asked to preach, and who will perform a public duty, but it is hard for them to do the little duty that is seen in secret by them and God alone. And so we are asked to contribute our tithes and offerings, not only because the Church needs money to build itself, but also that they might be tested.

The Lord apparently realized that some men can give service easier than money or goods. We have the lesson of the rich young man who came to the Master inquiring what he might do to inherit eternal life. He was told that he should "keep the commandments," to which he replied: "All these things have I kept from my youth up: what lack I yet?" (See Matthew 19:16-20.) We are told in Mark's account: "Then Jesus beholding him loved him." (Luke 18:22.) He loved him for the good things he had done and sought to show him the way to perfection, so he answered: "If thou wilt be perfect, go and sell that thou hast, and give to the poor, and thou shalt have treasure in heaven: and come and follow me." But the young man turned away sorrowful, "for he had great possessions." (Matthew 19:21-22.)

The prophet Malachi declared that in the last days the Lord should send his messengers to prepare the way before him, and he called upon Israel (and I interpret that to mean latter-day Israel) to return unto him and promised that he would return unto them. Then he said, "Will a man rob God? Yet ye have robbed me." They said: "Wherein have we robbed thee?" And he said: "In tithes and offerings, . . . for ye have robbed me, even this whole nation. Bring ye all the tithes into the storehouse, that there may be meat in my house."

And so the Lord proceeded to promise those who would bring their tithes and their offerings together that he would rebuke the devourer for their sakes, and that a book of remembrance should be written before him for them that feared the Lord. "And they shall be mine, saith the Lord of hosts, in that day when I make up my jewels; . . . Then shall ye return, and discern between the righteous and the wicked, between him that serveth God and him that serveth him not." (See Malachi 3.)

Now, the Master tells us that when he shall come in his glory and all the holy angels with him, and before him shall be gathered all nations, he shall separate them one from another as the shepherd divideth his sheep from the goats, and to them on his right hand he shall say: "Come, ye blessed of my Father, inherit the kingdom prepared for you from the foundation of the world:

"For I was an hungred, and ye gave me meat; I was thirsty, and ye gave me drink: I was a stranger, and ye took me in:

"Naked, and ye clothed me: I was sick, and ye visited me: I was in prison, and ye came unto me.

"Then shall the righteous answer him, saying, Lord, when saw we thee an hungred, and fed thee? or thirsty, and gave thee drink?

"When saw we thee a stranger, and took thee in? or naked, and clothed thee?

"Or when saw we thee sick, or in prison, and came unto thee?"

Then shall he say unto them: "Inasmuch as ye have done it unto one of the least of these my brethren, ye have done it unto me." (Matthew 25:31-40.)

I think it is a grand and glorious thing that the Lord has reestablished his church and that so efficiently, and without cost of administration, it is able to do so much to care for the unfortunate of its members.

The Master said, "My doctrine is not mine, but his that sent me. If any man will do his will, he shall know of the doctrine, whether it be of God, or whether I speak of myself." (John 10:16-17.)

I know this is a true promise, and it is true today. I have had the privilege of filling four missions for this church, and I have never hesitated to promise the people that if they would do the will of the Father, and would investigate our message and ask the Lord humbly, they could know for themselves that this work is of God and not of man.

I think the spirit of this work is the most wonderful thing in the world. We can make organizations; we can make programs; but unless God puts into them his Spirit, they will be of no avail. I have been with many of our young people in the mission field; I have labored with them; I have traveled with them; I have prayed with them; I have slept with them; and we have held testimony meetings together that have lasted for hours, when the influence and power of the Spirit of God filled every soul until there was not a dry eye in the meeting, and I know the joy of such experiences.

I shall never live long enough to forget one such meeting in the little country of Holland in Rotterdam when I was on my first mission. President Heber J. Grant was president of the European Mission and was present. There were more than one hundred missionaries there from Great Britain in addition to our own group, and missionaries from other lands.

We were there all day except for just a short recess for sandwiches, and every missionary had the privilege of bearing his testimony. When we were all through President Grant stood up and said, "Now, brethren, today you have tasted of the fruits of the gospel of Jesus Christ. You know what the Spirit of God is. Now, go out and give it to the world; and the more you give away, the more you will have left."

I have seen this verified many, many times; the more one gives away in service in this church, the more influence and power of that Spirit he enjoys himself. The Spirit of God is in the Church, and I thank him for it.

God help us to so live that we may enjoy his Spirit; that we may have influence and power for good in the world of men and in our own families and in the congregations of the Saints; that we may make our contribution to the establishment of latter-day Zion; that the commandment of God to the Prophet Joseph might be realized; that Zion might increase in beauty and holiness; that her borders might be enlarged and her stakes strengthened; yea, that Zion might arise and put on her beautiful garments.

24

The Spirit of Sacrifice

We have been taught all our lives that judgments should befall the nations until men's hearts shall fail them with fear. Notwithstanding these judgments, there is little any of us can do about it because the Lord is to continue his judgments among the nations until they shall beat their swords into plough shares and their spears into pruning hooks, and learn war no more.

Inasmuch as we can do little about this, we should be more concerned with the opposite force that is operating in the earth. We are not unmindful of the message of Mormonism to the world, that the Lord sent his messenger to prepare the way of his coming, and he shall come quickly to his temple, and he shall come cleansing and purifying as refiner's fire and fuller's soap. And so the thing that should concern us as Latter-day Saints, if we are in harmony with his great plan of preparation, is to prepare for his coming.

David saw this relating to our day and the great work that should come forth among the children of men:

"The mighty God, even the Lord, hath spoken, and called the earth from the rising of the sun unto the going down thereof.

"Out of Zion, the perfection of beauty, God hath shined." (Psalm 50:1-2.)

Our missionaries have been called into the earth from the rising of the sun unto the going down thereof, declaring that the mighty God hath spoken. And how has he shined out of Zion, the perfection of beauty? By sending forth his ambassadors of eternal truth to the nations of the earth to bear witness of the restoration of the gospel of the Lord Jesus Christ.

"Our God shall come, and shall not keep silence; a fire shall devour before him, and it shall be very tempestuous round about him.

"He shall call to the heavens from above, and to the earth, that he may judge his people.

"Gather my saints together unto me; those that have made a covenant with me by sacrifice." (Psalm 50:3-5.)

Not only were our pioneer fathers and mothers required to sacrifice in order that they might prove themselves worthy to stand among the saints of God who are to be gathered in these latter days, but we are required to make sacrifices also. We may not be required to forsake our homes and go into new lands; we may not be required to lay our loved ones away by the side of the road; we may not be driven out by friends and ridiculed and reviled, but the Lord nevertheless expects sacrifices at our hands. And I think the Lord does not let such sacrifices go unrewarded.

I recall reading with interest the book published by J. Will Knight on the Knight family. If you have read it, you will recall that Brother Jesse Knight's mother had been married before she married Jesse's father, and after becoming a widow and burying two children, she gathered with the Saints in Kirtland. As she arrived there, the brethren were trying to gather contributions from the scanty means of the Saints in order to be able to liberate the Prophet Joseph. Sister Knight turned her purse upside down and gave them all she had—I think some fifty dollars. The Lord of Israel and the angels of heaven could not overlook a sacrifice of that kind.

She later married Jesse's father and raised a family. Then her husband died and she moved to St. George. When she visited Jesse on one occasion, she failed to say anything to him about becoming active in the Church. For many years he had done very little, and finally, when she was about to return, he said: "Mother, how is it you are not preaching to me as you usually do?"

She answered: "Jesse, I have prayed in the temple for my children many times, and on one occasion the Lord made known to me that I was not to worry about you anymore, that you would one day understand for yourself—and I never intend to argue again with you about religion."

And you know how literally this promise was fulfilled, for soon after that Jesse did understand, and he rendered a great service to the Church.

There is hardly a family among the Saints that could not testify of the sacrifices that have been made for the gospel in this last dispensation. I remember working with a young man before I went on my first mission. He had been driven from his home and his young wife had deserted him because as he was passing a street corner one evening in an eastern city, on his way home from work, he had stopped at a street meeting and listened to the testimonies of our missionaries and their explanation of the doctrines of the Church, which he said pierced his heart like a two-edged sword. He joined the Church, and his people cast him out. I was with him when he received a telegram announcing the birth of his child. He did not have the spirit of hardness or retaliation. He said, with feelings of emotion and tears in his eyes, "The only desire I have in my soul is someday to stand on that same street corner and proclaim to the people of my own town the restoration of the gospel of the Lord Jesus Christ."

We may not have to make such sacrifices as have

been made in years gone by, but as I travel through the Church and witness the marvelous manifestations of the faith of the Latter-day Saints, I feel impressed that the Lord truly has gathered his Saints who have made a covenant with him by sacrifice. In all the auxiliary organizations of the Church we see how people give of their time and their talents for the building up of the kingdom. The sacrifices made for missionary and temple work are marvelous. There is a spirit of sacrifice in the heart of every true Latter-day Saint who has been touched with the testimony of the Holy Ghost, the power by which this work is moving onward in the world.

In the third chapter of Malachi, which I feel relates to this people in our day and time, we read how the Lord was to send his messenger and prepare the way for his coming. Then he indicates that from their fathers' days they had departed from him, and when they asked how, he says: "In tithes and offerings. Ye are cursed with a curse, for ye have robbed me, even this whole nation," meaning the nation of Israel.

Then, after promising to pour out the blessings of heaven upon them if they will return unto him, he states:

"Your words have been stout against me, saith the Lord. Yet ye say, What have we spoken so much against thee?

"Ye have said, It is vain to serve God. [Have you ever heard such a conversation in the midst of the Latter-day Saints?]

". . . And what profit is it that we have kept his ordinance, and that we have walked mournfully before the Lord of hosts?

"And now we call the proud happy; yea, they that work wickedness are set up; yea, they that tempt God are even delivered."

We often hear people remark that the wicked are blessed even above many of the faithful saints, and that is what Malachi of old heard.

"Then they that feared the Lord spake often one to another: and the Lord hearkened, and heard it, and a book of remembrance was written before him for them that feared the Lord, and that thought upon his name.

"And they shall be mine, saith the Lord of hosts, in that day when I make up my jewels; and I will spare them, as a man spareth his own son that serveth him.

"Then shall ye return, and discern between the righteous and the wicked, between him that serveth God and him that serveth him not." (Malachi 3:8-9, 13-18.)

Those of us who have labored in different parts of the Church and have faith in the promises of the prophets have, I am sure, a desire that when the God of Israel fulfills this promise, when he makes up his book of remembrance, when he writes therein the names of his jewels, we wish to see recorded therein the names of those whom we love and among whom we have labored.

I think back to the time when I labored as a missionary as a young man in Holland, to the kindness of those Dutch people and their faithfulness in keeping the commandments of the Lord; and I am sure that if it shall ever be my privilege to enter into his presence, where the book of remembrance shall be opened and his jewels shall be remembered, I would not be happy if my Dutch friends were not there. And I feel the same about the Saints among whom I have labored as a bishop in three different wards, and as a president of a stake in California, and the good Saints in the South, where I had the privilege to preside.

As I travel through the stakes of Zion and see the people come from great distances to listen to the representatives of the General Authorities who are sent unto them, I feel to say, God bless the Latter-day Saints. They truly are evidencing their faith in God and in his great latter-day work by the sacrifices they are willing to make.

Some years ago I heard President Heber J. Grant

in a priesthood meeting promise the Latter-day Saints that if they would pay their tithes and their offerings, the Lord would bless them with increased power and leadership in their own families. I was in the stake of Zion where a bishop was released after a service of twenty-three years, and when we called him to speak, he told of the great joy he had had in witnessing the blessings of the Lord upon the members of his ward because of their faithfulness. He told of one brother and sister who had paid their tithing conscientiously and regularly for all those years, and he said they have a posterity of more than eighty, and there is not one but pays his tithing and keeps the Word of Wisdom.

When I was president of the Rotterdam Branch in Holland many years ago, a sister came to me after the meeting one Sunday morning and said, "Brother Richards, I have only earned a quarter this week. [That was the equivalent in American money.] Should I pay tithing on it?"

I looked at her for a minute, and then said: "Sister, if this were my church, I would not take your tithing. But it is not my church; it is the Lord's church, and tithing is a principle upon which blessings of the Lord are predicated. And sister, if you have only earned twenty-five cents this week, I surely do think you need a blessing, so I would advise you to pay your tithing and be blessed." And I wrote her a receipt for two and a half cents (we happened to have a coin of that denomination in Holland). She later immigrated to Utah and raised a fine family.

Many of those people lived under very meager circumstances and could not save anything from week to week. And when we brought them the gospel, they would say, "You would not expect us to pay tithing, would you?" And I would give them the same answer. I have seen family after family immigrate to America, own their own homes, drive their own automobiles, educate their children, and send their boys and girls on missions. I want to tell you that the spirit of sacrifice has not gone out of this church.

I once stood on the porch of a beautiful home in Idaho, surrounded by 160 acres of as fine irrigated land as I ever saw, and the good brother, a convert to the Church, said to me, "My wife said, 'Father, if the Church asked for it, would you give it to them?'" And he straightened up and said, "I replied: 'Yes, Mother, and there would not be a penny against it either.'" Surely the Lord has been gathering his saints together unto him, those who have made covenant with him by sacrifice.

God bless the Latter-day Saints. God bless you, my brethren and sisters. This is his work, and he is busy preparing the way for his coming. It is important that we harmonize our lives with his great program of preparation and, when the voice of the Lord comes unto us, that we heed it and follow the leadership of those who are sent to guide us in the way of eternal truth. May the Lord bless every man and woman in the Church for their sacrifices for the building up of the kingdom of God.

25

Testimony of the Spirit

I wondered if, in the Church as a whole, we realize the value of the testimony of the Spirit. It was Moroni who said that by the Holy Ghost we might know the truth of all things. In our church we are rich with knowledge and testimony through the Holy Ghost.

Jesus said to his disciples: "It is expedient for you that I go away: for if I go not away, the Comforter will not come unto you." (John 16:7.) He said: "And I will pray the Father, and he shall give you another Comforter, that he may abide with you for ever; Even the Spirit of truth; whom the world cannot receive, because it seeth him not, neither knoweth him: but ye know him; for he dwelleth with you, and shall be in you." (John 14:16-17.) Then we are told that he shall teach us all things and that by the Holy Ghost we might know the truth of all things.

Nine years after my grandfather, Franklin D. Richards, had been baptized a member of the Church, during which time he had filled five missions in the United States, had come up through the grades of the priesthood to the office of high priest, and was then serving as a member of the presidency of the European Mission, he records in his journal the following: "Most of all things, this day, I desire the Holy Spirit, which giveth life, yea, life more abundantly to both body and spirit." This is the power by which this kingdom grows.

You will remember how Peter denied the Christ thrice before he received the Holy Ghost, but after he received the Holy Ghost, when he was commanded that he should no more preach Christ in the streets of Jerusalem, Peter replied, "Whom shall men obey? God or man?" And he considered himself not worthy to be crucified as was his Lord. This is the testimony of the Spirit and the power by which this kingdom is growing in the earth.

You will recall the admonition of the apostle Paul to his brother Timothy, when he put him in remembrance that he should stir up the gift of God, which he had received by the laying on of his (Paul's) hands. Was this idle talk, or do we receive the Spirit of God by the laying on of hands of his servants? If so, should we not all seek to stir up the gift of the Spirit that he might guide and direct us?

I cannot conceive that any Latter-day Saint can be without a testimony of the divinity of this work if he will but consider what has been accomplished in the Church because of the gift of the Spirit of God which is in it.

It is said that during the twenties, when the elders were being persecuted in Great Britain, the government sent an officer to Utah to investigate the "Mormon problem" and see what it was that made the Mormons so determined to carry their message to other nations. When he returned, his report was that the "black secret" of Mormonism was the individual testimony of its members. And surely this is true. You can travel throughout the wards and stakes of Zion and the missions of the Church, or go where you will, and wherever you find Latter-day Saints who have received the gift of the Spirit by the laying on of hands, this spirit is evidenced through their activities in the Church. A power is there that just cannot be found anywhere else in all the world.

We once received a letter at the Presiding Bishop's Office from a young man who had been converted to the Church through meeting our boys in the armed forces. He sent in a substantial amount of tithing. Then he bore his testimony in his letter. He wrote: "Before closing I would like to mention that I have gained a very strong testimony of a very many great, wonderful, and glorious things since being baptized. I could not make this letter long enough to bear my testimony, but I would like to say that I *know,* with all sincerity, that I have God's blessing upon enclosing this money. It is a glorious inspiration when you see the road of life, the light of eternal darkness, the direction of God's path, and the beam of his eternal goodness. These things I have; these things I shall never forsake. With these, I have eternal happiness. Although this money which I am sending is termed in the thought of 'coins,' I know—we know—that actually it is a symbolic but compact measurement of one-tenth of what the Lord has given and provided me as a blessing in life. Although this measurement is earthly, it has a spiritual meaning, the same as all of God's ordinances. This ordinance I feel pleasured, humble, and privileged to offer and perform."

The Lord said that he has never given a temporal commandment unto his children, that all of his commandments are spiritual, and this new convert to the Church felt the power and the spirit of it.

While in the mission field, Sister Richards and I were invited by a member of another church to attend a lecture by an itinerant preacher who was going through the land explaining to the churches how they could get out of debt. His program was that they should turn to the Lord's way of paying their tithes and their offerings, and if they would just do it for ten months, their churches could all get out of debt. After the meeting I had the privilege of being introduced to him, and I told him I would like to bear testimony that he was getting near the truth, that we had been preaching that law all our lives. Then I added, "But what I cannot understand, Reverend, is that if tithing is the Lord's law of blessing his people, why you do not ask them to pay their tithing all their lives, so that they can have the blessings of the Lord, instead of for only ten months." He replied, "Mr. Richards, we cannot go quite that far yet."

Now this is the difference between a man-made system and one where the Lord puts into it the breath of life, the Spirit of God, the Spirit by which we know the truth of all things. We have ministers come in our offices to inquire how we run the tithing system in our church, and when we tell them that all the wards and branches send in all the money they receive to us and we send back what their allowance is, they shake their heads and say, "They wouldn't do that in our church. The local organizations would take out what they need first, and if there were any left, they might send it to headquarters."

Well, that same spirit carries through in all the activities of the Church. The testimony of the Spirit of God is the most marvelous thing I know of in this world, and I would rather see that testimony planted in the hearts of my children than anything I know of.

Brother Melvin J. Ballard used to tell about the colonizer in the Northwest who had learned what a marvelous work we had done in colonizing, and then he came down here to write a treatise on it, to see if he could make it work. After he had prepared his report, he said, "Mr. Ballard, you tell me what is wrong with it. You read it over. I have tried it, but it just will not work for me." Brother Ballard read it and said, "You have here a perfect corpse. If someone would just breathe into it the breath of life, it would work." Now, we know what the breath of life is.

At a meeting in the temple, a mission president told how his father was sent up to Canada when he was a mere lad, by the president of the Church, to colonize.

He wanted to return for years, and his son asked him why he did not come back. He said, "I cannot return until the president of the Church gives me my release."

I have met many others who have had similar experiences. When they came to Utah in the early days of the Church, they would have gladly remained in Salt Lake City with the body of the Church and the brothers and sisters they had known, save for one thing: the testimony of the Spirit of God. When they were called by his servants to settle other localities, they were true to their call. This is the spirit by which the Church has accomplished so much.

Many thousands of missionaries have gone out for this church. I dare say that out of those thousands you could not find half a dozen who would desert their missionary call for all the money in this world or for any position that might be offered to them. Is there any power in the world that can plant such feelings in the hearts of the children of men? Do you think Joseph Smith could have done it, that Brigham Young could have done it, that any prophet could do it? No, that is the power of the testimony of the Holy Ghost.

Some of my Dutch friends came into my office—a man and his wife—and they said, "Brother Richards, we have filled one mission together, but we would surely like to go on another." Then he said, "If we sell our home and our automobile, we can finance ourselves." Is there any other cause in this world for which men would ask for the privilege of selling all they have—even their homes—other than that they might bear witness to the truth of this great latter-day work?

President Heber J. Grant told how he was offered a salary of forty thousand dollars to affiliate himself with an insurance company in the East, when he was but a young man. But he was called of God to be an apostle of the Lord Jesus Christ, and he could not accept. I want to tell you that some of our leaders today have given up positions that were worth just about ten times as much as the allowance they are getting from the Church to live on. They did not ask for the privilege to thus serve, and they did not ask what they were going to receive. They were called by the voice of the Lord's anointed and that is all that mattered, because in their soul was a testimony of the Spirit of God.

May God help us to so live and labor and teach that this testimony may ever live in the hearts of our boys and our girls, the youth of Zion.

26

Other Than by Hearsay

The story is told of a new minister who moved into the community where Carlisle lived, and he went to the office of Carlisle and asked this question: "What do the people of this community need more than anything else?" And Carlisle's answer was: "They need a man who knows God other than by hearsay."

You know, I have thought a lot about that. I think what this world needs today more than anything else is to know God other than by hearsay, to know why he created this earth and why we are here, where we are going and how to get there, so that we know what life is really for. I have come to feel that one of the greatest necessities even in the Church is that we have a strong testimony, the power of conviction. As I read the Holy Scriptures, it seems to me they make it very plain that we, his children, through obedience can know God other than by hearsay. Jesus said: "My doctrine is not mine, but his that sent me. If any man will do his will, he shall know of the doctrine, whether it be of God, or whether I speak of myself." (John 7:16-17.)

This is a promise to all men, and that promise is just as binding today as when Jesus spoke it: if we will do the will of the Father, we may know other than by hearsay that his message is from God, the Eternal Father.

Then you will remember he said: "And this is life eternal, that they might know thee the only true God, and Jesus Christ, whom thou hast sent." (John 17:3.) There is a promise that we might know him, or at least it infers that we might know him other than by hearsay.

You remember when Nicodemus came to Jesus by night; he indicated that he knew he was a prophet sent of God, for no man did the things that he did save God was with him. Then after he had explained to Nicodemus the message of baptism and to take upon him the name of Christ, Nicodemus could not understand him; and Jesus said, after repeating it, "Art thou a master of Israel, and knowest not these things?" (John 3:10.) He said: "We speak that we do know, and testify that we have seen; and ye receive not our witness." (John 3:11.) Every true servant of God who is sent in his name to administer the holy ordinances of the gospel speaks that he does know, and testifies that he has seen.

A few years ago a group of ministers who were passing through Salt Lake en route to Los Angeles to attend a ministerial convention stopped over in Salt Lake City. They wanted to ask some questions about our teachings, and arrangements were made for them to meet one of the Twelve in the conference room in the Church Office Building. After that apostle had answered their questions, he bore his solemn witness that he knew that Jesus was the Christ, that Joseph Smith was his prophet, that the Book of Mormon was true. He knew it other than by hearsay. Then, when he closed his testimony, he turned to those ministers and said, "Which one of you can testify that you know that you have the truth?" After a brief pause, the leader of the group said, "Well, we *hope* we are right."

When I was a missionary over in Holland, in the city of Utrecht, there was a seminary where young men were trained for the ministry. They used to come and attend our meetings, and then they would remain afterwards and discuss religious principles with us. One night I proved to one of those young men that they were not teaching the principles of the gospel of the Lord Jesus Christ, and he turned to me and said: "Do you think the Lord will hold us responsible for teaching things that we know are not fully in accord with the scriptures?" I said that I would rather let the apostle Paul answer that question, for Paul said; "But though we, or an angel from heaven, preach any other gospel unto you than that which we have preached unto you, let him be accursed." (Galatians 1:8.)

I would just like to remind you now of the experience of the apostle Paul. You will remember how he persecuted the saints, and then on the way to Damascus for the same purpose, a light appeared brighter than the noonday sun, and those who were with him all fell to the earth and a voice from heaven said, "Saul, Saul, why persecutest thou me? it is hard for thee to kick against the pricks." And he said, "Who art thou, Lord?" "I am Jesus whom thou persecutest." (Acts 26:14-15.) Then we follow Paul's great ministry, as described by the Savior, and he was persecuted as were no others of the brethren. He was flayed and stoned; then he stood before the great governor Festus and King Agrippa, in bonds, at Rome, and they desired to hear from him.

There Paul related his marvelous experience, for he knew other than by hearsay that Jesus was the Christ. When he had finished his testimony, Festus said: "Paul, thou art beside thyself; much learning doth make thee mad," to which Paul replied: "I am not mad, most noble Festus; but speak forth the words of truth and soberness." And then Agrippa replied: "Almost thou persuadest me to be a Christian." And then you remember Paul said, "I would to God, that not only thou, but also all that hear me this day, were both almost, and altogether such as I am, except these bonds." (Acts 26:24-25, 28-29.)

There is another great story that all the world ought
to know, one that is comparable to the story of the apostle Paul, and that is the story of Joseph Smith, who in
his youth saw the confusion in his community and knew
not which church he should join. Then he read the words
of James: "If any of you lack wisdom, let him ask of
God, that giveth to all men liberally, and upbraideth not;
and it shall be given him." (James 1:5.)

He said that he realized that if any man needed wisdom, he did, and he went into the woods to pray. And
just like that glorious light that shone over Paul, brighter
than the noonday sun, after he had had the powers of
darkness fall upon him until he felt as if his very life
would be crushed from his body, a light appeared to him
brighter than the noonday sun. God was repeating, in
substance, an experience such as Paul had, to usher in
this, the dispensation of the fulness of times. For Joseph
Smith saw in that light two glorious messengers, the
Father and his Son. Then he bore his testimony after
he was told by Jesus that he should join none of the
churches, because they all taught for doctrine the commandments of men.

Joseph Smith said he felt like Paul of old. He could
not understand why people would persecute him for telling the truth. You know, he was in prison some thirty
times, and he finally sealed his testimony with his blood.
He said he knew that he had seen a vision, he knew that
God knew it, and he dared not deny it because he
knew that by so doing he would offend God and come
under condemnation. (Joseph Smith 2:25.)

I was back in Washington holding a conference a
few years ago and we had over 2,000 present in that
building. We heard from the stake president, a multi-
millionaire. He stood before those people and told
them that the greatest thing he had and owned in all
this world was his witness that this is the truth and that
Joseph Smith was a prophet of God. The next man we

called was the head of one of the government organizations in Washington. He bore the same testimony. Then
we called the president of a great university, and he bore
the same testimony.

Then we called a new convert, a young mother with
two children, and she stood there and said that when the
missionaries came to her home, they read to her the
promise in the Book of Mormon that if she would read
it and ask God, the Eternal Father, in the name of
Christ the Lord, that he would manifest the truth of that
book unto her by the power of the Holy Ghost. She
said she got down on her knees and asked God if it were
true, and then she read it, and she said her whole soul
was illumined.

Then we called on a returned missionary who had just
spent three years in the mission field. I had talked with
him before the meeting. I had said, "Did you feel that
the time you spent in the mission field was a waste of
time, that you should have been home getting your
schooling and getting ready to marry?" "Oh," he had
said, "Bishop, if the brethren want to make me happy,
just let them load me on a plane in the morning and send
me back to the Argentine." Then I said to that great audience of over 2,000: "Which one of you, if called upon,
could come and occupy this pulpit and testify that you
know beyond any shadow of doubt that this work is
divine, that it is the work of God the Eternal Father,
that Jesus is the Christ, and that Joseph Smith was his
prophet?" As far as I could tell, there wasn't one hand
that didn't go up.

Jesus once asked his disciples: "Whom do men say
that I the Son of man am?" They said, "Some say thou
art . . . one of the prophets." "But whom say ye that I
am?" And Peter answered, "Thou art the Christ, the Son
of the living God." And then Jesus said, "Blessed art
thou, Simon Barjona: for flesh and blood hath not revealed it unto thee, but my Father which is in heaven."

(Matthew 16:13-17.) By that same power we know other than by hearsay that this work is divine, and that is my witness to you in the name of the Lord Jesus Christ.

27

A Testimony, Sacred and Dear

Sometime ago three Salt Lake girls wrote a song called "My Testimony." As I remember, the first line goes like this: "I have a testimony, sacred and dear to me." The one thing that I have that is sacred and dear to me, above all other things, is my testimony, and it has been a great guide in my life, and I have yielded to that testimony whenever a call has come to me to serve in the Church.

Sometime ago I had the experience of visiting the Samoa, Tonga, and New Zealand missions. After we left Auckland, New Zealand, by plane, headed for home, we had to travel sixty-five hundred miles over water. All we could see was water and clouds and sky, and the only way we knew that we were traveling in the right direction was the setting of those instruments in the cockpit. And I thought at the time how dependent we were upon the accuracy and the dependability of those instruments.

I will give you another illustration. Sister Richards and I have a son-in-law who made the trip to the Antarctic with Admiral Richard E. Byrd. And they used to take their provisions and cache them in the snow and then go on for a hundred miles or so with a dogsled, and then come back and pick up those provisions. In a few minutes after they had left, their tracks were obliterated by the wind and the snow, and the only way they could find their provisions was through the accuracy of their instruments.

Those experiences impressed me greatly, and I have compared them to a testimony. The instruments are true and they can be depended upon, and when we have a testimony—a real testimony—that is "sacred and dear to us," we can depend upon it.

I read a little story some years ago about a group of boys who were trying to decide whether there was a God or not, so they asked a man about it. He said he did not know anything about such things, and so they went to the schoolteacher, and the schoolteacher said she did not know, that "some say there is and some say there isn't." One of the boys asked his parents, and the mother said there was and the father said he did not know anything about such things. So he decided to write a letter to Frank Crane, who was then editor of the *Globe* in New York, and ask him if there was a God. Here is part of his answer to this boy:

Yes, my boy, there is a God. You cannot see or hear him, but I will tell you how you can feel him. Did you ever lie, or cheat or steal, or treat a smaller boy cruelly, or be a coward when you should have been brave? If so, you have felt a hurt inside your mind, a miserable feeling in your heart as if you were sick at your stomach, or as if you had struck your finger with a hammer. It is God that so makes you hurt.

It is not the police that protect your lives, my boy, only a few wicked men come into conflict with the policeman. But there is something that holds every man back from cruelty and uncleanness, that stays the murderer's arm, and causes many a woman to drown herself rather than be vile. That something is God.

Such feelings are put in the heart of every man and woman. The apostle Paul put that same thought in words like this: "For this is the covenant that I will make with the house of Israel after those days, saith the Lord: I will put my laws into their mind, and write them in their hearts. . . ." (Hebrews 8:10.)

God has put his laws into our minds and written them in our hearts. And Paul further tells us that some would have "their conscience seared with a hot iron." I take it that is just another way of expressing the thought that we often hear, that "vice is a monster of so frightful mein, As to be hated needs but to be seen; Yet seen too oft, familiar with her face, We first endure, then pity, them embrace." (Alexander Pope, "An Essay on Man.") We cannot embrace sin until that which God has put in our minds and in our hearts, our conscience, is seared with a hot iron, so to speak, so that we do not feel the seriousness of the things that we do.

I think of when I was a young boy on the farm, and one of our neighbor boys, who was considerably older than I, came over one day and suggested to my younger brother and me that we go and steal some strawberries. We went up around the back way to get to the strawberry patch, and he went in first and got some berries and came out. I suppose it would have been my turn next, as I was the next oldest, but by that time the owner of the berry patch had seen us and so we left in a hurry. We went directly home. Mother was sick in bed with a new baby. I did not go into the bedroom to see her as I usually did. She did not know I had been out stealing strawberries, but I had a sick feeling in my stomach, and I felt as if I had hit my finger with a hammer. I think that is what Frank Crane meant when he said, "It is God that so makes you hurt." When you do that which is wrong, it does not need to be publicized; the world does not need to know it; but there is someone up there who knows it, and he has written his law in our hearts and in our minds so that that testimony should be our guide and our director to restrain us from doing the things that are displeasing to the Lord.

You remember the story about the man who took his son to steal corn. They each had a sack, and when they arrived where the corn was, the father looked in all directions and could not see anybody coming. Just as he went to reach for the corn, his boy said, "Daddy, you forgot to look up." Now there is someone up there who has a powerful influence upon our lives and our hearts and our minds, and when we do good it is just wonderful how we feel. And he knows how to direct us to the good feelings. He said to his apostles when he was about to be offered up: "Herein is my Father glorified, that ye bear much fruit," and then he added, "These things have I spoken unto you . . . that your joy might be full." (John 15:8, 11.) You see, when you do good and you bear much fruit, then you have a fullness of joy; and when you do bad or evil, then you have that sick or hurt feeling.

That is what I think a testimony is for, to guide and direct us to do the things that will bring us true joy and happiness. If we apply this in our lives we will know how wonderful it is when our testimony is such that it enables us to walk above the things of the world and the weaknesses and wickedness of the world, so that we can look all men in the face and fear no man because we are walking in the ways of the Lord and keeping his commandments. That is when our instrument is set true; that is when our testimony is working in our mind; that is when we land in San Francisco instead of in South America when we are traveling, and we are all traveling the road to eternal life and exaltation. But there are many by-ways and highways and detours, and it is an unfortunate thing that many people find themselves on these detours.

I give you as another illustration of the value of testimony the story we read in Holy Writ about the great man Joseph, one of the twelve sons of Jacob, the one that we look back to with pride when the patriarch tells us that we are of his lineage. You remember when he was tempted by Potiphar's wife. She did everything she could to try to seduce him until, as he fled from her on the last occasion, she grabbed his cloak. He knew that she would use that as evidence against him, that it might cause him imprisonment or death, and he was imprisoned and barely escaped being put to death; but when he fled from that wicked woman, he was just following his testimony, that little instrument set in his heart and in his mind by the Lord, which taught him right from wrong. And he fled from her with words like this upon his lips: "How could I do that wicked thing and thus offend God?" You see, he was not thinking of injury to his body; he was thinking of the estrangement between him and the Lord and of that sick feeling he would have in his heart, so to speak, and in his mind, if he had permitted himself to lower his standards to the point that he could do that which his testimony told him could not be done and still maintain his full friendship with the Lord.

When one of our sons returned from the Navy, I said to him, "I do not know whether your mother and I have been duly expressive of our appreciation of the fact that you came home clean instead of taking up the habits of the men you were associated with." "Well," he said, "Father, you do not need to thank me. All I had to do was to think of you and Mother and my brothers and sisters, and I wanted to be like you." It is a marvelous thing when in one's youth he can plant a testimony in his heart so that regardless of what the temptations are, he has the power to resist the same, having set his instruments true so that they keep him in the proper channel and on the proper path.

I would not have you think that I do not believe in forgiveness of sin. That I do with all my heart. But how marvelous it is when young men and women starting out on the journey of life can avoid the pitfalls, and when their testimony is so true within them that they can avoid the things that will mar their lives and bring them sorrow. We have many people come to us with their sorrows and we wish we could blot them out of their minds. They say, "Why didn't we think farther and faster, and why didn't we realize what this would mean?" These hurt feelings will sometimes follow people all through their lives. To illustrate:

I had a letter from a woman who said that in her youth she made a mistake. She said, "I have suffered from that all my life. I have raised six children. I have been president of the MIA and president of the Relief Society, and every time the bishop has asked me to serve I have told him that I was not worthy, but I did not have the courage to tell him why. Now," she said, "how can I get rid of that feeling?" You see, she had that hurt feeling as if she were sick to her stomach. If people really want to be happy in life, they must avoid these experiences in their youth. Their testimonies should enable them to do so.

I had a letter from a woman written while she was sick in the hospital. She did not know whether she would live or die, but she had something she wanted to get off her mind. People come to us with their troubles. Now, it is a wonderful thing to try to help people when they are in trouble, and I would go a long way to help them, and the Lord will. He has even promised that ultimately he would blot their mistakes out of his remembrance. But how much better if we, as leaders in Israel and of the youth of Zion, can help them to increase their testimonies to the point where they can resist temptations to do wrong and stand up for what they know is right, that they will have none of these sorrows and regrets to worry about later on.

A testimony not only enables us to live properly, but it also impels us to great service. It enables us, in the words of the Savior, to put the seeking of the kingdom of God first in our lives, for he promised that "all other things will be added thereunto."

When I courted my wife, I had been on a mission and had learned to love the Lord and his church so deeply that I told her there would always be one that would come ahead of her. Then I had to explain that my duty to the Lord and his church would have to come first, but she accepted me on those terms. That is what a testimony will do for a person. It is God who creates such feelings in the human breast and makes one want to live to enjoy his divine approval.

There is a short passage of scripture that, to me, is one of the most marvelous things in the scriptures; it is in Hebrews, where Paul tells of the things that have been accomplished by faith. And then he says that by faith Enoch received a testimony before he was translated, "that he pleased God." (Hebrews 11:5.) His testimony enabled him to so live while he was yet here in mortality that he obtained the assurance from God that his life was acceptable to him. I do not know what a testimony could do for a person that would be more wonderful than that.

As we travel in the Church we witness the sacrifices that are being made for the gospel's sake. And we realize that all this is due to the testimony of the individual. We had one missionary with us in the South who had left his wife and four kiddies at home. He became discouraged and homesick, and he wrote his wife that he was coming home. She wrote back and said, "If you come back you will not have a home to come to." She said, "You cannot have me, and you cannot have the children and you cannot come in this house until you have filled an honorable mission and you are honorably released." He settled down and went to work and became the president of one of our districts, and he is a great leader in the Church. That is what a testimony will do.

I think of when I was called on my second mission to preside over the Netherlands Mission. I took Sister Richards and three children with me. We brought back four with us, but they were all ours. When we returned home they could not talk English, and our folks had the thrill of their lives listening to them rattle off the Dutch. When I received that call I was just ready to start in the lumber business, and I had a friend, not a member of the Church, whom I had worked for, who was putting up $50,000. We had bought the ground and were all ready to start when the President of the Church asked me if I would go to Holland. If I had loved the things of this world I could not have afforded to give up that business opportunity, but I turned that aside and went to Holland. While I was gone, my friend invested his money elsewhere so we did not go into the lumber business.

Later, when I was in business in Salt Lake City, President Heber J. Grant called for a thousand short-term missionaries, experienced men. "And," he said, "bishops and stake presidents are not exempt." I was then the bishop of a ward. My testimony impelled me to go to my stake president, and I said, "There isn't any man in my ward better able to go financially than I am, and if you want me I will go." Well, to make the story short, I left my wife and seven children, and the business in the hands of my employees, and went on another mission.

Then I had a call to go to California and preside over a stake. People do not know it, but the President of the Church sent my father over to my office to see how I would like to go down there, and I said, "Well, Father, I do not know what I would do for a living down there. I have ten men and two girls working for me, and they depend upon me for a living. And my children are just at the mating age, and I would not like to take them away from their friends. You had better tell the President that I do not know what I would do for a living, but I love the Church enough to go anywhere they want me to, and if he wants me to go I will go down and look around." And the President said, "Tell him to go look around." And in sixty days we had sold our business and had moved to California. Again, that is what my testimony did for me.

I think now of Brother Ezra Taft Benson. When he was called to be a member of the Twelve, nothing was said to him about whether he would get an allowance to live on. I was in his stake to attend a conference; I knew him well, and he said, "LeGrand, do they make any provision for the General Authorities to live?" "Well," I said, "they give you a living allowance, but you will not live like you are living here unless you have something tucked away that you can draw on." I happen to know that Brother Benson had an offer for just about ten times as much per month as the allowance that the brethren gave him. Why did he not take that offer of ten times as much? Because of his testimony. His instrument was set loyal and true to the Church, "the Church and the kingdom of God first," as President Taylor used to say, and so you know what happened.

When I chose Bishop Thorpe B. Isaacson to be my counselor in the Presiding Bishopric, it was the same thing. His tithing had been just about the same each year as his allowance was later as a member of the Presiding Bishopric. In fact, when he got his first six months' checks he turned them right into the cashier and said, "Credit these back. I have never been on a mission—it is about time I was doing something for the Church." When President George Albert Smith asked him, in my presence, if he would be willing to serve as my counselor, thinking of that fine business he had, he said, "Yes, President Smith, but I would like to go back to South Bend, Indiana, to see if the president of our company will let me appoint a manager, so I can save some of my business. You know, in the insurance business so much of it is renewals, and you receive in the future the reward of your labors of the past. But," he said, "if they will not let me do it, I will tell them to take the business."

Think of the testimonies of the apostles of old, which led every one of them to give their lives for their testimony, except John, who was privileged to tarry until the Savior should come again. I have had many a Mormon elder under my supervision in the mission field who, under the influence of the testimony that God had planted in their hearts, would have given their lives for their testimonies, and no human being can put such feelings in the human heart.

One missionary who was there on his second mission told of an experience. While on his first mission he and his companion held a morning meeting and then went home to have lunch with a family. While they were eating, a man rode up on horseback and asked if they were not going to hold an afternoon meeting.

"No," he said, "we had not planned on it."

"Well," the man said, "the people thought you were, and the church is full and they are all waiting for you."

The missionary said, "All right. We will be right over."

When the missionaries arrived, there was a whole bevy of men on horseback with lassoes and their pistols strapped on them, and they said, "We have had enough of you Mormons. We are going to get rid of you. We are going to hang you up to this tree."

This missionary was a bit witty and said, "Well, that is all right. We have got to die sometime—we might just as well die now as any time—but there is really no hurry about it, is there? Come on inside and let's talk it over."

The result was that he was invited to go home with the leader of the mob and stay the night. They did not hang him to the tree. He could easily have given his life for the testimony the Lord had planted in his heart.

I love the Church. I love God the Eternal Father with all my heart and all my soul, and I thank him for the testimony that burns in my heart, and I thank him that I have had it since I was a boy, so that I have been able to avoid the pitfalls and the evils that could have marred my life. And if I had the power, I would burn such a testimony within the heart of each member of the Church, that no one would ever need to fear that he might have to look back upon his youth with regret, but he would find himself ever traveling onward and upward to the great goal that God has prepared for those who love him.

28

The Sacrament Meeting

When Jesus was among men, he said that the gospel was the pearl of great price, and one seeking goodly pearls would sell all that he had in order that he might acquire the pearl of great price. And then he indicated that if we would seek first the kingdom of God and his righteousness, all other things would be added unto us.

One of the means by which we can increase our spirituality and appreciation of the gospel is by doing what the Lord has suggested in a revelation to the Prophet Joseph Smith: "And that thou mayest more fully keep thyself unspotted from the world, thou shalt go to the house of prayer and offer up thy sacraments upon my holy day." (D&C 59:10.) Is there any true Latter-day Saint who would not like to keep himself more unspotted from the world? Is there any father or mother in Israel who would not like his or her sons and daughters to keep themselves unspotted from the world?

Jesus said, "Where two or three are met together in my name, there will I be also." Wouldn't you like to go where he is? Wouldn't you like your children to go where he is, where they can visit with him through his holy Spirit and feel his power? I do know that when men and women meet together in his name, there he is present at least by the power of his holy Spirit.

Brothers and sisters, I do not think there is anything more important, if we would find joy and peace and the happiness the gospel has to give, than that we as Latter-day Saints form the habit of attending our sacrament meetings and taking our children with us. I think the Church has a right to expect that of us.

Jeremiah of old, speaking of our day, said, "Turn, O backsliding children, saith the Lord, for I am married unto you: and I will take you one of a city, and two of a family, and I will bring you to Zion:

"And I will give you pastors according to mine heart, which shall feed you with knowledge and understanding." (Jeremiah 3:14.)

Many of us have spent many years of our lives inviting backsliding Israel, the children of God, to come to Zion, and when they arrive, marvelous is the organization of the Church and the priesthood quorums and the auxiliaries that the Lord has provided to feed them with knowledge and understanding if they will only come and attend their meetings; but if they do not, how can the Lord feed them with knowledge and understanding as he has promised?

I remember reading the remarks of President Heber J. Grant when he said he knew Saints in foreign lands who would walk miles and miles to be able to attend a sacrament meeting because they loved the truth and they loved the Church; but when they came to Zion, that love waxed cold and they would not even walk across the street; and then he indicated that just as the body without food will wither and die, so also will the spirit of man wither and die without spiritual food. And I could not help but think of the words of Jesus, when, after he had fasted forty days, the devil came to tempt him and, pointing to the stones, said, "If thou be the Son of God, command that these stones be made bread." But Jesus rebuked him in the words of Isaiah, saying: "It is written, Man shall not live by bread alone, but by every word that proceedeth out of the mouth of God." (Matthew 4:3-4.) We must go where the words of God are to be heard if we would not wither and die spiritually.

Brigham Young said, "Whether we be poor or rich, if we neglect our prayers and our sacrament meetings, we neglect the spirit of the Lord and a spirit of darkness comes over us." We do not want to neglect our prayers; we do not want to neglect attendance at our sacrament meetings. We do not want a spirit of darkness to come over us. I want to bear testimony, as a result of my own experience and training, and that of my children, that I know of no other way that we can keep the spirit of God burning in our souls and in their souls like attending sacrament meetings. When I walked out of our fast meeting one day with my son, who was a teacher in the Aaronic Priesthood, he turned to me and said, "Daddy, if the bishop had not announced the closing song just when he did, I could not have kept my seat another minute." And I thanked the Lord that my boy was there to feel that spirit and that power, for "where two or three are met together in my name, there will I be also."

When I think of how marvelously the Lord has provided for our spiritual growth and edification and advancement, and how dilatory some of us are in accepting his invitation, I feel as I imagine Alma did of old when he said, "O, that I were an angel, and could have the wish of mine heart, that I might go forth and speak with the trump of God, with a voice to shake the earth," that I might be able to make the Saints realize the importance of their responsibilities in these matters. I wonder, when Jesus does meet according to his promise, and there are groups of two or three where there might be tens or hundreds, if he does not feel as he did when he stood overlooking Jerusalem and cried out, "O Jerusalem, Jerusalem, thou that killest the prophets, and stonest them which are sent unto thee, how often would I have gathered thy children together, even as a hen gathereth her chickens under her wings, and ye would not!" Then he adds: "Behold, your house is left unto you desolate. For I say unto you, Ye shall not see me henceforth, till ye shall say, Blessed is he that cometh in the name of the Lord." (Matthew 23:37-39.)

May we accept his invitation, mingle with the Saints, strengthen the meetings of the wards wherein we reside, that we may not have a spirit of darkness come over us and that our houses may not be left desolate unto us.

29

Blessings Through Tithe Paying

It is reported that one of the Presidents of the United States made the statement that he considered the Mormon Church the greatest organization in the world for the development of the individual, and we know this to be true.

Let us first consider the development of one's talents. Think of the experience afforded our young people to take active part in our auxiliaries and priesthood organizations; seminaries and institutes and Church schools; talks in Sunday School; participation in drama, public speaking, dance, and athletic activities in MIA; the training of our boys in the Aaronic Priesthood; home teaching; speaking in public meetings; administering the sacrament; activities of our boys in Scouting.

During the war, some of our soldiers were stationed on Catalina Island off Los Angeles. A Catholic priest was sent there to conduct services for the Catholic boys at that base. In a meeting of all the servicemen, he asked for volunteers to set up his altars ready to serve mass on Sunday. Three boys volunteered, and when the work was completed the priest said, "I will see you boys at mass in the morning." One of the boys replied, "I guess not, Father." Then the Father wanted to know why, to which the Mormon boy replied, "Well, we are Mormon boys." The Mormon boys are so accustomed to doing church work that it was just natural for them to volunteer.

During the war, we were told by an officer that Mormon boys were the only boys in the service who could hold their own meetings, do their own preaching and praying, and perform their own ordinances without the help of a chaplain.

We send our young men into the mission field as boys, and in two years or more they return as matured men. These experiences prepare our young men to be better husbands, better fathers, and better citizens; and our young women likewise are better prepared to be wives and intelligent mothers and to assist in the great work of the Church, particularly with the youth of Zion.

Not only are we taught to use our talents for the building of the kingdom of God in the earth, for the blessing of his children, and for the honor and glory of his holy name, but we are also taught to give freely of our substance for the same purposes.

When Jesus said, "No man can serve two masters: for either he will hate the one, and love the other; or else he will hold to the one, and despise the other. Ye cannot serve God and mammon" (Matthew 6:24), he realized that in his church there would have to be a principle to test people's faith, to see which they loved most: God or mammon.

Therefore, before the Lord needed money for the building of his kingdom he gave the law of sacrifice to Adam and his posterity, and you remember that Cain's offering was rejected. These offerings were burned as burnt offerings because the Lord did not need them for his church at that time, but Cain and Abel needed to be tested.

Consider now the experience of the rich young man who came to Jesus. "And, behold, one came and said unto him, Good Master, what good thing shall I do, that I may have eternal life?

"And he said unto him, Why callest thou me good? there is none good but one, that is, God: but if thou wilt enter into life, keep the commandments.

"He saith unto him, Which? . . ." (Matthew 19:16-18.)

Then Jesus enumerated most of the Ten Commandments, to which the young man replied, "All these things have I kept from my youth up; what lack I yet?

"Jesus said unto him, If thou wilt be perfect, go and sell that thou hast, and give to the poor, and thou shalt have treasure in heaven: and come and follow me.

"But when the young man heard that saying, he went away sorrowful: for he had great possessions." (Matthew 19:20-22.)

It should be noted that the rich young man asked, "What good thing shall I do that I may have eternal life?" Then it was that Jesus told him to keep the commandments. When the young man informed him that he had done this from his youth, Mark tells us that "Jesus beholding him loved him." (Mark 10:21.) How wonderful! I have always thought that this rich young man might have become one of the Savior's chosen Twelve if he had had the faith to part with his earthly possessions in favor of his love for his Master. Everyone will have to be put to the test to prove which he loves most, God or mammon.

In the restoration of the gospel to the Prophet Joseph Smith, the Lord gave to the Prophet the law of tithing in answer to his inquiry, "O Lord, show unto thy servants how much thou requirest of the properties of thy people for a tithing." Then, after giving the law of tithing, the Lord adds: "And I say unto you, if my people observe not this law, to keep it holy, and by this law sanctify the land of Zion unto me, that my statutes and my judgments may be kept thereon, that it may be most holy, behold, verily I say unto you, it shall not be a land of Zion unto you." (D&C 119:6.)

To the prophet Malachi, the Lord declared the time when he would send his messenger to prepare the way before him, when he would come swiftly to his temple in the latter days, and this messenger was to call his people back to the worship of the Lord and keeping of his commandments. Listen to the words of this prophet:

"Even from the days of your fathers ye are gone away from mine ordinances, and have not kept them. Return unto me, and I will return unto you, saith the Lord of hosts. But ye said, Wherein shall we return?

"Will a man rob God? Yet ye have robbed me. But ye say, Wherein have we robbed thee? In tithes and offerings.

"Ye are cursed with a curse; for ye have robbed me, even this whole nation." (Malachi 3:7-9.)

The Lord calls us back to serve him in the payment of our tithes and offerings, indicating that if Israel would return unto him, he would return unto them. Then the Lord, through the prophet Malachi, further states:

"Bring ye all the tithes into the storehouse, that there may be meat in mine house, and prove me now herewith, saith the Lord of hosts, if I will not open you the windows of heaven, and pour you out a blessing, that there shall not be room enough to receive it.

"And I will rebuke the devourer for your sakes, and he shall not destroy the fruits of your ground; neither shall your vine cast her fruit before the time in the field, saith the Lord of hosts.

"And all nations shall call you blessed, for ye shall be a delightsome land, saith the Lord of hosts." (Malachi 3:10-12.)

The faithful Latter-day Saints have accepted this invitation from the Lord to return unto him in the payment of their tithes and their offerings, and they have realized the promised blessings that the Lord gave, and they are a blessed people.

We read further in that same chapter the following:

"Your words have been stout against me, saith the Lord. Yet ye say, What have we spoken so much against thee? Ye have said, it is vain to serve God: and what profit is it that we have kept his ordinance, and that we have walked mournfully before the Lord of hosts?

"And now we call the proud happy; yea, they that work wickedness are set up; yea, they that tempt God are even delivered.

"Then they that feared the Lord spake often one to another: and the Lord hearkened, and heard it, and a book of remembrance was written before him for them that feared the Lord, and that thought upon his name.

"And they shall be mine, saith the Lord of hosts, in that day when I make up my jewels; and I will spare them, as a man spareth his own son that serveth him.

"Then shall ye return, and discern between the righteous and the wicked, between him that serveth God and him that serveth him not." (Malachi 3:13-18.)

So, in our youth program we require that the boys and girls should be full tithe payers in order to get their achievement awards—not that we are particularly interested in increasing the income to the Church, but we want all the young men and young women in Israel to have their names recorded in this book of remembrance, that they might be numbered among his jewels when he would come to claim his own.

Prophets and Patriarchs

30

The Need for a Prophet

Recently I read an article in a national magazine, written by the senior editor, under the title "The Battle of the Bible." The whole article was devoted to the failure of the churches to perform what the churches should do in the world today. Here are just two sentences from that article: "You feel religious restlessness everywhere you go. The big denominations, long placid, are suddenly possessed by turmoil." "Many Protestant leaders believe that the church will not survive as it is."

Now think of that! Then think of the words of Paul of old when he said that perilous times should come:

"This know also, that in the last days perilous times shall come.

"For men shall be lovers of their own selves, covetous, boasters, proud, blasphemers, disobedient to parents, unthankful, unholy." (2 Timothy 3:1-2.)

In the face of such declarations, what is the remedy? I have come to think that there is only one remedy, and that is the voice of a living prophet. I thank God that we believe in a living prophet, that we have a living prophet to guide us in these latter days.

Many thinking people in religious circles in the world today believe that we need the voice of a prophet.

When I was down in the South as a missionary, there appeared an article in the *Atlanta Constitution,* reporting a Methodist conference where Bishop Ainsworth discussed the conditions existing in the churches relative to the alarming conditions observed today and urged the churches and people of all faiths to engage in a crusade to save civilization from moral decadence; then he added: "Never in the nation's history was the arresting voice of a prophet of God more needed than it is today."

Now it is wonderful if people begin to realize the need of the arresting voice of a prophet of God.

In an article in the Luton (Bedfordshire, England) *Saturday Telegram,* the Reverend James A. Sutherland discussed the need of a prophet:

> We all recognize that something has got to be done for at the moment we are in a plight. Where our earthly leaders falter, our people drift and die. We cannot forget that when the blind set out to lead the blind, chances are that both will find themselves in a ditch. A dictator being out of the question, WHAT ABOUT A PROPHET?
>
> The Prophet never is self-appointed. It is well to keep that in mind. Nor is he chosen of his fellows. Always he is Heaven sent. Yet I am cheered at the thought that he has a knack of appearing at the right time. That being so, I incline to the belief that our Prophet must surely be getting ready for us. Let us not forget that; hope and pray as we will for his coming. Men have an old habit of greeting the true prophet with stones. We need not be surprised if an old-fashioned welcome awaits the Prophet of our day. No one can say when such a prophet will come, but of our need of him, there is no question.

Isn't it wonderful to think that spiritual leaders are beginning to recognize their failure, that they need the word of living prophets? As Amos of old said: "Surely the Lord God will do nothing, but he revealeth his secret unto his servants the prophets." (Amos 3:7.)

An article in the Atlanta *Journal* quoted Bishop Warren A. Candler of the Methodist Church. He discussed the decadent condition of the Christian world, and said: "The whole world, especially our own country, needs a revival of genuine religion." After discussing that need, he said: "We need the reappearance of prophets sent from God."

I think that it is a wonderful thing that these men recognize that they don't have what it takes!

In the Alabama *Christian Advocate* I read a poem titled "The Cry for Prophets":

> O timorous Church of Christ,
> Cease counting your gain and losses.
> The future, imperiled is calling
> With the voice of a million crosses!
> *Calling for faithful Prophets and Seers,*
> To rise up and prophesy—
> To kindle a fading vision afresh,
> Lest a visionless people die.
>
> Our sins are many, our needs are sore;
> *O, Prophet, show us the roll—*
> Take up the scales of God once more,
> And weigh the things of the soul.
> Point not alone to the Patriarchs
> For the leading we need today—
> Scrolls of the Ancients we cherish,
> But the Prophets must lead the way.

Another statement came from one of the leaders of the Methodist Church, Dr. John Lidgett, as follows: "It is undoubtedly true that we need a revival of religion, but such a revival cannot be man-made. It must be God-given. We must pray for it, work for it, but that alone will not make it possible. *It must come from God.*"

As already indicated, when a true prophet is sent, an old-time welcome will await him. This thought is also expressed in Giovanni Papini's *Life of Christ,* in these words:

All the prophets who have ever spoken upon the earth were insulted by men, and men will insult those who are to come. We can recognize Prophets by this, that smeared with mud and covered with shame, they pass among men, bright-faced, speaking out what is in their hearts. No mud can close the lips of those who must speak. Even if the obstinate Prophet is killed, they cannot silence him. His voice multiplied by the echoes of his death will be heard in all languages and through all the centuries.

It is the mission and the privilege and the responsibility of the Latter-day Saints to bear witness to all the world that the God of heaven has raised up a prophet in our day to usher in the restored gospel of his Son, Jesus Christ, and it is our responsibility to bear that message.

Peter, the apostle, said: "And he shall send Jesus Christ, which before was preached unto you: Whom the heaven must receive until the times of restitution of all things, which God hath spoken by the mouth of all his holy prophets since the world began." (Acts 3:20-21.)

How can there be a restitution of all things spoken by the mouths of all the holy prophets since the world began without a living prophet upon the earth, a person unto whom such a restitution can be conveyed by the powers of heaven? No man, no prophet of God, is ever self-sent; he must be called and sent by our Father in heaven.

When Moroni the prophet, who lived upon this American continent four hundred years after the birth of the Savior, visited the Prophet Joseph Smith as a messenger from heaven, a resurrected being, he visited him three times during the night and again the next morning. Joseph was then only eighteen years of age, and Moroni told him that his name would be had for good and evil among every nation, every kindred, and every people.

We sing, "Praise to the man who communed with Jehovah, Jesus anointed that prophet and seer," while the world has denounced him as a false prophet, and he was put to death with his brother Hyrum. He said that he felt much like the apostle Paul when he made his defense before King Agrippa; and I read you his testimony:

. . . I had actually seen a light, and in the midst of that light I saw two Personages, and they did in reality speak to me; and though I was hated and persecuted for saying that I had seen a vision, yet it was true; and while they were persecuting me, reviling me, and speaking all manner of evil against me falsely for so saying, I was led to say in my heart: Why persecute me for telling the truth? I have actually seen a vision; and who am I that I can withstand God, or why does the world think to make me deny what I have actually seen? For I had seen a vision; I knew it, and I knew that God knew it, and I could not deny it, neither dared I do it; at least I knew that by so doing, I would offend God and come under condemnation. (Joseph Smith 2:25.)

The evidence that Joseph Smith was a prophet of God is seen on every hand in the great organization of The Church of Jesus Christ of Latter-day Saints and its great achievements and accomplishments. It has been said that one of the presidents of the United States said that this was the greatest organization in the world for the development of men and women. And we know that that is true. Men not of the Church have even borne testimony, while thousands of members have had planted in their hearts by the power of the Holy Ghost a witness that Joseph Smith was a true prophet of God. And that, after all, is the best knowledge that one can get.

The Prophet Joseph Smith has given to the world more revealed truth than any prophet who has ever lived upon the face of the earth, aside from Jesus Christ the Lord, as far as any records we have today give evidence.

Many thinking people who are not members of the Church have recognized in Joseph Smith a puzzle, and have wondered where his power came from. A writer for the New York *Herald,* who had visited with the Prophet Joseph Smith back in 1842, published this:

> Joseph Smith is undoubtedly one of the greatest characters of the age. He indicates as much talent, originality and moral courage as Mohammed, Odin or any of the great spirits that have hitherto produced the revolutions of past ages. . . . While modern philosophy, which believes in nothing but what you can touch, is overspreading the Atlantic states, Joseph Smith is creating a spiritual system, combined also with morals and industry, that may change the destiny of the race—we certainly want some such

prophet to start up, take a big hold of the public mind, and stop the torrent of materialism that is hurrying the world into infidelity, immorality, licentiousness, and crime.

It is a prophet, the voice of a prophet, that this world needs today.

Now you remember the statement contained in the book *Figures of the Past* by Josiah Quincy, the former mayor of Boston, when he said:

It is by no means improbable that some future textbook for the use of generations yet unborn, will contain a question something like this: "What historical American of the nineteenth century has exerted the most powerful influence upon the destiny of his countrymen?" And it is by no means impossible that the answer to that interrogatory may be thus written: "Joseph Smith, the Mormon prophet" and the reply, absurd as it doubtless seems to most men now living, may be an obvious commonplace to their descendants.

A college president who taught down at the Brigham Young University just a short time ago made this statement at the close of his service there: "It may well be that the Mormon people have the key that will eventually save this country."

Men do not make statements like that without some reason for it. He had seen the lives of the people, and he knew something of the accomplishments of this church.

Here are a few comments from a few of the visitors to our exhibition at the 1964-65 New York World's Fair, and this is just an inkling of the marvelous comments of people who wrote in those books there: "There is hope for the world with people like you." "More of this, no doubt, shall save our world." "Have seen nothing equal to it as far as religion is concerned."

We have similar statements from people who have visited our Welfare Square in Salt Lake City, where the Church has made preparation to take care of under-privileged and needy people. I read you a few of those statements: "It is a pattern for our Federal government to attempt to follow." "This is the most wonderful thing I have ever seen, and I hope to come back again." "This, to my way of thinking, is a real religion." "We believe your church and its members are doing the great deeds that may someday achieve a true brotherhood of man."

We knew that, but we are grateful to know that other people are finding it out!

Besides the great organization of the Church, we have the Book of Mormon, a tangible evidence, and that evidence is something that the world is beginning to recognize, even some of the ministers. No man would dare write a book of five hundred pages and put in it such a promise that if you would ask God, the Eternal Father, in the name of Christ, he would manifest the truth of it unto you by the power of the Holy Ghost. (See Moroni 10:4.)

A minister who visited our exhibit at the World's Fair in New York wrote this: "I am reading the Book of Mormon, and it is a revelation, and I believe it is the truth."

Sometime ago a minister wrote and said that he had had a Book of Mormon in his library for years and had never read it. He said, "Recently I started reading it." And in this letter he referred to Alma, Mosiah, and King Benjamin and their wonderful teachings, and he said, "I am quoting from them in my sermons to my people."

A minister of the gospel toured Temple Square some years ago. He wrote a letter later and said that he had been a minister of the gospel for thirty-seven years and that he had acquired a library that had cost him over twelve thousand dollars (and that was when money was money; it would cost him a lot more now!). Then he said, "But I have in my library a book that is worth more than all the other books, because it is the word of God." And he mentions it as the Book of Mormon.

People don't need to be in the dark. If they are just willing to be open-minded and will investigate the truth

that we have to offer, they cannot help but know that
this is the work of God, the Eternal Father.

I say to all of our friends who are not of us, of
every church and every creed, in the words of our song:

> Come, listen to a prophet's voice,
> And hear the word of God,
> And in the way of truth rejoice,
> And sing for joy aloud.
> We've found the way the prophets went
> Who lived in days of yore;
> Another prophet now is sent
> This knowledge to restore.
> —*Hymns,* No. 46

That is our testimony to the world: we *do* have a
living prophet.

31

"A More Sure Word of Prophecy"

The greatest even in recorded history of all time was the life and the mission of the Redeemer of the world.

His work is not yet finished. We read in the Book of Mormon that "my work is not yet finished; neither shall it be until the end of man, neither from that time henceforth and forever." (2 Nephi 29:9.)

I think of him as the Creator of worlds unnumbered to man: ". . . but all things are numbered unto me," the Lord said. ". . . by the Son I created them." (Moses 1:35, 33.)

I think of his great atonement and of the promises that yet await us. You remember when he stood before Caiaphas, the chief priest of the Jews, and Caiaphas said, "I adjure thee by the living God, that thou tell us whether thou be the Christ, the Son of God." And Jesus answered, "Thou hast said." Then he added, "Hereafter shall ye see the Son of man sitting on the right hand of power, and coming in the clouds of heaven." (Matthew 26:63-64.)

It is this "coming in the clouds of heaven" and the work that is necessary to be done to prepare for his coming that I would like to explain here. Let us turn to the Holy Scriptures for the promises of the resurrection.

Think of getting our bodies back out of the grave and being reunited with our loved ones; read the testimony of John, when he was banished upon the Isle of Patmos, describing that time: "And God shall wipe away all tears from their eyes; and there shall be no more death, neither sorrow, nor crying, neither shall there be any more pain: for the former things are passed away. . . . He that overcometh shall inherit all things; and I will be his God, and he shall be my son." (Revelation 21:4, 7.)

Then we read further that it is they who die in Christ who shall come forth in the morning of the first resurrection, but that the rest of the dead live not again until the thousand years are ended.

What is there in this world that we could do to repay for the privilege of coming forth in the morning of the first resurrection and receiving our loved ones and being united with them and with the servants of the living God, and with the Redeemer of the world, when he comes in the clouds of heaven?

If we understood really what the gospel is, we would know why Jesus said that the merchant man seeking costly pearls would sell all that he had in order that he might acquire "one pearl of great price" (Matthew 13: 45-46), and we would also understand what he meant when he said, "For what is a man profited, if he shall gain the whole world, and lose his own soul? or what shall a man give in exchange for his soul?" (Matthew 16:26.)

We just do not have the capacity to appreciate the great blessings that await the faithful, for the Lord said to the Prophet: "For great shall be their reward and eternal shall be their glory." (D&C 76:6.)

I have great faith in the fulfillment of prophecy. I think of the words of Jesus as he walked along the way to Emmaus following his crucifixion, when the eyes of the two disciples were holden that they could not recognize him; and as he heard them talking of his crucifixion, he said, "O fools, and slow of heart to believe all that the prophets have spoken." He explained to them from the scriptures the words of Moses and the prophets, how they had all testified of him and of his work. Then, we are told, he opened their understanding, "that they might understand the scriptures." (See Luke 24:13-53.)

We also have the words of Peter in which he said, "We have also a more sure word of prophecy; whereunto ye do well that ye take heed, as unto a light that shineth in a dark place, until the day dawn, and the day star arise in your hearts;

"Knowing this first, that no prophecy of the scripture is of any private interpretation.

"For the prophecy came not in old time by the will of man: but holy men of God spake as they were moved by the Holy Ghost." (2 Peter 1:19-21.)

And that is what makes the word of prophecy more sure than anything else in all this world.

We ought to analyze the prophecies with respect to this great latter-day dispensation and the preparation for the coming of the Son of Man.

We find people today who say, "We could accept your message, but we cannot believe that Joseph Smith was a prophet." If they were to believe in the preexistent life, they could then understand. When Jeremiah was called as a boy to be a prophet, he could not understand it, and the Lord said to him, "Before I formed thee in the belly I knew thee; and before thou camest forth out of the womb I sanctified thee, and I ordained thee a prophet unto the nations." (Jeremiah 1:5.)

The Lord not only knew Jeremiah, but he also knew Joseph Smith. Three thousand years ago the Lord revealed unto Joseph who was sold into Egypt that in the latter-days, out of his loins, would be raised up a choice seer and a prophet like unto Moses.

We read in Holy Writ that there was no prophet in all Israel like unto Moses, because Moses talked with God face to face. That is the kind of a prophet the Lord promised Joseph he would raise up out of his loins in the latter-days, and that Joseph Smith was this promised prophet is our testimony to the world. The things that Jesus and the prophets declared would have to be accomplished before his coming could not be accomplished without a prophet through whom the Lord could work.

We read in Malachi where through his prophet the Lord said that he would send a messenger to prepare the way for his coming. Who but a prophet could be this messenger? Has there ever been a time that the Lord came swiftly to his temple? How could the world be prepared for his coming without a prophet? This promise has reference to his second coming, for Malachi adds: "But who may abide the day of his coming? and who shall stand when he appeareth? for he is like a refiner's fire, and like fullers' soap." (Malachi 3:2.)

So in his last coming, he will come swiftly to his temple. He will come to sit in judgment in the great and dreadful day of the Lord, in the latter days when "all the proud, yea, and all that do wickedly, shall be stubble: and the day that cometh shall burn them up, saith the Lord of hosts, that it shall leave them neither root nor branch." (Malachi 4:1.)

And then he goes on to say that before that day he would send Elijah the prophet to turn the hearts of the fathers to the children. (Malachi 4:5.) We bear witness that Elijah did come, and because of the knowledge and the information he brought, we continue to build temples and do the great work of the Lord.

When Peter was speaking to those who had put to death the Christ, he said, "Repent ye therefore, and be converted, that your sins may be blotted out, when the times of refreshing shall come from the presence of the Lord;

"And he shall send Jesus Christ, which before was preached unto you.

"Whom the heaven must receive until the times of

restitution of all things, which God hath spoken by the mouth of all his holy prophets since the world began." (Acts 3:19-21.)

How can one believe the Holy Bible and not believe that one of the preparatory things for the coming of the Redeemer of the world would be a "restitution of all things which God hath spoken by the mouth of all his holy prophets since the world began"?

Daniel saw in the last days that a kingdom that would be set up should become as a great mountain and fill the whole earth, and how could that be without a prophet of God?

Then there was the record of Joseph that was to come forth to be joined with the record of Judah, according to the command the Lord gave to Ezekiel, and how could that be without a prophet who should do this work? The Lord works through his servants, the prophets. We bear witness to the world that the Prophet Joseph Smith, raised up of the Lord, was in very deed the instrument that the Lord had in waiting through the centuries, in the preexistent state.

Jesus knew that he would work through the instrumentality of his servants, and that is why he said, as he stood overlooking Jerusalem, "O Jerusalem, Jerusalem, thou that killest the prophets, and stonest them which are sent unto thee, how often would I have gathered thy children together, even as a hen gathereth her chickens under her wings, and ye would not!

"Behold, your house is left unto you desolate.

"For I say unto you, Ye shall not see me henceforth, till ye shall say, Blessed is he that cometh in the name of the Lord." (Matthew 23:37-39.)

We have had some wonderful testimonies of people who have understood the great work that the Prophet Joseph has done. The world is beginning to recognize the power and the spirit that is in this work, a power that causes every man to be willing to devote himself to the building of the kingdom; this is the kind of power and influence that can overcome the world and establish God's kingdom in the earth.

I bear you my witness that this is in very deed the work of the Lord and that he is at the helm.

32

Turn to the Prophets

I think one of the most important things in life is to be able to properly evaluate things and put first things first and second things second. Many people reverse the procedure. When I was in Holland on a mission, I went to the great Rijks Museum in Amsterdam, and I led one of our Mormon missionaries up to a small oil painting a little over a foot square. I said, "What would you give for that?"

"Well," he said, "if I had to take it home and hang it up, I don't think I'd give over ten dollars for it."

And I imagine that if it were passed around in the West where we have been so busy subduing the wilderness to make it blossom as the rose, it might pass many a home without getting an offer of more than ten dollars. But the National Art Museum paid 350,000 guilders for that little piece of art, which at that time was the equivalent of $120,000 of American money. Now why would the missionary not pay more than ten dollars? Because he didn't have the capacity to comprehend, understand, and appreciate art. In that same sense, we trample many wonderful things under our feet because we don't have the capactiy to appraise them properly.

I was in the Tabernacle in Salt Lake one day at an

organ recital, and the lady sitting next to me turned to me and said, "Mister, where's the choir?"

I replied, "There isn't any choir here today. That's just the organ."

"No, listen," she said. "I can hear the choir singing."

And I looked around. Some people were just sitting there on the edge of their seats drinking it in, and others were sitting there snoozing, waiting until it was over so they could go to something more interesting. Now, I think the important thing in life is that we learn to appreciate the things that are really worthwhile and that determine not only our happiness here in this life, but throughout the eternities that are to come.

Just a few years ago as we went through the Church holding our conferences, we had a film entitled *The Search for Truth*. It was built largely around the testimonies of scientists, both members and nonmembers of the Church, indicating why they believed there was a God. One man by the name of A. Cressy Morrison, at the head of a national scientific organization in New York, said that there wasn't one chance in billions that this universe came into existence of its own accord. He said there had to be a master intelligence back of it.

I have a copy of an article that appeared in the *Reader's Digest* where Morrison gave seven reasons why he believes there is a God simply from the observable things about him that he could analyze. (See *Reader's Digest,* October 1960.) Then I say to myself, "Well, the scientists can tell us that there is evidence of a master intelligence back of all of this, but they can't tell us why. For that, we have to turn to the prophets."

Whenever you see evidence of intelligent organization, you know that there was a purpose back of it. Some years ago, President J. Reuben Clark, Jr., in talking to the seminary and institute teachers, titled his subject "Man, God's Greatest Miracle." Just stop to analyze the human body for a few minutes. Think what it would be if you didn't have an elbow. How could you feed yourself? How do you suppose that elbow got there? What if you didn't have any fingers? How could you play the piano or use the typewriter or things like that? Think of all the bones, sinews, and the nerves in your body; then think of what you take inside of you each day. There is literally a chemical laboratory that goes to work. You don't have to turn a switch or push a button. Without even thinking about it, it takes out all of the life-giving elements, puts them in the bloodstream, and throws the waste away. And the fool says in his heart, "There is no God."

Just think of being able to create the vision of an eye or the hearing of an ear or being able to talk. I started quoting a little poem just recently that I had learned over seventy years ago. If I could tuck things away in my office like that, that would be wonderful. And then, when you are so tired and worn out that you think life isn't worth living, you lie down to rest for a few hours. Then the Lord gives you a little hypo that puts you to sleep so that you don't know what is going on while he works you over; he even gives you a little television set (you know, the dreams that keep you interested while he is making you over for the next day's work). Even after I have analyzed all of that, however, I say to my wife, "Yet the most wonderful thing that God created is the feeling of the human breast." That's why Jesus could say that this is the first and the great commandment, that thou shalt love the Lord thy God with all thy might, mind, and strength. (See Luke 10:27.) And if he hadn't put that kind of feeling in the human breast, you couldn't do it. Yes, all of that is just a part of this marvelous creation of the Lord.

I was in a meeting up in Portland just a couple of weeks ago. There were over 1,500 people there, and about 250 nonmembers of the Church. It was a missionary meeting, and they wanted me to talk to them. So I made a little statement like this. I said, "If I were to ask you

here tonight what's the most wonderful event that has
transpired in this world in the last 150 years, what would
you say?" And then I added, "I imagine that most of you
would say, 'When the astronauts landed upon the moon.'
Truly that was a great event. Just imagine our being
able to sit in our front rooms and turn on our television
sets and watch them land, watch them walk when they
could hardly put their feet down on that dust that they
found up there, and to hear them speak clear from the
moon back here to the earth. What a tremendous achievement in the days in which we are privileged to live!
And yet, I don't know how much good that is going to
do the world. Maybe you do. Maybe you scientists do."
Then I added this to that group: "But there was an event
that transpired 150 years ago that transcends that moon
landing in my ability to appreciate and understand. And
that was when Joseph Smith went out in the woods to
pray, and God the Father and his Son Jesus Christ
descended in a pillar of light."

Now, when the astronauts landed on the moon,
everybody in the world stood in awe, waiting for their
landing to prove successful. Wouldn't it be wonderful
if in the same spirit the whole world could have witnessed the coming of the Father and the Son in that pillar
of light, just as the Savior appeared to Saul on the way
to Damascus, and know what it really meant? I doubt if
any of us have the capacity to comprehend and understand the full magnitude of that event. It opened the
door to what Paul called the dispensation of the fulness
of times, in which period he said that the Lord had revealed the mystery of his will to him, that in that dispensation he would bring together in one in Christ all that
which is in heaven above and which is in the earth beneath. (See Ephesians 1:10.) That is what the true gospel
of the Lord Jesus Christ is for. The scientists can tell
us that there is evidence of a master intelligence back
of it but they can't tell us why. For the meaning and

purpose we have to turn to the words of the holy prophets.

If the world just knew that and if they could just comprehend and understand why this world has changed so much since that event back in 1820 as compared with all the history of the world preceding that time, then they would realize that there is an intelligence that brought this universe into existence and gave man his body. When the Lord created the earth, he placed man on it and gave him dominion over the fish of the sea and over the fowls of the air and over every creeping thing upon the earth. In other words, every man is a god in embryo, a son of God. Man can become like his Father if he is willing to pay the price and to prepare himself for what the Lord has in store.

Thus the coming of the Father and the Son opened the way for the restoration of the gospel and the Holy Priesthood, the power that Jesus gave to his twelve when he said, "Ye have not chosen me, but I have chosen you, and ordained you. . . ." (John 15:16.) He also said, "Whatsoever ye shall bind on earth shall be bound in heaven." (Matthew 18:18.) That power was lost to the world during the Dark Ages. The world considered the heavens closed and sealed, and here came the Father and the Son to prove that the heavens are not sealed, that the words of the holy prophets should be fulfilled in the latter days. You remember, following the day of Pentecost, that Peter told the people that the heavens were to receive the Christ until the restitution of all things spoken by the mouths of all the holy prophets since the world began. (See Acts 3:19-21.) The world can't look for the return of Jesus when he will come in power and great glory until there is such a restitution, and that is our message to the entire world, introduced by the coming of the Father and the Son.

Back in 1934 there was a man here in America by the name of William A. Kennedy from Lima, Peru. He was here to gather funds for the establishment of a research university or seminar to study the early inhabitants of the Americas, particularly the Incan and Mayan civilizations. He had promises of enough money that, when matched by the small Americas, would total $30 million and the assurance that within ten years that amount would increase from $60 to $70 million. Then I said to myself: "Let them spend their $70 million and they will know mighty little about the early inhabitants of these lands of America. They may be able to dig out of the earth some of these pots and kettles and things of that kind, but compare that with the Book of Mormon, over 500 pages, written under the inspiration of heaven by holy prophets, just as in the Bible, telling of the history of the people that God led to this land of America. We would give them a copy for fifty cents, and if they didn't have fifty cents, we would give them a copy for nothing."

If you would just stop to think a minute of what's happened in this world since the Prophet Joseph Smith had that marvelous vision and revelation, then you would realize that someone who had something to do with the creation of this world and with our being here has had something to do with the change in this world. In Isaiah 60 we read: "Arise, shine; for thy light is come, and the glory of the Lord is risen upon thee.

"For, behold, the darkness shall cover the earth, and gross darkness the people: but the Lord shall arise upon thee, and his glory shall be seen upon thee.

"And the Gentiles shall come to thy light, and kings to the brightness of thy rising." (Isaiah 60:1-3.)

That is what happened way back in 1820 when the Father and the Son appeared to Joseph Smith. Darkness covered the earth for century after century, and people lived upon the earth and they traveled in the same crude manner, having crude ways of communication. If you would just like to see an evidence of that, when you are

down in California, go to Sutter's Fort near Sacramento.
It has been restored as it was in 1847 when our pioneers
came into the Salt Lake Valley. See the kinds of carpets
on the floors and see the cooking utensils over the open
fireplace. See the kind of beds and the kind of chairs
and furniture that they had. Even in my day I remember
when we used to tuck the ticks full of straw and sleep
on them, and we used to sew the carpet rags in order
to make our carpets and put straw underneath them.
This world is so changed.

When I first went to Holland they were still cutting
their wheat with a sickle and a scythe and plowing with
oxen and donkeys. It was the same when I went to the
South. Well now, the light was to rise and shine. The
Lord said: "And it shall come to pass in the last days,
saith God, I will pour out of my Spirit upon all flesh:
and your sons and your daughters shall prophesy, and
your young men shall see visions, and your old men shall
dream dreams:

"And I will shew wonders in heaven above, and
signs in the earth beneath: blood, and fire, and vapour
of smoke—[airplanes, atom bombs, etc.]. . . ." (Acts 2:17,
19.)

The Lord has been pouring out his Spirit upon all
flesh. It isn't just because men and women are more
intelligent of themselves that all the world has changed
and so much progress has been made. It is because the
day has come when the Lord would pour out his Spirit
upon all flesh and they shall dream dreams and see
visions. I am impressed by a statement called "Sikorsky's
Dream" that I copied out of the *Reader's Digest* a few
years ago:

When I was about eleven years old, I had a wonderful
dream. I saw myself walking slowly along a narrow, luxuriously
decorated passageway, on both sides of which were walnut doors
similar to stateroom doors on a steamer or a railroad train. A
spherical electric light from the ceiling produced a pleasant bluish
illumination. I felt a slight vibration under my feet, different from

that of a steamer or a railroad train. It didn't seem strange to me in my dream that I was traveling on a large flying ship, although at that time no such thing existed.

Over thirty years later, in 1931, Sikorsky Aircraft delivered the first American Clipper to Pan American Airways. I had test-piloted this plane before it was furnished and decorated, and now Pan American officials invited me to accompany them on a flight over New York City.

I sat comfortably in the front cabin, watching the city in the setting sun. As it grew dark, I decided to see what was going on in the rear. While I was walking toward the smoking lounge, the steward turned on the lights. I stopped in surprise. I realized that I had seen all this a long time ago—the passageway, the bluish lights, the walnut doors and walls, the elegant entrance to the lounge. Finally I remembered my childhood dream.

It was the same scene in every detail. (Igor Ivanovitch Sikorsky, "Dream of the Future," *Reader's Digest,* June 1942, pp. 152ff.)

The Lord gave Sikorsky a dream thirty years before he made that airplane when there wasn't such a thing. And that's the way his Spirit has been moving upon all flesh in order to bring about the completion of this dispensation of the fulness of times that Paul spoke of. As I understand that, I think it meant that everything that was created in its crude form ultimately to serve the use of man should be brought forth during that dispensation.

Ripley's *Believe It or Not* a few years ago had this statement:

Believing that nothing more remains to be invented, the head of the Patent Office in 1830 [that's when the Church was organized] suggested his office be closed. Since then, more than 2½ million patents have been issued! Today American industry is investing $10 billion yearly in research for new ideas that will mean more jobs, whole new industries.

The first federal patent act was passed in 1790 and from 1790 to 1830 (40 years) 6,500 patents were issued or an average of 161 per year. From 1830 to 1958 (128 years) 2,853,187 were issued, or an average of 22,290 per year.

Now you can say that just happened so. Well, why didn't it happen 500 years ago or 1,000 years ago? Isaiah said, "Darkness should cover the earth, and gross darkness the people"; and when gross darkness rested upon the people, things didn't happen—but a new day has come. The dispensation of the fulness of times was ushered in. If the world knew that that was the cause of this great intellectual progress the world has made, humanity would get down on its knees and beg for an opportunity to be taught the gospel as we have it restored by holy angels.

I know this work is divine. I know that God the Father and his Son Jesus Christ did visit this earth; he did open the dispensation of the fulness of times; and you and I are honored and privileged to be able to live in this enlightened period such as the world has never known. And this is because of the restoration of the gospel.

33

The Patriarchal Calling

In restoring the gospel to the earth in these latter days, the Lord again gave unto the members of his church evangelical ministers, or patriarchs.

"It is the duty of the Twelve, in all large branches of the church, to ordain evangelical ministers, as they shall be designated unto them by revelation."

In this revelation, the Lord further indicated that "this order was instituted in the days of Adam." (D&C 107:39, 41.)

The importance of this calling is evident from the fact that the Lord, by revelation, took Hyrum Smith, the brother of the Prophet Joseph, out of the First Presidency of the Church and called him to be the Patriarch to the Church. (D&C 124:91-93.)

To understand and appreciate the calling of a patriarch, one must understand the principle of the pre-existence of spirits. From the book of Abraham in the Pearl of Great Price, we obtain such a clear understanding of this principle.

"Now the Lord had shown unto me, Abraham, the intelligences that were organized before the world was; and among all these there were many of the noble and great ones;

"And God saw these souls that they were good, and he stood in the midst of them, and he said: These I will make my rulers; for he stood among those that were spirits, and he saw that they were good; and he said unto me: Abraham, thou art one of them; thou wast chosen before thou wast born." (Abraham 3:22-23.)

While the Lord stood in the midst of these spirits, indicating that there were many noble and great ones whom he would make his rulers, none of these spirits brought with them into this world a knowledge that they were among the noble and great spirits and that they would be called by the Lord to be leaders among his people. This knowledge had to come to them later. The scriptures give us many illustrations of this fact.

While Jesus was the creator of this earth and all things pertaining thereunto (see St. John 1:1-3, 14), nevertheless, he was born as other children and had to learn to walk and talk, but the Lord revealed unto him, as he increased in years, who he really was and what his mission in life was to be.

"But with the precious blood of Christ, as of a lamb without blemish and without spot:

"Who verily was foreordained before the foundation of the world, but was manifest in these last times for you." (1 Peter 1:19-20.)

At the age of twelve, Jesus was reasoning with the wise men in the temple; we read: "And Jesus increased in wisdom and stature, and in favour with God and man." (Luke 2:52.)

Had he brought with him all the knowledge he had when he was with the Father and was the Creator of this earth, he would not have had to increase in wisdom and stature and in favor with God and man.

Later we hear Jesus say: "I came forth from the Father, and am come into the world: again, I leave the world, and go to the Father." (John 16:28.)

"I have glorified thee on the earth: I have finished the work which thou gavest me to do.

"And now, O Father, glorify thou me with thine own self, with the glory which I had with thee before the world was." (John 17:4-5.)

Just as Jesus was sent at the particular time appointed by the Lord to do the work for which he had been foreordained, so were many of the "noble and great spirits," among whom the Lord stood when he said, "These I will make my rulers," such as Jeremiah.

"Then the word of the Lord came unto me, saying,

"Before I formed thee in the belly I knew thee; and before thou camest forth out of the womb I sanctified thee, and I ordained thee a prophet unto the nations." (Jeremiah 1:4-5.)

But Jeremiah did not have this knowledge and, therefore, had to be told. This was also true with the apostle Paul. While he went about persecuting the saints, he was sincere in his belief that he was doing God's service. So the Savior appeared to him on the road to Damascus to let him know how wrong he was. And when the Savior told Ananias to go to Paul, he could not understand, because he knew of Paul's activity in persecuting the saints; so the Savior said to him: "But the Lord said unto him, Go thy way: for he is a chosen vessel unto me, to bear my name before the Gentiles, and kings, and the children of Israel." (Acts 9:15.)

Just as Paul was a "chosen vessel," so have been many who have been sent at the time before appointed by the Lord to do the work for which they were called before they were born.

Such was the case with the Prophet Joseph Smith. As Lehi told his son Joseph in the wilderness, the Lord promised that in the *latter days* he would raise up a prophet, from the loins of Joseph who was sold into Egypt, like unto Moses (we read in the scriptures that there was no prophet in Israel like unto Moses, because he talked with God face to face), who would bring forth his word and bring men to conviction of his word, which had already gone forth among them, and would bring men unto salvation and would be great in his eyes. (See 2 Nephi 3:1-15.)

This prophet was Joseph Smith, and the Lord had him in waiting for his day and time, just as he has had many other of the "noble and great" spirits.

The apostle Paul understood this when he said: "And hath made of one blood all nations of men for to dwell on all the face of the earth, and hath determined the times before appointed, and the bounds of their habitation." (Acts 17:26.)

The patriarch, through the spirit of revelation to which he is entitled through his ordination, should be able to reveal in his blessing some of the special qualifications and purposes for which the individual member has come into the world at this particular time. No doubt many of us in our blessings have been told that we have not come upon the earth by chance, but in fulfillment of the decrees of the All Mighty, to perform the mission for which we were foreordained.

As I read my blessing given to me by my father, then a stake patriarch, when I was only eight years old, it is a miracle to me that he should have been able to so fully indicate my mission and calling in life. It seems to me like writing history in advance.

The patriarch is also expected to define the lineage through which we are born.

In addition to this, he can remind those who receive blessings at his hands of the wonderful promises of the Lord to his saints of this dispensation through the keeping of his commandments. For example:

"For thus saith the Lord—I, the Lord, am merciful and gracious unto those who fear me, and delight to honor those who serve me in righteousness and in truth unto the end.

"Great shall be their reward and eternal shall be their glory.

"And to them will I reveal all mysteries, yes, all the hidden mysteries of my kingdom from days of old, and for ages to come, will I make known unto them the good pleasure of my will concerning all things pertaining to my kingdom.

"Yea, even the wonders of eternity shall they know, and things to come will I show them, even the things of many generations.

"And their wisdom shall be great, and their understanding reach to heaven; and before them the wisdom of the wise shall perish, and the understanding of the prudent shall come to naught.

"For by my Spirit will I enlighten them, and by my power will I make known unto them the secrets of my will—yea, even those things which eye has not seen, nor ear heard, nor yet entered into the heart of man." (D&C 76:5-10.)

He may also warn them of the judgments of the Lord if they fail to keep his commandments. President Brigham Young once said: "If we neglect our sacrament meetings and our prayers, the spirit of darkness will come over us, and the Spirit of the Lord will withdraw himself."

The Lord said in a revelation through the Prophet Joseph Smith: "I, the Lord, am bound when you do what I say; but when you do not what I say, ye have no promise." (D&C 82:10.)

The stake patriarch is authorized to give blessings to members of his stake upon a recommend signed by the bishop. He may also give blessings to members of other stakes upon a recommend signed by the bishop and stake president. He may give blessings to members of missions upon receipt of a recommend signed by the branch and mission president. And he may give blessings to his own blood relations.

The Patriarch to the Church may give blessings to any Church member when properly recommended.

A devoted husband, father, and family man, Elder LeGrand Richards enjoys a rich association with children, grand-children, and great-grandchildren. This family picture was taken on April 6, 1952, the day Elder Richards was sus-... tained as a member of the Council of the Twelve Apostles.

When he was first called as Presiding Bishop of the Church, Elder LeGrand Richards had as counselors in the Presiding Bishopric, Bishop Marvin O. Ashton, left, and Bishop Joseph L. Wirthlin, center.

At the time he was called to the Council of the Twelve, Elder LeGrand Richards had as counselors in the Presiding Bishopric, Bishop Joseph L. Wirthlin, left, and Bishop Thorpe B. Isaacson, right.

Elder LeGrand Richards wears the ceremonial headdress of the Catawba Indian tribe, almost all of whom joined the Church. Here he is shown with Chief Blue of the tribe.

This photograph of Elder LeGrand Richards and his wife Ina Ashton Richards was taken in January, 1915.

Elder LeGrand Richards, seated in the center, was presiding over the Netherlands Mission when this photograph was taken with some of his missionaries in March of 1914.

As Presiding Bishop and a member of the Council of the Twelve Apostles, LeGrand Richards has traveled millions of miles in all parts of the world in fulfillment of his calling.

One of the significant contributions made to the Church by Elder Le-Grand Richards has been his book, A Marvelous Work and a Wonder. *Hundreds of thousands of copies have been sold, and many converts have come into the Church because of it. In the true spirit of missionary work, Elder Richards has not taken any royalty payments.*

LeGrand Richards at age 26.

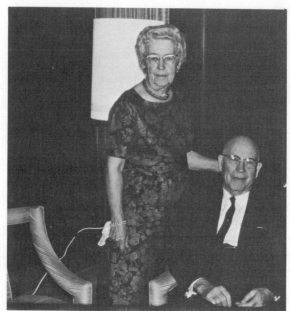

Elder LeGrand Richards and his wife Ina on the occasion of their 60th wedding anniversary.

FOUR GENERATIONS: Elder LeGrand Richards, his son G. LaMont Richards, a grandson G. LaMont Richards, Jr., and a great-grandson David LaMont Richards.

The Promise of Eternal Life

34

The Resurrection

Of all the blessings and privileges the gospel of Jesus Christ has to offer its faithful members, the promised resurrection from the dead is one of the greatest, for it opens the door to an eternal association with loved ones and friends, which condition we have the capacity to understand and appreciate at least in part.

Jesus was the greatest person who has ever lived upon the earth, for he was not only the Creator of this world, but of "worlds without number" (Moses 1:33), and he came into the world of his own free will and choice and gave his life to atone for the sins of the world, so that what man lost through the transgression of Adam he might regain through Christ's great atoning sacrifice.

"For as in Adam all die, even so in Christ shall all be made alive." (1 Corinthians 15:22.)

The angels proclaimed the birth of Jesus as Israel's promised Messiah; he demonstrated in all his teachings and the miracles he performed that he was the Son of God, and that all power was given unto him in heaven and upon earth, even the power to lay down his life and take it up again. (John 10:17-18.) But the final proof of all his claims came when the stone was rolled away from the door of the sepulchre, notwithstanding the presence of the Roman guard, and his body came forth after three days, as he had said; and when the women approached the sepulchre and found the stone rolled away, and "found not the body of the Lord Jesus," they were much perplexed, and two men stood by them in shining garments and said: "Why seek ye the living among the dead? He is not here, but is risen."

When the women reported this experience unto the apostles, "their words seemed to them as idle tales, and they believed them not."

Even though Jesus had told his apostles that "the Son of man must be delivered into the hands of sinful men, and be crucified, and the third day rise again," they could hardly believe. How then could the world be expected to believe? "That we should live again is no more a miracle than that we live at all."

Upon receiving the report from the woman, Peter "ran unto the sepulchre, and stooping down, he beheld the linen clothes laid by themselves, and departed, wondering in himself at that which was come to pass." (Luke 24:1-12.)

As the apostles were gathered together, "Jesus himself stood in the midst of them, and saith unto them, Peace be unto you.

"But they were terrified and affrighted, and supposed that they had seen a spirit.

"And he said unto them, Why are ye troubled? and why do thoughts arise in your hearts?

"Behold my hands and my feet, that it is I myself: handle me, and see; for a spirit hath not flesh and bones, as ye see me have.

"And when he had thus spoken, he shewed them his hands and his feet.

"And while they yet believed not for joy, and wondered, he said unto them, Have ye here any meat?

"And they gave him a piece of a broiled fish, and of an honeycomb.

"And he took it, and did eat before them." (Luke 24:36-43.)

Without his body of flesh and bone, Jesus would not have eaten the fish and honeycomb. What greater proof could he have given of his resurrection?

Following his resurrection, Jesus "shewed himself alive after his passion by many infallible proofs, being seen of them forty days. . . .

"And when he had spoken these things, while they beheld, he was taken up; and a cloud received him out of their sight.

"And while they looked stedfastly toward heaven as he went up, behold, two men stood by them in white apparel;

"Which also said, Ye men of Galilee, why stand ye gazing up into heaven? this same Jesus, which is taken up from you into heaven, shall so come in like manner as ye have seen him go into heaven." (Acts 1:3, 9-11.)

It seems incredible that, in the light of this plain and convincing evidence of his resurrection, "by many infallible proofs" lasting over a period of "forty days," men should believe today that Jesus is a spirit or essence everywhere present. This would imply that he had died a second death, that his spirit and body were again separated, else how could he be now but a spirit?

It was in this glorified, resurrected body that Jesus appeared unto the Nephites in the land of America (see 3 Nephi 11), and unto Joseph Smith while he was but a boy, in the woods on his father's farm at Palmyra, New York.

To further prove that the resurrection would come to all men because Jesus was victor over death and the grave, we read:

"And the graves were opened; and many bodies of the saints which slept arose,

"And came out of the graves after his resurrection, and went into the holy city, and appeared unto many." (Matthew 27:52-53.)

If the resurrection were to be but a spiritual resurrection, as some teach and believe, there would have been no need of the graves having been opened, and this account would not have stated "and many bodies of the saints which slept arose." Thus the bodies and spirits were again united.

The Lord revealed unto the Prophet Joseph Smith that when the body and spirit are separated they cannot receive a fulness of joy. "For man is spirit. The elements are eternal, and spirit and element, inseparably connected, receive a fulness of joy; And when separated, man cannot receive a fulness of joy." (D&C 93:33-34.)

There were also those who were resurrected among the Nephites in America, following his resurrection. (See 3 Nephi 23:9-13.)

That is why Paul tells us that Christ was the "first fruits" of the resurrection.

"But every man in his own order: Christ the firstfruits; afterward they that are Christ's at his coming." (1 Corinthians 15:23.)

We should mention his second coming, to which the apostle Paul refers.

All through his earthly ministry, Jesus looked forward to and taught his disciples of his second coming. For example, his parable of the five wise and five foolish virgins. "Watch therefore, for ye know neither the day nor the hour wherein the Son of man cometh." (Matthew 25:13.)

His declaration:

"When the Son of man shall come in his glory, and all the holy angels with him, then shall he sit upon the throne of his glory;

"And before him shall be gathered all nations: and he shall separate them one from another, as a shepherd divideth his sheep from the goats." (Matthew 25:31-32.)

His disciples fully understood from his teachings that he would come again. When "he sat upon the mount of Olives," they "came unto him privately, saying, Tell us, when shall these things be? and what shall be the sign of thy coming, and of the end of the world?" (Matthew 24:3.)

Of course, they had reference to his second coming, for he was already with them. And while Jesus gave them many signs of his coming, he informed them, "But of that day and hour knoweth no man, no, not the angels of heaven, but my Father only.

"But as the days of Noe were, so shall also the coming of the Son of man be." (Matthew 24:36-37.)

Then we have his final testimony as he stood trial before the chief priests and elders:

"But Jesus held his peace. And the high priest answered and said unto him, I adjure thee by the living God, that thou tell us whether thou be the Christ, the Son of God.

"Jesus saith unto him, Thou hast said: nevertheless I say unto you, Hereafter shall ye see the Son of man sitting on the right hand of power, and coming in the clouds of heaven." (Matthew 26:63-64.)

When John, the beloved apostle of our Lord, was banished upon the Isle of Patmos, the angel of the Lord showed him many things from before the foundation of the world to the winding-up scenes when we would have a new heaven and a new earth, and among other things he was shown the coming of the Savior and the resurrection of the worthy dead at his coming, and when Satan would be bound for a thousand years:

". . . and they lived and reigned with Christ a thousand years.

"But the rest of the dead lived not again until the thousand years were finished. This is the first resurrection.

"Blessed and holy is he that hath part in the first resurrection: on such the second death hath no power, but they shall be priests of God and of Christ, and shall reign with him a thousand years." (Revelation 20:4-6.)

What a promised privilege to the faithful! Think of
being associated with him in his ministry for a thousand
years with our resurrected bodies, while he is over-
coming all his enemies and preparing his kingdom to be
delivered unto his Father. As Paul explains:

"Then cometh the end, when he shall have delivered
up the kingdom to God, even the Father; when he shall
have put down all rule and all authority and power.

"For he must reign, till he hath put all enemies
under his feet.

"The last enemy that shall be destroyed is death."
(1 Corinthians 15:24-26.)

If we had the capacity to understand the magnitude
of these promises, it would seem that none should falter
but that each would so live that he would be worthy to
have part in the first resurrection, and that we would all
do all in our power to help our loved ones and friends to
live to be worthy of these blessings, remembering the
words of our Savior:

"Because strait is the gate, and narrow is the way,
which leadeth unto life, and few there be that find it."
(Matthew 7:14.)

The apostle Paul tells us: "But the natural man receiveth not the things of the Spirit of God: for they are
foolishness unto him: neither can he know them, because
they are spiritually discerned." (1 Corinthians 2:14.)

It is because the natural man cannot understand the
things of God that we read such statements as this:

In Senator Albert J. Beveridge's book *The Young
Man and the World,* the senator quotes the following
statement made to him by a man whose name is known
to the railroad world as one of the ablest transportation
men in the United States: "I would rather be sure that
when a man dies he will live again with his conscious
identity, than to have all the wealth of the United States,
or to occupy any position of honor or power the world
could possibly give."

Measured by this man's appraisal, how rich and favored we are, for this is common knowledge to a Latter-day Saint.

From a revelation to the Prophet Joseph Smith, we read:

"When the Savior shall appear we shall see him as he is. We shall see that he is a man like ourselves.

"And that same sociality which exists among us here will exist among us there, only it will be coupled with eternal glory, which glory we do not now enjoy." (D&C 130:1-2.)

We have never seen a person who has been clothed with "eternal glory," but the Prophet Joseph Smith described such a man, Moroni, who appeared to him. After giving a detailed description he stated:

"Not only was his robe exceedingly white, but his whole person was glorious beyond description, and his countenance truly like lightning." (Joseph Smith 2:32.)

When the angel of the Lord showed John the Revelator, who was banished upon the Isle of Patmos, many wonderful things, John was so impressed with his personage, for he had been endowed with "eternal glory" just as Moroni had, that he fell down to worship at the feet of the angel:

"Then saith he unto me, See thou do it not: for I am thy fellowservant, and of thy brethren the prophets, and of them which keep the sayings of this book: worship God." (Revelations 22:9.)

Thus this angel and Moroni were real men who had lived upon the earth and had been resurrected and were continuing in the service of the Lord as we will all be privileged to do, if we are faithful, and the same "sociality" which exists among us here will exist among us then.

The prophet Isaiah saw the time when we would have a new heaven and earth; he declared:

"For, behold, I create new heavens and a new earth:

and the former shall not be remembered, nor come into mind. . . .

"And they shall build houses, and inhabit them; and they shall plant vineyards, and eat the fruit of them.

"They shall not build, and another inhabit; they shall not plant, and another eat; for as the days of a tree are the days of my people, and mine elect shall long enjoy the work of their hands.

"They shall not labour in vain, nor bring forth for trouble; for they are the seed of the blessed of the Lord, and their offspring with them." (Isaiah 65:17, 21-23.)

Note how Isaiah makes plain the fact that "they shall build houses, and inhabit them, and they shall plant vineyards, and eat the fruit of them." Who shall do all this? Families, of course, just as they do now, for as Isaiah stated, "they are the seed of the blessed of the Lord, and their offspring with them."

In this new world, therefore, there is a continuation of family organization after the resurrection, a truth the Lord has made so plain through his revelations to the Prophet Joseph Smith, in this new gospel dispensation.

What a glorious day it will be, therefore, when the trump of God shall sound if we are worthy to come forth in the morning of the first resurrection, to receive and be united with our loved ones, when the graves are open and they come forth through the power of the atonement wrought for us by the Redeemer of the world. (D&C 29:13.)

35

The End of the Journey

No matter what adventure in life one may embark upon, it is natural that his devotion thereto may be measured by the end he expects to attain. The farmer, day after day, gives his physical strength for the harvest he expects to gather. The student leaves loved ones and friends to attend college and burns the midnight oil that his quest in preparation for a more abundant and remunerative life may not be in vain. Our Pilgrim fathers, with their families, left their beloved homes, not in search of gold but in search of God, that they might be privileged to worship him according to the dictates of their own conscience. Our pioneer fathers took to the wilderness, with their families, that they might find a haven of peace and rest beyond the reach of their enemies.

The motivating power in the lives of most Christian people, causing them to interest themselves in religious matters, deals not so much with what religion can do for them in this present life, but what it has to offer after death.

What is the end of the journey? Many and conflicting are the philosophies and explanations given in answer to this question. The church should explain, since the church is to bring to us the word of the Lord, the plan and purpose of life. The church should be able to speak in definite terms. Why should not a son of God know what is at the journey's end to safeguard him against a life of failure and to inspire him to a life of devotion? We must know where we are going. Without this, religion would be very incomplete. To the lack of this information must be attributed much of the unbelief in the world today, and much of the inactivity in religious matters.

Salvation to most Christians means the escape from eternal burning. Hence the statement so often heard among them: "I am saved." One prominent minister stated that a person could be saved just like that, with which he gave a snap of the fingers. Thus, the end of the journey to such people is an escape from eternal punishment. No constructive program as to how we are to spend our time has been advanced.

If there is a church other than The Church of Jesus Christ of Latter-day Saints that believes and teaches that the family unit of husband, wife, and children shall endure in organized form beyond the grave, it has not been my privilege to contact the same. During a conversation with a very prominent minister, he admitted that his church did not hold out a promise or assurance of the continuation of the marriage tie or family unit but, he stated: "In my own mind I find stubborn objections."

A minister asked the question: "Can a person be saved in this life or must he die to be saved?" To which I replied: "If you will tell me what you mean by being saved, I will answer your question," and when he seemed lost for an answer, I explained to him that the Latter-day Saints believe that salvation is not an end but a process; that the Prophet Joseph Smith taught that "we are saved no faster than we gain knowledge." I called attention to the fact that we received our bodies because we were faithful in the life we lived before we came upon this earth; that those who were not faithful were denied this privilege and we know them as Satan and his angels.

Thus, because we were once faithful, we are privileged to come upon this earth and enjoy it in possession of a body, and because Satan and his angels were not faithful, they were cast out of heaven (see Revelation 12 and Isaiah 14) and the only bodies they can have are the ones they are able to take possession of that belong to their brothers and sisters who were faithful.

It is comforting to know that we kept our first estate, and above all things we should now desire to know the way so we will not be deprived of blessings within our reach.

Through the Prophet Joseph Smith, we received the Book of Abraham, from which I quote:

". . . and we will make an earth whereon these may dwell; and we will prove them herewith, to see if they will do all things whatsoever the Lord their God shall command them; And they who keep . . . their second estate shall have glory added upon their heads for ever and ever." (Abraham 3:24-26.) It is good to know that we are to be added to and not subtracted from, if we keep this second estate, which means: "As in Adam all die, even so in Christ shall all be made alive." We may lose our bodies for a brief span, but they will be returned to us more beautiful than we have ever known them before, and they will be as real and tangible as they are now.

"When the Savior shall appear we shall see him as he is. We shall see that he is a man like ourselves. And that same sociality which exists among us here will exist among us there, only it will be coupled with eternal glory, which glory we do not now enjoy." (D&C 130:1-2.)

In Alma 40:23 we read: "The soul shall be restored to the body, and the body to the soul; yea, and every limb and joint shall be restored to its body; yea, even a hair of the head shall not be lost, but all things shall be restored to their proper and perfect frame."

We have never seen a person who has been clothed with eternal glory, but the Prophet Joseph describes such a man, Moroni, when he appeared to him, in these words: ". . . immediately a personage appeared at my bedside, standing in the air, for his feet did not touch the floor. He had on a loose robe of most exquisite whiteness. It was a whiteness beyond anything earthly I had ever seen; nor do I believe that any earthly thing could be made to appear so exceedingly white and brilliant. His hands were naked, and his arms also, a little above the wrist; so, also, were his feet naked, as were his legs, a little above the ankles. His head and neck were also bare. I could discover that he had no other clothing on but this robe, as it was open, so that I could see into his bosom. Not only was his robe exceedingly white, but his whole person was glorious beyond description, and his countenance truly like lightning." (Joseph Smith 2:30-32.)

When Adam and Eve were placed in the garden, the earth yielded to their touch without the resistance of thorns and thistles with which the earth was cursed when they were driven from the garden to earn their bread by the sweat of their brow. (See Gen. 3:17-19.) But since the atonement of the Savior was complete, not only is man to be resurrected, but the earth is to be restored to her original status. Speaking of this time, Isaiah states:

"And they shall build houses, and inhabit them; and they shall plant vineyards, and eat the fruit of them.

"They shall not build, and another inhabit; they shall not plant, and another eat: for as the days of a tree are the days of my people, and mine elect shall long enjoy the work of their hands.

"They shall not labour in vain, nor bring forth for trouble; for they are the seed of the blessed of the Lord, and their offspring with them." (Isaiah 65:21-23.)

When the millennial reign is ushered in, the righteous dead who have died in the Lord will come forth, and men and women, both those who have remained upon the earth and those who are to come forth from the grave, will live in organized society, just as real as they do now, except the kingdom of God will bear rule, to which all other kingdoms will be subjected. The family unit shall continue to exist and the relationship of husband and wife will be as necessary then as it was before death came into the world and the earth was cursed.

That thousand years will be the greatest working period the kingdom of God has ever known, for the King himself shall preside until all enemies are placed under his feet and the kingdom is prepared as a bride for her bridegroom, to be delivered up unto the Father. The Lord will continue to work through men and women then as he does now. Parents will receive their children in the resurrection and husbands and wives will be restored to each other providing they have observed the law that entitles them to this blessing, just as those who had observed the law receive bodies in this life. When the Master comes, he will bring with him those who have been faithful and true, who have learned of his work and are prepared to assist him in preparing the king-dom to deliver up unto the Father. This is more than escaping eternal burning, which people have in mind when they say they are saved. This is a life of activity. Is it worth being faithful in this life that we may be called forth to a life of activity with him, our Master and Redeemer, as against waiting in the grave until the thousand years are ended to come forth and receive ac-cording to our work?

That all shall not receive alike is clearly evidenced by the statement of the Master: "In my Father's house are many mansions: if it were not so, I would have told you" (John 14:2), and the statement of Paul: "There is one glory of the sun, and another glory of the moon, and another glory of the stars: for one star differeth from another star in glory. So also is the resurrection of the dead . . ." (1 Corinthians 15:41-42). Who then, except ourselves, shall determine to which glory we shall go?

Men everywhere should be happy to accept such a philosophy if they but understood it. Thus the end of the journey is to be added upon. We shall lose nothing, but gain much, if we are faithful in keeping our second estate. It must have been Paul's understanding of this philosophy which caused him to declare: "Eye hath not seen, nor ear heard, neither hath it entered into the heart of man, the things which God hath prepared for them that love him," and "O death, where is thy sting? O grave, where is thy victory?"

36

Messages of Hope and Comfort

From the funeral services of Heber Moon and his wife, Ruby E. Pierce Moon, January 27, 1950:

The Prophet Joseph tells us that when the Savior appears, we shall see that he is a man like unto ourselves, except he has been endowed with eternal glory, which glory we do not now possess; and that the same sociality which exists among us here will exist among us there. We are not able to fully understand what it means to be endowed with eternal glory as Jesus was when he came forth from the tomb. If you will read the description the Prophet Joseph gave of Moroni when he appeared to him three times during the night, you will see that the Prophet said that he defied all description. He was a man like President Moon, who had been faithful in all things and had received his body, and it had been endowed with eternal glory.

When John the Revelator was banished on the Isle of Patmos, the angel of God showed him everything from before the foundation of the world until the winding-up scenes thereof, when there should be no more death and no more pain or sorrow, for all former things should be done away and we should no more need the sun by day nor the moon by night, for the glory of God should be upon us and upon the earth. John was over-whelmed with it all and was about to kneel down to worship the angel when the angel said, "See thou do it not: for I am thy fellowservant, and of thy brethren the prophets." (Revelation 22:9.) Thus we see the angel endowed with eternal glory, which glory we do not now possess, but which we may all possess through our faithfulness.

The Prophet Alma indicated that we are not all born at the same time, and that mattereth not; neither do we all die at the same time, and that does not matter. If President and Sister Moon had been sent on a mission to England we would have been happy and would have felt that it was the will of the Lord; if the Lord had a work for them to do in the spirit world, should he not be just as able to call them there as in a mission field here upon this earth? Who are we to understand and know the providences of the Almighty? They did not know the sting of death. They passed from life to life. Jesus said, "God is not a God of the dead, but of the living, for they live all unto him." So President and Sister Moon are not dead, but they live unto their Father in heaven.

From the funeral services of Kate Woodhouse Kirkham, October 19, 1946:

If I were asked to define a successful man or woman according to my measure, I would know of no better way than to point to Brother and Sister Kirkham. Their family is a credit to them. They have the kind of faith that will bring honor and glory to their name forever and forever. They have done their work well. They will not have to apologize when they meet their Maker. They have made many, many friends and many converts, and they have done the temple work for many, many who have gone beyond, and have gathered the genealogy for many, many more that their children can continue to work for. So, from every angle that the Lord has of measuring success in this life, they have been successful.

Some people spend all their time trying to acquire wealth. Brother Ashton used to tell a homely little story of the funeral cortege leaving the meeinghouse. Two friends were sitting on the ditchbank whittling, and one of them turned to the other and said, "Did he leave anything?" "He left everything" was the reply. With some people they leave everything. When others die they take practically everything with them, because they have been gathering and garnering and laying aside, as Jesus taught: "Lay not up for yourselves treasures upon earth, where moth and rust doth corrupt, and where thieves break through and steal: But lay up for yourselves treasures in heaven, where neither moth nor rust doth corrupt, and where thieves can not break through nor steal: For where your treasure is, there will your heart be also." (Matthew 6:19-21.)

Brother and Sister Kirkham have devoted themselves to the gathering of treasures in heaven and have laid them safely away. Their whole lives have been full of the spirit of service unto their fellowmen.

From the funeral services of Sister Billie Palmer

We thank the Lord at times like this that we have a knowledge of the gospel and that we do not have any uncertainty of the future and the life hereafter as many people do. I know of no other church in the world that teaches that the family relationship and family unit will project itself into the eternal worlds. The ministers say as part of every marriage ceremony, "until death do you part." That is as far as their promise of being together goes. It really is a bill of divorcement at the death of either party. But we have the word of the Lord and the promise of the Lord that the marriage covenant performed in the holy temples of the Lord in his church are eternal and that men and women so married are sealed together for time and all eternity and their children will be theirs in the hereafter, just as they are on this earth. Eternity is a long time. It is longer than we can feel or even imagine.

Paul says: "For we know in part, . . . But when that which is perfect is come, then that which is in part shall be done away. . . . For now we see through a glass darkly; but then face to face: now I know in part; but then shall I know even as also I am known." (1 Corinthians 13:9-12.)

When the time comes that the veil of forgetfulness is rolled back, we may have many happy memories of hours and days and years spent with each other and of things that happened in the spirit world before we came to this earth. Childhood brings its satisfaction. Youth has its joys and appreciation for the privileges and friendships created in young manhood and womanhood; then we enter into marriage, which is the sweetest thing in the world when proper and clean, and children come along like angels from heaven, and then the grandchildren come. These are the experiences that we would not want to be without. But we do not want to go back and do them over again. We realize that in this life each step is a step ahead in the accomplishment of life's mission and in bringing us closer to God as we travel along the road of eternal progression. Each new experience will add its joy, for, as the Lord has promised, we will be added upon forever and ever. In this program of being "added upon," probably the greatest promise the Lord has made that we have the ability to understand and appreciate is the promise that the family ties that bind us here will bind us in the eternal worlds, where love will fill our hearts for each other, and all selfishness will cease. I would not give very much for the salvation offered by any other church, because they cannot give us assurance that we can enjoy the association of our loved ones during eternity.

God has restored the power of the priesthood to bind families together for time and all eternity, but sometimes there is a situation of remorse; family ties have been broken because members have not kept the commandments of the Lord. I cannot think of anything finer for a husband and wife than to have a family following in their footsteps because their lives have been worthy for their sons and daughters to follow.

From the funeral services for Herman Van Braak, July 31, 1944

I cannot say anything to add to what Brother Van Braak has done, for he has preached his own sermon in the life that he has lived; but I would like to say a few words about Brother Van Braak today and tomorrow and in the future until we see him again, and in order to illustrate what I am going to say, I am going to report to you a few of the words that Brother Heber C. Kimball spoke at the funeral service of Jedediah M. Grant.

Jedediah M. Grant was President Heber J. Grant's father and a counselor to Brigham Young, and Heber C. Kimball was also a counselor. Brother Kimball visited Brother Grant shortly before his death. He said that Brother Grant was so weak he could not speak, and he laid his hands upon his head and blessed him, and then the Lord gave him increased strength and Brother Grant talked for over an hour. He said, "Brother Heber, I have been into the spirit world two nights in succession, and of all of the dreads that ever came across me, the worst was to have to again return to my body, though I had to do it."

That sounds a little strange, but remember that we have not seen what is there. Didn't Paul tell us, "Eye hath not seen, nor ear heard, neither have entered into the heart of man, the things which God hath prepared for them that love him"? (1 Corinthians 2:9.) We have not the ability in mortal life to look beyond the grave. But even in this life it is possible for men to taste of the powers of the world to come; and of the heavenly gifts and those that enjoy such precious privileges and then fall away, Paul indicates it is impossible to renew them unto repentance. Brother Van Braak has had the privilege here in mortality of tasting of some of these powers of the world to come.

When Jedediah M. Grant looked back and beheld his body after what he had seen, he was disappointed to have to return to it, though he had to do it. "But, oh!" said he, "the order and government that were there. When in the spirit world, I saw the order of righteous men and women. I beheld them organized in their several grades, and there appeared to be no obstruction to my vision. I could see every man and woman in their grade and order. I looked to see if there were any disorder there, but there was none. Neither could I see any death nor any darkness, disorder or confusion."

You remember that when the disciples came to Jesus and said, "Master, teach us to pray," the first thing Jesus taught them to ask for, after duly saluting the Father in that marvelous prayer, was, "Thy kingdom come. Thy will be done in earth, as it is in heaven." (Matthew 6:10.) We have never seen such a condition yet. We have never seen his will done in earth as it is in heaven. If all were like Brother Van Braak, we would be nearer there. That is the pattern, and here on earth we have been attempting to establish an order and organization such as exists there, and that is what President Jedediah M. Grant saw when he saw the organization of families and the perfection of organization that existed there. He said that the people he saw were organized in family capacities, and when he looked at them he saw grade after grade. All were organized and in perfect harmony. He would mention one item after another and say, "Why, it is just as Brother Brigham says it is. It is just as he has told us many a time."

President Grant said he had studied the gospel by day and by night in his travels by land and by sea for twenty-one years, just as thoroughly as any man ever studied any branch of science, and he said that his studies had brought him only to the ABC's, that such a study would lead into the eternities. Then Brother Grant said he saw his wife, Caroline, there and that she was holding in her arms their infant child who died on the plains and whose body was eaten by the wolves. He said, "You see, the wolves didn't hurt her, did they." Then Brother Grant asked her where Brother Joseph and Brother Hyrum were. She replied, "They have gone away ahead to transact and perform business for us."

This reminds us of the words of the Savior: "In my Father's house are many mansions: if it were not so, I would have told you. I go to prepare a place for you . . . that where I am, there ye may be also." (John 14:2-3.) So Joseph and Hyrum had gone on to prepare the way for those who were associated with them. Then he spoke of the buildings he saw and said that Solomon's temple was much inferior to the most ordinary building he saw in the spirit world. Then he commented on the gardens: "I have seen good gardens on this earth, but I never saw any to compare with those that were there. I saw flowers of numerous kinds, and some with fifty or a hundred different colored flowers growing on one stalk." After seeing all these things, Brother Grant said he felt extremely sorrowful at having to leave so beautiful a place.

Brother Van Braak believed in eternal life. You and I believe in eternal life. Have you ever stopped to figure what eternity means? We are told that time is measure only to man, that by God there is no time. It is one eternal round. . . .

Brothers and Sisters, if the veil were rolled back

and we could see what eternity really is, as Paul has seen, and Brother Jedediah M. Grant has seen, and other of the brethren, and could taste a little more of the powers of the world to come, we would be more willing to do the things we are asked to do here upon the earth.

37

To Build the Kingdom of God
(Remarks at the Los Angeles Temple Dedication, March 13, 1956)

I desire to express my feelings, the feelings of my heart here today, to you brethren and sisters, in the words of the song that we have just heard, "I Know That My Redeemer Lives." I know that he lives; I thank God for being one of his children, one of his humble servants with my Brethren with whom I am associated. I love them; I love the Lord; I love his work, and I love the Saints. I think they are wonderful.

I have sat through these sessions and thanked the Lord for your faith, for the things which you have done for the glory of the Lord here in this part of his vineyard. Some of you know that I had the privilege of presiding over the Hollywood Stake when there were two stakes in all the Southern California area, and now there are eighteen covering the same territory. We worked for that and we prayed for it, and we thank God for the great success the work has had. This beautiful temple erected here in honor of the Lord is an evidence of your love and your faith, coupled with all the other fine things you have been doing here in this locality.

We have had many people come here to see the temple and they have admired it; they have admired the architecture, the artistry, the decorations and the paintings, the beauty of this structure. As we drove around it the other night, floodlighted as it was, it seemed almost ethereal, as if it had been dropped down from heaven. You could not go anywhere and find anything that looked so beautiful, at least to the Latter-day Saints. While I was riding on the train to Salt Lake a couple of weeks ago, the conductor, who lives in Los Angeles, said, in talking of the tourists on the train who had been visiting here in California, that they were out-spoken in the thought that the Mormon Temple was the most interesting thing that they had seen. Then when you read the words of the Lord to the Prophet Joseph, even before the Church was organized, when he said that "a marvelous work is about to come forth among the children of men," and how he would give his ser-vants the power "to bring it forth out of obscurity and out of darkness," it makes one rejoice to live to see his promises being fulfilled.

It is a wonderful thing to be living in the day when the Church is making such rapid progress. Now, if we love the Lord and love his children, we are not only interested that they should admire the architecture, the artistry, and the beauty of the building, but our hearts go out to them and we wish that they might be able to share with us the spiritual implications and what this temple stands for, that they might realize what the Lord really has done in our day and in our time.

I desire to read a few words spoken by President Brigham Young at the laying of the cornerstone of the Salt Lake Temple. He said, "This morning we have as-sembled on one of the most solemn, interesting and joyful and glorious occasions that have ever transpired or will transpire among the children of men while the earth continues in its present organization and is oc-cupied for its present purpose, and I congratulate my brethren and sisters that it is our unspeakable privilege to stand here this day and administer before the Lord

on an occasion which has caused the tongues and pens
of prophets to speak and write for many scores of centuries which are past." That was the feeling of this great
leader of the Church when the cornerstone was laid for
the Salt Lake Temple, and when he said it had caused
the tongues and pens of prophets to speak and write for
many centuries that had past, he no doubt had in mind
how the Lord let the prophets of old see our day and
see the temples built in the tops of the mountains. You
will recall the words of Isaiah and Micah that in the
latter days it would come to pass "that the mountain of
the Lord's house shall be established in the top of the
mountains, and all nations shall flow unto it," and they
would say, "Come ye, and let us go up to the mountain
of the Lord, to the house of the God of Jacob, and he
will teach us of his ways, and we will walk in his paths."

Brethren and sisters, where in all the history of the
world could you find anything that approximates a fulfillment of that great prophecy like the gathering of the
saints of Zion from almost every land under heaven to
the valleys of the mountains? They have come to learn
of his ways and walk in his paths, and many of us are
descendants of those pioneers who built that great temple
unto the Lord.

Then I think of the words of the apostle Paul when
he said the Lord had made known unto him "the mystery
of his will [something the world did not understand]
. . . That in the dispensation of the fulness of times
he might gather together in one all things in Christ,
both which are in heaven, and which are on earth"
(Ephesians 1:9-10), and where in all the world could you
go to find an appropriate place to unite heaven and
earth such as you find in this church where we do a
great work for the living and the dead, to unite the
fathers who have gone beyond with the children who
are here? I think these are the things President Brigham
Young had in his mind.

Three thousand years ago the Lord permitted Isaiah to see our day and these accomplishments, and now we have this great program of uniting fathers to their children. President Joseph Fielding Smith spoke on that subject and how marvelously this spirit of turning the hearts of the fathers to the children and the children to their parents has rested upon people all over the world in establishing genealogical societies, in doing research since Elijah came. I think that is another great thing that Brigham Young had in mind, the coming of Elijah the prophet. Is there anyone in the world that can tell us about Elijah and his coming except The Church of Jesus Christ of Latter-day Saints? So we thank the Lord for the great knowledge that has come through the restoration of the gospel and through these holy prophets, and we would share it with all the world that they might also understand these glorious truths with us. The Savior said that the hour was coming and was nigh at hand when the dead would hear the words of the Son of God and they that would hear should live. We also have the testimony of Peter that when the Savior was put to death he went and preached to the spirits in prison, and then he tells us that "for this cause was the gospel preached to them that are dead, that they might be judged according to men in the flesh, but live according to God in the spirit." (1 Peter 4:6.)

Now isn't it marvelous to think that we can do a work here in the temples of the Lord that makes it possible that our loved ones who have gone beyond without having heard the fullness of the gospel as it has been restored in these latter days might live "according to God in the spirit" because we are able to administer for them the holy ordinances of the gospel which cannot be administered in that spirit world to which they have gone?

I have talked of the necessity of gathering genealogy and doing this great work. If the veil were just rolled back and we could see our loved ones there, knowing how eagerly they might be waiting for the work to be done, I wonder if this great and important mission of the Church might not seem of greater importance to us than it does at the present time.

I think at the present time of the testimony borne by President Wilford Woodruff in the conference at Salt Lake as reported in 1898 where he tells us about George Washington and the writers of the Declaration of Independence, and he said they were the choicest men the Lord could find upon the face of the earth, and then he said this: "Another thing I'm going to say here because I have a right to say it, every one of those men that signed the Declaration of Independence with George Washington called upon me as an Apostle of the Lord Jesus Christ in the Temple at St. George on two consecutive nights and demanded that I should go forward and attend to the ordinances of the House of God for them."

Think of that for a moment. How important these ordinances must be! These great men whom God sent in their day and time to give us this great Constitution under which we live, and then how the Lord permitted them to come back and ask for these ordinances so that they might "live according to God in the spirit," as Peter tells us, the reason for which the gospel was preached to them. They did not come back to inquire how the United States of America was getting along, the thing for which they had given their lives and devoted their energies. They wanted these ordinances . . . that are administered in the house of the Lord. When the Savior gave unto his apostles the Holy Priesthood, the power to bind on earth and it would be bound in heaven, it seems to me that it is of great significance to think that there are things that can be bound here on this earth that shall be bound in the heavens, and that must be done by the power of the Holy Priesthood.

So as we contemplate the restoration of the gospel, we are grateful that the Lord sent back men who bore that Holy Priesthood, that it has been committed to men here upon this earth, and that these holy temples are being erected and have been up to the present time in order that we might discharge the great responsibility that rests upon us that, in the words of Paul, we might "gather together in one all things in Christ, both which are in heaven and which are on earth."

If we just knew those who have gone beyond—our loved ones, who they are, a little more about them— we might be more interested in them. I was reading in the history of the Richards family recently, and I found that many of our ancestors were ministers of the gospel, and some of the tributes that were paid to these men, who did not have the privilege of knowing the truth as we know it, would make you think they could have been leaders of the Church had they lived today. In fact, I would like to read a few words from the description of one of the ministers by the name of James Richards. When I read this, I thought that it was about what we would all say about Stephen L Richards, my cousin, a member of the First Presidency. We could hardly find words more appropriate. This is what is said after speaking of others: "But among all, I say it with the earnestness of thorough conviction, there is not one to whom my mind reverts with a deeper and more filial reverence than to James Richards. He was so wise, so judicious, so prudent. His counsel, in those days, was as if a man inquired at the oracle of God. Everywhere, in the pulpit, the lecture room, the parlor, and the market place, he was the same upright, dignified, consistent Christian minister. Especially did his excellencies shine out as a member of our Church judicatories. The amenity of his manners, the clearness of his reasoning, and the solidity of his judgment, gave him an influence which could not but be felt. I look back upon him with mingled feelings of love and veneration."

If we had just known men like that, our loved ones

and our ancestors, it seems to me it might have made a difference. It makes one feel sad to realize how few of our Father's children have had the privilege of embracing the gospel. It is hard to believe that there are not many great and noble men among them who will accept the gospel when it is preached to them in the spirit world in order that "they might live according to God in the spirit," as Peter said. It is necessary that we have these holy temples in which the work can be done for them.

I was in a conference the other day in a stake near here, where a large group of singers, young people, sang "Open the Gates of the Temple." When my turn came to speak I said to those young people, "I'm sure it must be pleasing to the Lord to hear that prayer sung unto him, and I hope you all live so that when the time comes for your marriage, you can go into the gates of the temple." And I was reminded then that we are the ones who determine our worthiness to enter, just like when John was banished upon the Isle of Patmos, an angel representing himself to be the Master said, "Behold, I stand at the door, and knock; if any man hear my voice, and open the door, I will come in to him, and will sup with him, and he with me." (Revelation 3:20.) But you see, we have to open the door; we have to make our lives conform to these things that are necessary in order that the gates of the temple shall be opened. As I go through the Church I tell the Saints our first great responsibility is to build the kingdom of God in the earth, and the second is a companion unto it, to build our own kingdoms. And when I think that our young men and our young women, without being married in the temple, cannot lay the foundation of a kingdom that will project itself into the eternal worlds, I join with my brethren in pleading with all Latter-day Saints to plant deep in the hearts of your children as they grow into manhood and womanhood an earnest desire to be worthy of marriage in the house of the Lord.

I leave you my love and my testimony. I love the people here in these parts. I thank the Lord for the great work you are doing. I thank him for this temple. I thank him for all you have done to make it possible, for your kindness to us while we have been with you. I pray God to grant unto those of you who are here to attend these services from day to day the righteous desires of your heart, that you may grow in knowledge and understanding and faith, in good works and in preparation for eternal glory in the presence of the Lord, which I pray for each of you in the name of the Lord Jesus Christ. Amen.

38

"Out of Zion, the Perfection of Beauty"
(Remarks at the Oakland Temple
Dedication, November 19, 1964)

Brothers and sisters, I feel humble in standing here this day upon this holy and sacred occasion and in your presence and in the presence of our Prophet.

Each of the brethren who has spoken has expressed his gratitude to the Lord that President McKay has been privileged to be with us and participate in these dedicatory services. I am sure that each of us has had a prayer in his heart for a long time that he would have this privilege, and the Lord has magnified him, and for that we thank him.

I feel to extend my congratulations to all of you good people and those whom we have met prior to this session and those who will follow for your contributions to the erection of this magnificent edifice to our Father in heaven.

I think of the words of the Psalmist—all of the prophets have seen our day—and in the fiftieth Psalm we read these words: "The mighty God, even the Lord, hath spoken, and called the earth from the rising of the sun unto the going down thereof.

"Out of Zion, the perfection of beauty, God hath shined." (Psalm 50:1-2.)

Brother Monson has indicated the impression that

this building will make upon the minds of the people. Just think of the hundreds of thousands who have been here to inspect it. Think of the millions who have been to the Church exhibit at the New York World's Fair. The attitudes of people are changing. "Out of Zion, the perfection of beauty," God is shining to the world in the accomplishments of his people and in such things as the building of these holy temples and the great work of our missionaries. . . .

I think the temple in Salt Lake is "the mountain of the Lord's house" referred to by Isaiah, and all these other temples that have been added since, and those that will be added, are but an expansion of the work that this great prophet must have seen would cause men to gather from all over the world to the holy temple, the house of the God of Jacob, for the blessings they might receive in that temple. (See Isaiah 2:2-3.)

Remember when Nicodemus came to Jesus by night and said: ". . . we know that thou art a teacher come from God: for no man can do these miracles that thou doest, except God be with him." (John 3:2.) Jesus didn't start on some great oration of life. He said, "Except a man be born again, he cannot see the kingdom of God." (John 3:3.) And Nicodemus could not understand. You remember his statement. And then the Savior repeated, "Except a man be born of water and of the Spirit, he cannot enter into the kingdom of God." (John 3:5.) And then Nicodemus couldn't understand, and Jesus said, "We speak that we do know, and testify that we have seen; and ye receive not our witness. If I have told you earthly things, and ye believe not, how shall ye believe, if I tell you of heavenly things?" (John 3:11-12.)

The entrance into the kingdom is what Jesus described as the earthly things, being born again of the water and of the Spirit; and here in these holy temples we learn of the "heavenly things" that have been revealed to contribute to our exaltation. You recall when the apostle Paul was caught up into the third heaven and the paradise of God, he was not permitted to write the things that he saw, but he did say, "Eye hath not seen, nor ear heard, neither have entered into the heart of man, the things which God hath prepared for them that love him." (1 Corinthians 2:9.)

No man can conceive here in mortality what God has prepared for those who love him, and in his holy temples are where we learn of the heavenly things that will prepare us to enter into that third heaven that Paul spoke of, and it is a marvelous thing when you think of how broad the gospel plan is.

Jesus, remember, said that "the hour is coming, and now is, when the dead shall hear the voice of the Son of God: and they that hear shall live." (John 5:25.) And then he goes on, "Marvel not at this; for the hour is coming, in the which all that are in their graves shall hear his voice. And shall come forth. . . ." (John 5:28-29.) . . .

Now in these dedicatory services, our worthy President has expressed the thought that there are unseen visitors here—the prophets who have lived in this dispensation, maybe our loved ones. And he has indicated that the veil might be very thin, and I want to bear my testimony to you that I think the unseen powers that are operating in this world to help to bring about the fulfillment of the Lord's promises are far beyond our ability to comprehend and understand. The old prophets said that in the latter days the Lord would pour out his Spirit upon all flesh, and the young men should see visions and the old men should dream dreams. And so think of what has happened since the Father and the Son appeared to the Prophet Joseph Smith by the pouring out of his Spirit upon all flesh in order to bring about his purposes so that we could do the things that we do now. Think of our means of travel, our means of communication—these microphones here that carry the voice, and now carry it all over the world. I have a little thing here in my pocket that is to me a miracle. See that little film. On that film is the entire Bible, over twelve hundred pages. Think of what that means in this great microfilming program of the Church to gather together all the records of the world where we can put them away in our libraries, and then by blowing them up, we can read everything that is on them. It is a marvelous work and wonder.

Now I like also to think of how marvelously the Lord has moved upon the hearts of the children of men all over this world since Elijah came to turn the hearts of the fathers to the children, and the hearts of the children to the fathers, to gather genealogy, and to write records. We are told that at that time there were no genealogical associations and libraries except for royal families, and now records are being written by the thousands and the hundreds of thousands, and many of us have had our own personal experiences. I would like to relate a few that have come to my attention.

When I went on my first mission to Holland, there were three of us who went to that land—myself, a brother from up in Idaho, and one from down in Spanish Fork. We landed in Rotterdam. One of them was sent up to the north, and I'll talk of him because he had a German name, and when he was called to go to Holland his people were disappointed, feeling that he ought to go to Germany where he could look up the genealogy of his father's people. And when he arrived in the northern part of Holland, what we call Groningen, he was sent out into the little city of Veendam, and he and his companion went looking for a place to live, furnished rooms. This young man said to his companion, "This looks like a nice place. Let's go in here." And after he had been there a few weeks, he found that a record of his father's people had been brought across the border out of Germany, and the father's family never knew that their people had ever been in Holland. Think of the inspiration of God that led the president to send that boy to Holland, and the inspiration that guided the president of the mission to send him up into the north, and the inspiration that guided the district president to send him to the little city of Veendam, about 60,000 people at that time, and the same inspiration that led him and his companion to the very house where he found that record.

He died over there with smallpox. I was present at his burial, and the city was going to burn the book. The district president said, "If you do, it will cost you five hundred dollars." They said no book is worth that much, but they fumigated it page by page in order that the work could be done, and that is in the hands of the family.

When I went on a short-term mission back in the East a few years ago, one of my companions out of Idaho was set apart for his mission by my father, and among other things Father told him that he would not only do a great work for the living, but that he would also do a great work in gathering genealogy of his father's people. Now that was a statement to make, wasn't it? And after we had been there a little while, we had a storm, and it surely does know how to storm back there. I said, "I guess we better go in the library and see what we can find about your father's people." We found a book there with thousands of names in it that had been gathered. His name was Wadsworth and went back into the Longfellow family. Then we went up into Boston to try to find a copy. The publishing house had gone out of business. We went to a second-hand bookstore with high walls and a ladder running along it. The owner said, "I believe I have one of those books." He crawled up the ladder, brought the book down, dusted it off, and for twenty dollars this boy got a record of his people with thousands of names. Do you think that those things are just accidental or just happen?

Under the inspiration of the Almighty we brought in a new convert down in the South while I was there. He went into the library in Jacksonville to look up the record of his people. He found a book that had been published by a judge in Texas by his name. The foreword said: "This book has been published at great expense and time on the part of myself and my wife, and why we have done it we do not know, but we trust that in the providence of the Almighty it may sometime serve a useful purpose."

When I was president of the stake in Los Angeles, we had a meeting of our stake genealogical committee. The chairman of the Los Angeles library was there, and we talked about gathering genealogy. He said, "I don't know what it is. I have spent thousands of dollars gathering genealogy of my people. I have my vaults full of parchments and records." He said, "I don't know what good they will ever be, but I have a mania to do that," and I took the privilege of explaining to him that someday he would realize that he had been a partner with Elijah the prophet, and he hadn't known how much his influence had spread over this earth and had moved upon him.

I met a man up in Portland, Oregon, who had traveled all over the United States gathering genealogy of his people. He said, "Why I have done it I do not know."

We have a record prepared by the Richards family back in the East containing pictures of our grandfathers and thousands of names they have gathered, and you can read the history of these men and their genealogy and what they have accomplished. Many of them were ministers, and I have compared them at times with such men as my cousin, Stephen L Richards; and as President Joseph Fielding Smith said in his talk here the other day, many of them were noble and great men that God raised up as great leaders among his people before the gospel was here, who will be waiting to have their temple work done for them.

We have been in the old home town in Holland of our pilgrim fathers before they came to this land that they might worship God according to the dictates of their own consciences.

Isn't it wonderful that the Lord has made provision that the temple work can be done vicariously for such faithful people who showed such great love for the Lord, and that, as the old Prophet has indicated, we can become saviors upon Mount Zion? What will it mean when we stand in the presence of our loved ones and know that we have been privileged to be saviors unto them?

May God help you now to realize what this building means to each of you who have contributed to it, that you may come often, that you may get the dividends on your investment, and may God bless you for all you have done, I pray and leave you my blessing in the name of the Lord Jesus Christ. Amen.

Index

292